GOLDSTRUCK

STEPHEN WEBSTER

GOLDSTRUCK

A LIFE SHAPED BY JEWELLERY

SALMA

MARMITE

title page The Japanese Kabouki Mask Ring made and worn by SW since 1998

previous spread Doing the thing I do best. Making jewellery in the basement of our first boutique, 1a Duke Street, c.1998

opposite Watercolour and ink artwork of the Africa Cuff

overleaf Rory Dobner pencil drawing of various Stephen Webster creations

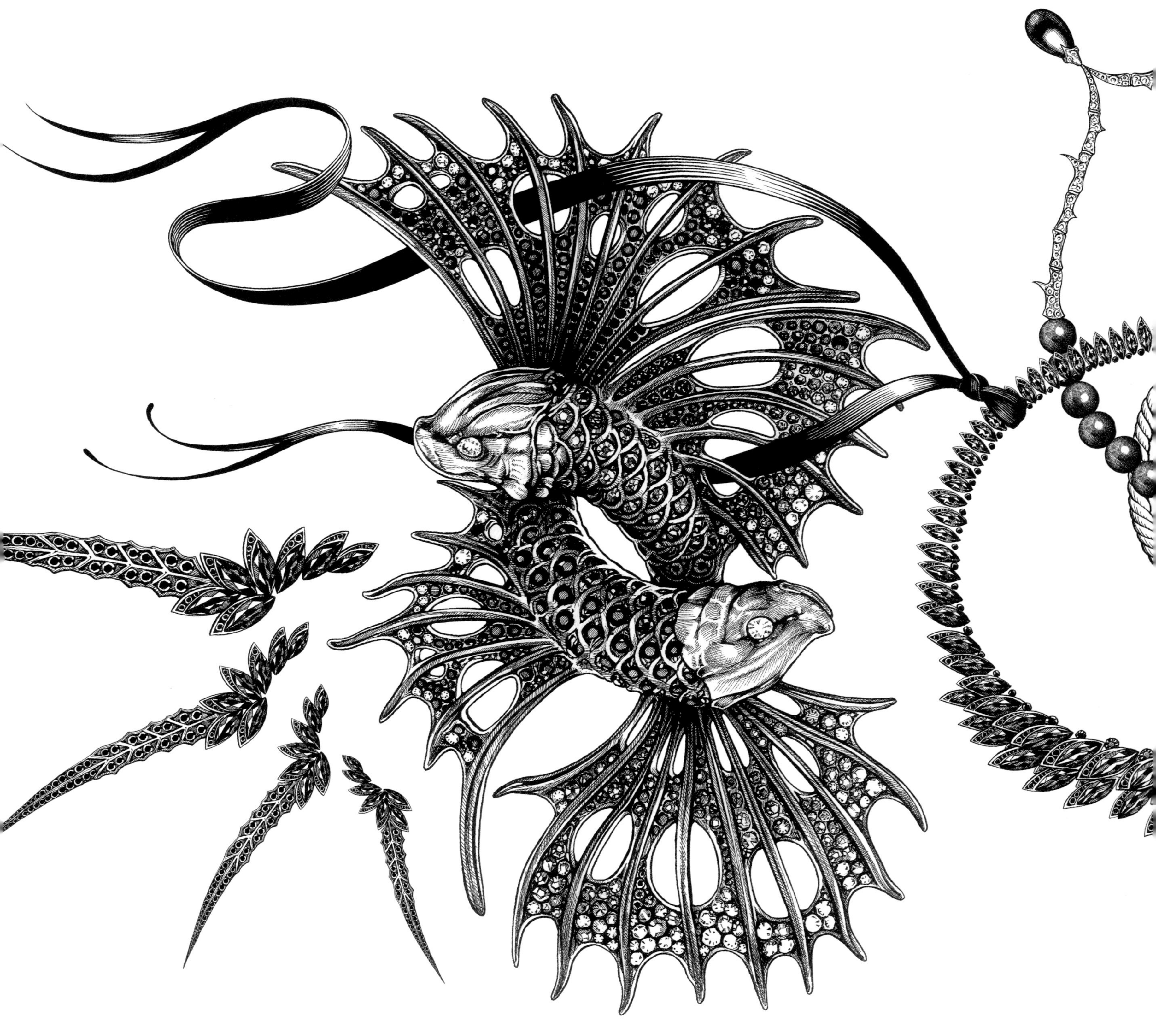

Ken Dodd, or David Essex, a portrait of Stephen Webster by Tracey Emin, a gift for being her guest columnist, 2005

FOREWORD

by Tracey Emin

There are very few people who can work with magic and make it become something real. My friend Stephen is one of those rarities. Our paths have crossed on many occasions from the Atlantis nightclub in Margate in the '70s to being students at Medway College of Design. A criss-cross of friendship and history, which is now exploding into a crescendo of a working collaboration. For years Stephen and I have often talked about combining our creative talents and now we are finally doing it. The culmination of both our creative minds and Stephen's skill; a 32 piece jewellery collection will be unveiled in 2016.

Stephen's world is fish, glass, beautiful things, animals, star signs and tropical worlds, nature all mixed up with a million different alloys. If I think about Stephen's mind I imagine it to be like a giant colour wheel with shapes and forms exploding like a magical planet.

From the Baroque to the incredibly beautiful, wild, rock and roll, punk sophistication, Stephen has found a niche that has escaped any other jeweller. From the points on the back of his rings that give an elegance and understated sexiness to the tiny tags on the clasps of his chains, and to the individual soldering of every tiny link, poetic attention to detail. This is how Stephen is with everything.

He is undoubtedly one of the funniest people I know. A really good dancer with a unique amount of style. But also he is a boy from Kent. You meet some people in life and immediately there is something innate and wonderful and you know that you are going to know them forever. I felt this when I first met Stephen.

He is really honest and totally loyal. On a good day he looks like a young David Essex, on a bad day, like Ken Dodd. Stephen's creativity is impish and kind, using gold and silver and diamonds and other precious stones; he is a true alchemist. He travels every corner of the globe pedalling his wares, a true gypsy king! Not bad for a boy from Kent.

There are some people in your life that you refer to as golden but Stephen truly is gold.

GOLDSTRUCK

INTRODUCTION

HOW I MET MADONNA

One of the most important phone calls of my life very nearly went unanswered. I had been away, on an extended trip to Santa Barbara, California and returned to a series of messages that started off polite and business-like but grew increasingly despondent and incredulous: "Hi, this is Madonna's assistant. Madonna has seen a catalogue of your work, can you come around next Wednesday to show her some pieces?" Beeeep. Next message: "Hi, this is Madonna's assistant, checking you are coming to the house tomorrow?" Beeeeep. Last message, preceded by an audibly resigned exhalation: "Hi, well I guess you are not coming. Thank you." I was beside myself. I had missed my big break. Madonna was showing interest in my jewellery and now it seemed as if I had well and truly blown my chance.

As so many of my best stories, it all started at a party. I was attending a friend's wedding when I met Brian, the groom's best man and an accountant at EMI. Brian told me how two guys had recently approached him from Oxford who asked him to join their management company and help look after Brit Poppers Supergrass and a relatively unknown outfit called Radiohead. Brian knew I loved music and asked me what I thought of the idea. I told him that Radiohead, who had just released their album *The Bends*, were amazing—the most exciting new band of the decade. Brian—whose favourite band was Status Quo—made the move to the music business and became a very good friend too.

Some years later Brian had reason to take a meeting with Madonna and offered to take one of my jewellery catalogues with him. I didn't think anything would come from showing my work to the world's most famous pop star and fashion icon, but what harm could it do? I left my business card with my mobile phone number on it in the package and flew to America. Back then, before mobile phones got smart and slim they were really big. They had bendy aerials and needed charging a lot. They also didn't work abroad, which is exactly where I was when Madonna's people called, three times.

Back in the UK, I took a deep breath, called back, got the assistant on the line and arranged to visit Madonna at her London home the very next evening. Because Brian was the one who had made the original introduction, I took him with me. To steady the nerves, we had a couple of large gins in the pub by Madge's house beforehand.

At first, it was a strange experience. Waiting in a reception room at Madonna's house we could smell something burning.

Watercolour and ink artwork of the Magnipheasant Collar

Concerned, I popped my head around the door in time to see Madonna herself walking up the staircase, cloaked in wisps of thick black smoke. Wow, I thought, is this how Madonna always enters a room? She apologised and explained that she had just burnt some toast. The notion of Madonna doing something as mundane as making toast proved to be an icebreaker. We laughed and got down to business. Madonna looked through my roll of rings, trying one on each finger and asked if she could walk around her house with them on for a while. Strange, I thought but why not? She came back and settled on two. One was a *Crystal Haze* classic and the other a *Rose & Crown*.

As we were packing up there was a knock on the door. A chap was shown in and introduced as her friend Guy. News had not yet broken that Madonna was dating the hot new film director, Guy Ritchie, later to become her husband.

The next day I received a call. Madonna had decided to keep the *Crystal Haze* ring while the other would be returned; and then... nothing. This time I kept my phone fully charged and on constant alert but for weeks, months even, I didn't hear another thing from Madonna or her assistant. In fact, I'd almost given up on the idea of Madonna as my dream brand ambassador until a cold Friday night in Kent. My wife Assia and I were at our house by the coast. I was out picking up a Chinese takeaway and noticed a copy of the *Daily Mirror* on the counter. Flicking through, I came across an almost full page, colour photo of Madonna and Guy, at very close quarters, looking as though they were having fun. She was holding a glass of champagne and wearing the *Crystal Haze* ring—my *Crystal Haze* ring!—on her index finger. I dashed home with the paper to show Assia. This was the first time I had seen my jewellery on anyone so famous and it just happened to be the most famous woman in the world.

What happened next was crazy. First thing on Monday morning I got a call from Marion Fasel, the jewellery editor of *InStyle* magazine in the States. The picture of Madonna and Guy had spread like wildfire, she explained. It was now official—they were an item. Marion knew my work from the Vegas trade shows and wanted to confirm that Madonna's ring was one of mine. She then interviewed me about Madonna, the ring, and how she was wearing it on her index finger.

Next it was American *Vogue* who ran a full-page story: "The new face of British jewellery," "The man who reinvented the cocktail ring." Michelle Kessler who wrote the piece was also one of New York's *it girls* and pretty soon all her *it girl* friends, including a young Tory Burch, were ordering the *Crystal Haze* ring too. Lydia Slater from the *Daily Telegraph* interviewed me in the Builder's Arms pub next door to the shop. The subsequent article portrayed me as not just a jeweller but a controversial figure in what was perceived to be a rather serious business.

Journalists who came to my shop around this time were surprised at being met by me personally, clearly expecting jewellers to be elderly, super serious, sober types who dealt with the gentry, handled heirlooms and items of great value. Instead they got me, Stephen, a Sex Pistols fan from Gravesend, Kent. Once these stories were published, Bergdorf Goodman, New York contacted me. Two buyers made an appointment to visit our tiny boutique in London. They walked away with half of my stock. Madonna had changed my life and she hadn't finished yet.

left First photograph of Madonna and Guy Richie together. Madonna is wearing the silver Obsidian Crystal Haze Ring on her index finger

right Rankin portrait shot for the "Lord of the Rings" article for *The Sunday Times Style* magazine

A couple of years later, with the Stephen Webster brand now at the centre of what was becoming a very different jewellery landscape—jewellery and its personalities being talked about, magazines rediscovering this forgotten luxury, a synergetic buzz generated between fashion and diamonds—I got another call from Madonna's assistant. Could I come to see her in Los Angeles this time? Madonna needs a special ring. Surely, that could only mean one thing?

This time, in a bid to save money, I stayed with my parents-in-law, in Redlands, San Bernardino County, some distance away from Hollywood. This was also where I kept my beautiful jalopy, a 1959 Thunderbird that had been a spontaneous roadside purchase made after our most successful Vegas show earlier that year. In my infinite wisdom, I decided to drive the 80 or so miles to my appointment with Madonna in *the bird*.

Now, unless you have several days spare, may I advise you to never drive anymore than 20 miles in an unrestored, 40 year-old car to an important meeting—especially in the searing heat. As soon as I entered the inevitable Los Angeles crawl, the temperature gauge in the car started to strain against the red pin. Like the rumblings of a post-vindaloo intestine, the noises from under the hood suggested things were going to blow. I pulled over just before the bird decided to discharge most of its bodily fluids. Knowing I was going to be late I called ahead to inform Madonna's people. All was cool, "see you when you arrive." Several hours later, I pulled into the recording studio for our rendezvous. Madonna had long gone but I could leave the designs for her with the assistant's assistant. All that way to Los Angeles and I had missed my moment! So, I flew home and waited.

Sure enough, I got the call. Madonna made her choice and I got to work making a wedding band for her fiancé. I was also told to expect a call from Guy regarding a ring for Madonna, and that I was to act surprised. Like a true ham, I feigned all ignorance when the *Lock, Stock* director came in to the shop to talk about it.

Needless to say, there was a great deal of interest in the Madonna/Ritchie wedding. The press knew that the venue was Skibo Castle in the Scottish Highlands and that Stella McCartney was making the dress, but I had been asked to keep quiet about my involvement until after the ceremony. *The Sunday Times* wanted to run the story of the wedding rings—Rankin took my portrait—with the sworn promise that no would escape until the following day. This meant *The Sunday Times* was taking it pretty seriously. As press goes, this was probably as good as it gets. "Lord of the Rings" was a double page spread in *The Sunday Times Style* magazine, whilst the wedding party was still going on by the time the paper hit the newsstands.

Now our phones never stopped ringing—customers, buyers, private commissions, more celebrities and requests for interviews from magazines and newspapers from all over the world. To this day I don't think there has ever been such a fuss made over a couple of fairly ordinary wedding bands. A chance meeting at a quiet English wedding had resulted in me making the rings for the most publicised, high profile, rock 'n' roll wedding of the decade. My life had changed forever. Thanks Brian.

Thunderbird's inaugural trip
after a full restoration, 2005

At the bench, making yet another ring, 1999

CHAPTER I

A LIFE SHAPED BY JEWELLERY

This book is my story. A true story. The story of a life shaped by jewellery rather than simply a book about jewellery. It's the story of a life seen through the wondrously seductive, shimmering prism of precious stones via the glistering reflection of silver and gold.

Education; in my case, wasted on the young. From the first day I entered a jewellery workshop I knew that I had found my vocation; a job for life; a glittering career. Like a magpie, the gold and silver, the shiny and glistering entranced me. More importantly, a jeweller's workshop very definitely wasn't school.

Writing this some 38 years after leaving Springhead School for Boys in Gravesend, Kent, I struggle to recall much about the classroom. I look at my own kids' time at their respective schools and they both seem to have loved it. Me? I certainly didn't love it. Springhead was supposed to have been a good school, a *tech* or *technical school*. I definitely liked English and sport. I liked art so much that I sometimes used to participate in extracurricular activities with the ceramics teacher—we called it "pottery" back then. She would sometimes invite my best friend and me to her flat where we would listen to Bowie and T-Rex records, drink tea and talk about pots. It was all very innocent. Our pottery teacher was also a hippy and being something of a fashion fascist back then, I didn't like or trust hippies. But Miss Ceramics was a girl and we didn't get to meet, let alone talk to many girls at Springhead School for Boys.

Ours was also a footballing school. I liked football but wasn't good enough to be in the first or second teams—even the third wasn't an option—but I was rather good at running. In fact, I never stopped running. In the summer running was a hero sport. And, let me tell you, I was every inch the hero. One sports day I won not just the 100 metres, but the 200 and 400 metre races as well. Come the long winter months, I was in my element again with *cross country* running. My enjoyment of this sport, which was often used as the ultimate punishment for disruptive kids who'd repeatedly forget their PE kit, marked me out as something of a freak. Cross country may have been the detention of sports but I was in love with it, almost as much as I was in love with my pottery teacher.

Then there was my English teacher who would go to the Six Bells pub every lunchtime, never ate, not even crisps, but drank at least three pints of beer. This made the afternoon English lessons rather terrifying. Red in the face and full of best bitter, midway through an examination of Trollope, he

top Tom and Jean Webster and a budding jeweller, 1960

bottom Dave and I discussing the price of gold, c. 1964

would pitch a large wooden blackboard eraser that would come hurtling through the air toward any one of us speaking out of turn. If said eraser hit you on the head you would see stars. These scare tactics helped us remember passages of Chaucer word for word.

The technique must have worked because English was one of the few O-levels in which I received a half-decent grade. The others were art and religious education, the latter pleasing my mum but was something of an embarrassment to me. My RE teacher, who we nicknamed "Mumbling Moses"—he was definitely Old Testament—had also taught my father who had attended the same school as me some 30 years earlier. If Mumbling Moses were alive today, his religious convictions would probably be in turmoil, what with gay marriage and the re-emergence of the holy wars.

By the time I was 15 I was ready to leave school. This didn't play too well with Mum and Dad. My parents had been supportive of most things I had chosen to do, but deciding to quit school before the age of 16 wasn't one of them. Having managed to graduate out of the comprehensive and on to the *tech*, the assumption had always been that I would stay on until 18 and sit my A-levels. But the mere thought of another two years in that testosterone fuelled, blackboard jungle environment had me reeling in panic. So, to the disappointment of my parents, I made a date with the visiting careers officer.

The Websters had a small house on a small, two-passage suburban development known as Hever Court Estate. The two roads Sandown—ours—and Goodwood—the other—were both named after racecourses that didn't even have the decency to be local. I guess the developer had been a bit of a gambler, very much like my own granddad—more about him later.

Ours was a suburb of a town called Gravesend. Can you hear the ghoulish doom and gloom in that municipal moniker? Much later in life I would go on to write an article about towns with condemned names, one of which was my hometown. Gravesend, due to its 20-mile proximity to London, carried with it a myth that its name was derived from it being the final resting place for those who perished during the time of the Black Death or the great plague of seventeenth century London. Sadly, this is not true. That place was actually Blackheath, which while on the way and just as dark, is not as far along the river as Gravesend. Like all the Thames estuary harbours, downtown Gravesend was a hard and gritty place. Many of the old riverside pubs would, at one time or another, have doubled up as brothels. Bustling with commerce generated from the River Thames—the main

artery for trade into the city of London—everything passed by Gravesend. Further along the Thames in Chatham was the Royal Naval Dockyard, the largest employer in the area.

Dickens lived in and around Gravesend and seemed like something of a nomadic type to us cynical locals. Indeed, if all the "Home to the Writer Charles Dickens" signage was to be believed then Chuck must have had a horse drawn RV to get him around. The horrific, rotting, stinking hulks that were used as prison ships, described so colourfully in Dickens' novel *Great Expectations*, were anchored on the Thames off the Gravesend marshes. We even had a Dickens Estate, which was, somewhat appropriately, really, really rough. Even by Gravesend standards.

Another famous resident of the St. George's church graveyard, was the Native American Pocahontas. Contrary to popular belief the "savage princess," as she became affectionately known amongst the hoi polloi of early seventeenth century London, was not just a Disney cartoon. Pocahontas was brought to London by John Rolfe, her plantation-owning spouse, and paraded around town like some fashion accessory for a couple of years. She must have picked up something nasty in the West End however, because just before the couple's planned return journey to Virginia, Pocahontas popped her moccasins and had to be buried at the historic riverside town of Gravesend.

None of this was of much concern to my parents, of course. They married in 1953 and, after a spell living next door to a riverside brothel, moved out to one of the shiny, newly developed suburbs. At the time this would have been every young working class couple's dream; a house with an inside loo, a driveway and no noisy brothel to keep you awake at night.

Mum and Dad couldn't afford central heating until my brother David and I were in our teens. Until then we would happily get dressed in the only warm room in the house: the airing cupboard. All four of us loved it on the Hever Court Estate however; it had countryside, and the A2! A proper motorway that took you to the coast one way and all the way to London the other. In fact, our house was so close to the A2 that my Dad used to have to vacate our driveway at a rolling 70 mph, in the style of Lewis Hamilton leaving the Silverstone pits, just to join the flow of traffic.

Webster brothers pulling birds in Trafalgar Square in celebration of England having won the World Cup, 1966

Prosperous times for Alfred Webster, King of Northfleet Hill, 1926

Our Dad was a salesman. He had a company car and, when I think about it now, a lot of freedom, and plenty of time to spend being a great father to Dave and me. Dad had trained to be a draughtsman at Henley's, one of the big Thames-side engineering factories but soon after finishing his apprenticeship, he quickly realised that once you had drawn up one blueprint for an industrial pump—and the next one and the next one—each one looked the same. So Dad traded his pen for a classic, Issigonis-designed Mini van full of paintbrushes. The Mini had an unsecured wooden bench in the back for Dave and me, where we sat amongst the bristling, business ends of hundreds of Harris' finest one to seven inch products. We loved it. Our Mum? She was simply the greatest. Access to Jesus through some kind of divine intervention meant she could make very little go a very long way, and we never wanted for anything.

As kids, Dave and I learned that things could have been very different for my Dad and his two sisters. Their Dad—our Granddad—had at one time been rich. Unfortunately, his gains were ill gotten and he lost his fortune as quickly as he had made it. Sometime between the wars, probably mid-1930s, our simple labourer Granddad, who had left school at 13, noticed that the working class liked to gamble with the little they didn't have. With a keen eye for the horses he started running a book from the front parlour of 16 Buckingham Road, Northfleet, Gravesend. My Dad recalls that on Saturday mornings there would be a line of cloth-capped men stretching the length of the street, all waiting to give money to his father in exchange for a mysterious slip of paper. Then, in the same evening, a shorter line would be back to swap the slip of paper for some money. Pretty soon my Granddad had a network of runners visiting all the pubs on Saturday mornings, taking bets and carrying small Bakelite boxes containing three dice. The box had a mechanism that would tumble the dice like an early first incarnation of the One Arm Bandit or fruit machine that became a permanent fixture in pubs, arcades and gaming rooms everywhere.

From what I can gather Granddad didn't spread the wealth around too much. He had fast cars, fancy clothes, a few guns—for sport, not robbery—but didn't allow my Nan to splurge on a joint of meat for the family on a Sunday. He once shot my Dad's pet rabbit, skinned it and made my Nan put it in the pot for dinner. I have a painting of him made at the time. He looked like a character out of the TV show *Boardwalk Empire*; Savile Row suit, gold fob, big Cuban cigar, a 1927 Bugatti. My Dad says he could have bought the whole of Buckingham Road, which despite its fancy name, was actually just a terrace of workers cottages.

Granddad could have easily broadened his portfolio in the manner of his contemporaries, such as the legitimately successful *turf accountant* Joe Coral—who at one time was actually employed as one of his runners. Sadly, Granddad was vulnerable to the stream of bent coppers and other, more heavyweight criminals all determined to help relieve him of the onerous burden of extraneous cash. In the end, this semi-literate man who had, for a while, bettered himself returned to the type of hand-to-mouth existence enjoyed by the rest of the inhabitants of Buckingham Road.

As you can see, Gravesend was an interesting place to grow up. Character building, you might say.

Hard times for Alfred Webster, 1929

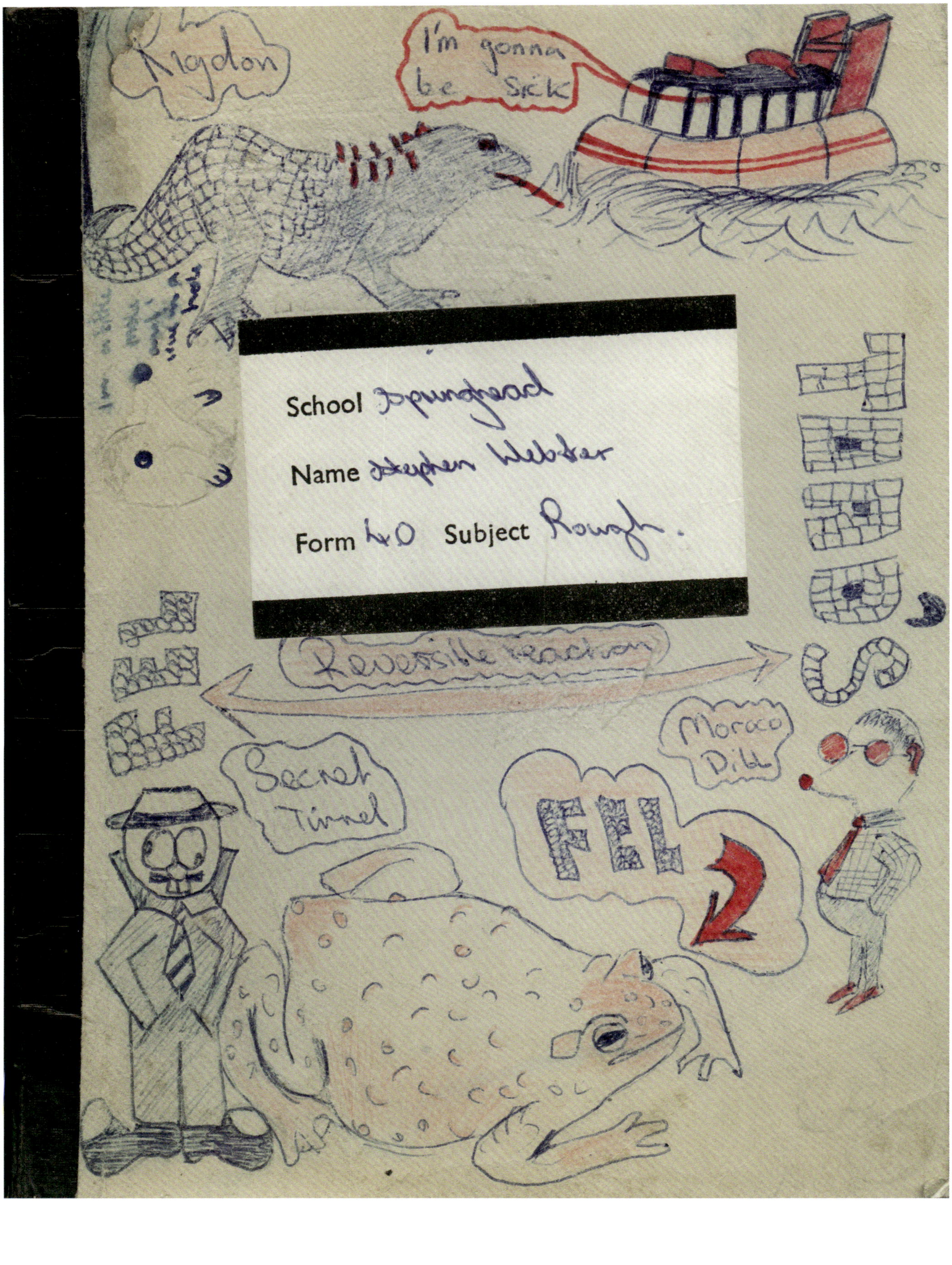

"Rough" being one of the subjects
I excelled in as a student at
Springhead School for Boys

CHAPTER 2

CAREER OPPORTUNITIES

A notice was pinned to the school notice board. For the following week a visiting careers adviser would be available to do just that—dish out career advice. Appointments had to be made. The only appointments I had ever made were with the family GP Dr Martin or our family dentist, Dr Antonovich who had a mean streak, an obsession for amalgam and a complete disregard for pain relief. Before I was 15 all my molars had been ground out, leaving fragile cusps of enamel and a smile akin to a bag of liquorice allsorts. Later in life, when my finances allowed, I worked my way back to a new set of Scandinavian crockery in a more desirable tone. Anyway, the careers advisor had been my first non-medical appointment, which only served to fuel my fear of appointments. Of course, I shouldn't have been worried. After all, I was already vigorously entrepreneurial, holding down three jobs—four if you count Sunday gardening for my Aunt Peg. I had two paper rounds and I did the bottling up in the evenings and weekends at my English teacher's local, the Six Bells. I always had money and I always spent it on clothes. I'm not saying I was the best dressed boy in Gravesend because there were a couple of rich kids in town whose mums bought them everything they asked for, but I was certainly up there with the local peacocks.

Every couple of months, from the age of 14, I would get the train to London and shop all day. I wouldn't eat or spend money on transport whilst I was there because every penny was dedicated to the task in hand—looking fashionable. At first it was Carnaby Street, then I migrated over to Chelsea's Kings Road. After that, Kensington High Street. Because of this, I wanted to be a designer, which is exactly what I told my careers adviser.

He had different designs in mind for me suggesting I consider a modern apprenticeship at the Royal Naval Dockyard in Chatham; boiler making, welding or fitting, perhaps. I wasn't convinced. Boiler making sounded hot and horrendous; welding was surely something you only did when you absolutely had to and certainly wasn't a career option for this fashionista; and fitting seemed a bad fit for me.

Then, a chink of light. A ray of hope. Chatham had an art school: Medway College of Design. What's more, Zandra Rhodes herself had attended the school at the start of her illustrious career in fashion. I told no one except my Mum and Dad that I was going to the open day but as I made my way to the fashion department, it occured to me that I hadn't thought this through.

The head of department met me. Wow. At this point in

top Mrs Webster's boys, 1975

bottom With my best friend, Andy Chevis, 1975

my life I don't think I had ever encountered an obviously gay man but had seen a brilliant TV drama about the famously flamboyant Quentin Crisp, an incredible story of a life that was tragic, but at the same time funny and heroic. This colourful queen chairing my appointment—camp, super friendly and welcoming—reminded me of the self-styled Naked Civil Servant. Medway College of Design, with its classrooms full of sewing machines, had such a different atmosphere to my butch, laddish school; and it had girls.

Continuing my tour with my camp head of department, I happened upon the jewellery department. This place was completely different. Noisy, slightly grubby, lit with orangey, naked flames—some small, others roaring like furnaces—and drills that looked worryingly similar to the torturous equipment favoured by the aforementioned Dr Antonovich. Everyone was working on something made of some kind of metal, either attending to tiny and intricate pieces, or manhandling large, silvery lumps. Later on I would find out that the courses and these workshops covered jewellery and silversmithing, hence the extremes and variations in the scale of the work undertaken. I'd seen enough. I wanted to continue my education in those workshops. I wanted to be a jeweller.

Still, not telling my art teacher—who was not, by the way, the foxy ceramics teacher, she had left by then—I arranged my own interview at the jewellery department. Prior to the interview, thinking that I would need to demonstrate my artistic skills, I sketched as many things as I could. I don't remember all the work I created for my portfolio but one piece was a study of my hand, another some flying mallards and, of course, my favourite subject to draw and paint, some fish; a cod for character and a mackerel for the colour.

Two Brians conducted my interview: Hill and May. The Brians were far more sober characters than the head of fashion I'd previously encountered. In fact, there was nothing remotely fashionable or overtly *creative* about them at all. The Brians were more like normal, corduroy-clad teachers that reflected the lack of connection between fashion and jewellery pervading the times. The interview went well. I was never quite sure if it had been the mallards or the mackerel, or, indeed, the cod, but there and then I was offered a place on the pre-apprentice course, starting in September 1976.

I was so excited that on the way home, by way of celebration, I stopped at the record shop and bought David Bowie's latest album, *Young Americans*. All that night—and for many more to follow—I was a Young American. The Thin White Duke would prove to be a major influence on my life. Ever since I had seen David Bowie—red spiky hairdo, platform-soled, knee-length boots, theatrical make-up, earrings, girly onesie—perform "Starman" on *Top of the Pops* in 1972, I knew there had to be other ways of earning a living; none of which involved fitting boilers, pumps or anything else to do with the heating, down pipes or drainage. As far as I was concerned, that day I had secured a place in the same star-dusted workplace as Bowie and his feather cut wingman Mick Ronson.

Back at school, first thing I did was to tell my art teacher. But instead of being pleased that at least one of his pupils was going to pursue a creative career, he threw a bit of a fit! Why had I not informed him that I intended to go to art school? What was he there for? To be honest, he was right, but I just didn't want to risk anyone else who might try to put me off. My parents, on the other hand, were just as excited as me. They had never seen me so enthusiastic about something educational.

That long summer of 1976 is still remembered as being the hottest since records began. It was also year zero for punk rock. For me, and many other boys of my age, punk changed everything. The first time I saw punks was on the floor of the Goldmine nightclub on Canvey Island—a soul boys' hangout. Jumping up and down on one another's shoulders, the punks looked as though they were fighting not dancing. DJ Chris Hill, the Goldmine's resident who specialised in spinning all the great US imported funk and rare groove, played a track by the Sex Pistols, and the place went mad. I was in amongst it. Chris, on the other hand, publicly smashed the vinyl 45, vowing never to play that "shit" again.

Within a week, gone was my Bowie inspired hair cut—even though I still loved Bowie—and the smooth soul boy clobber. In its place was a leather jacket and skinny, ripped black jeans. Later, the look would evolve into something altogether more colourful involving lime green trousers, a massive red mohair jumper from Vivienne Westwood's Seditionaries shop and plastic sandals from Acme Attractions on the King's Road.

My hair changed almost weekly. My girlfriend at the time, Jackie, was training to be a hairdresser and I was her perfect guinea pig. She usually started with a bleached blonde crop—some of which once ran onto my forehead and denuded half my eyebrow—then applied any dye she could lift from college; neon green, electric blue, shocking pink or scarlet. Whichever one she chose, the result was always eventful. I also had my second ear pierced. This schoolboy was a school leaver. I was ready to be an art student.

The department was split between the people on the foundation course, those taking the three year silversmithing course, the students on the three year jewellery course and us: 13 boys taking the pre-apprentice course, all of whom, without fail, would go on to become apprentices as either jewellers or silversmiths.

Our week was divided up between various practical disciplines; diamond mounting, diamond setting and modern jewellery—both making and designing—and silversmithing. Later, a couple of evenings a week, I took extra classes in chasing and engraving. The plan was that each student would gradually discover where their ability or preference lay, giving the teachers an idea of which apprenticeship they should pursue. Me? I loved them all. I couldn't believe how lucky I was that one of these deft and delicate crafts would serve as my future career but my enthusiasm had to be reined in a little. Mr Hill and I are great friends now and have been for many, many years but back in hot and sticky '76, things weren't quite so harmonious between us. My clothes may have been part of the problem.

During that last, long summer holiday, thrilled and emboldened that the next stage of my education—my life!—was to be art school, I burned my old school uniform and embraced the fashions that I loved so much. I recall that my chosen livery for my college debut was a pair of cherry red, 18-hole Dr. Martens boots, a black leather biker jacket—even though I only had a moped, not a motorbike—and a powder blue, vintage regulation US Air Force jumpsuit.

To my dismay, the jewellery and silversmithing department of Medway College of Design was far from the hotbed of dedicated fashion followers that I had anticipated. The other 12 pre-apprentice boys were a motley crew of the badly dressed. One had a ginger afro, flares and a ginger moustache, like an incandescent version of Jason King from the *Department S* TV series—that look may be Shoreditch hipster these days but back then it was bang out of order. This was profoundly disappointing for me, particularly after having been impressed by the note in Medway College's somewhat slim prospectus that name checked genius fashion designer and colour sergeant Zandra Rhodes, who would have grimaced had she walked into the jewellery department just a few years later and seen the sartorial disasters occupying the workshops.

Actually, my problem was not the other students, or their clothes; more that my carefully prepared first day attire had unwittingly drawn the attention of the teachers. I'm not saying this in any way went against me but I was certainly on their radar because of it.

Back to my friend Mr Hill. He was what you would call a stickler; a God is in the detail type. Later in my life I would discover there is a devil in the detail also, but for now, I needed to learn that in order to be an excellent craftsman/jeweller, being a stickler was key. It took me a while to find my rhythm. Some people are slow and methodical and others are not. Me? I never walked, I always ran. As for patience, I had none. The first 16 years of my life had been spent going at a full-tilt, pedal-to-the-metal pace, which, try as I might, I've never succeeded in calibrating.

Mr Hill taught diamond mounting, a skill that actually applies to jewellery making using *all* precious gemstones and not just diamonds. The mounter makes mounts covering all categories of jewellery—rings, earrings, bracelets etc.—which will be finished or *set* with precious gemstones. If a piece of jewellery is to be made using no gemstones then this craft is called "goldsmithing," which was Thursday's lesson. The long-established techniques employed in mounting are incredibly detailed, arcane, precise and absolutely rigid. There is no room for deviation or, God forbid, corner cutting when it comes to what is the fundamental basis of the craft of jewellery making.

First lesson we were all given a piece of nickel and tasked with making it perfectly square; simple enough you might think, but not when your teacher is eagle-eyed Brian Hill with his × 10 magnified loupe. Against all odds, eventually my piece of nickel was declared the thirteenth squarest thing in the jewellery department; which, I like to think, was also a nod to my dress sense as well as the other lads' abilities. With the first test completed, we could now move on to the real thing, right? I could hardly contain myself, but instead of a gold nugget, another piece of unglamorous nickel was provided, then another and another. I soon found out that piece after unfinished piece of our crude metal work was destined for the scrap pot and, testing my non-existent patience to its limit, it wouldn't be until a year later that any of us started to work with anything vaguely precious.

Next thing on the syllabus was a nine stone cluster. This is a classic style ring, based on a floral, Victorian design, which, prior to the moment when diamonds became a girl's best friend, was one of the most popular styles of engagement ring. The nine stones usually consisted of a central sapphire surrounded by eight diamonds of equal size. In the diamond-mounting class we focussed on the mounts but on Tuesdays our lesson would be spent learning diamond setting, a completely different skill dedicated to securing gemstones into the holes created by the mounter. Simple! Or perhaps not… After the eighth time of being told that one of my holes was out by a thousandth of an inch and that I had to start all over again, even the other boys began to notice that Mr Hill had taken issue with me. It could have been the hair, the earrings or the jumpsuit, I never did find out. What I do remember is gradually turning from eager beaver to somebody all together more cynical. Having fallen way behind the others, and with Mr Hill having become something of a mountain to me, I finally managed, on my ninth attempt, to get my nine holes in a configuration that must have been pretty close to perfection.

The other pieces we had to make throughout the year were: a solitaire mount, a coronet cluster—which is a kind of camped-up nine stone cluster—a line bracelet and a pearl snap. I never had to start one of these pieces again and Brian and I managed to move on from whatever it was that got us off to such a confrontational start—I'm positive it was the onesie. Much later, after he'd progressed to head of jewellery and silversmithing at the latterly re-branded University of the Creative Arts, Brian initiated me receiving an honorary MA before finally he retired from teaching in 2013. To mark the end of his career The Goldsmiths' Guild asked me to write an article about the person who I feel contributed more than anyone else to the UK's jewellery industry. I chose Brian.

There wasn't one subject included in the pre-apprentice course that I didn't love. Toward the end of year, having wholeheartedly embraced all aspects of its creativity, especially the brutality of silversmithing, I told Brian this was the field that I wanted to pursue most. He advised me not to, quite correctly urging me to go into jewellery. I had a gift, he told me. Silversmithing was an industry in decline. I could work well at a fast pace and this would become a valuable asset.

He was right. The jewellery industry, in London at least, seemed to be thriving. Each one of the 13 students were offered places within workshops, either in the Hatton Garden jewellery quarter or the jewellery houses surrounding the high end of Bond Street in the West End. I got an interview at Saunders Shepherd & Co Ltd in London and Brian offered to accompany me. Saunders Shepherd were goldsmiths, which meant that they made gold jewellery with no gems. But for me, the most important thing was the company's location: Hatton Garden, aka jeweller's nirvana, a place that was instantly magical to me.

Until the sixteenth century the Hatton Garden area was part of a beautiful estate inhabited by the Bishop of Ely. That was until a Christopher Hatton, a handsome aristocrat and nifty dancer from Northampton—also rumoured to be Queen Elizabeth I's boyfriend—took a fancy to the pile. There was understandable resistance to bounder Hatton moving in from the Bishop until Elizabeth waded in and threatened to unfrock him. Over the following centuries, people from all over Europe and the Middle East migrated to the city, attracted by the wealth but also the toleration and relative sanctuary to be found there. Many of these migrants brought with them their crafts and skills including, of course, those of the jeweller.

In 1977, when I first started my training in "the Garden" the area was a rabbit warren of jewellers' workshops and allied trades. Each building would contain dozens of setters, enamellers, platers etc., all of them a health and safety nightmare. Sometimes you could taste almonds in the air. This had nothing to do with toasted nuts, the distinct taste being the telltale sign of cyanide used by the electroplating boys. Everywhere were unregulated gas-fed open flames, soldering and melting molten precious metal all day and every day, and despite my endless tasks—being the last apprentice in—I loved every flaming moment of it.

Most days I didn't even get to sit at my bench until after lunch. I, of course, had to run and get this for everyone else, which alone took an hour and a half. Most of the other goldsmiths and employees were Jewish and they all had very specific requirements: hot salt beef sandwiches, bagels with smoked salmon etc., mostly purchased from the Yiddish-speaking Mrs Cohen's Kosher Café, which also doubled up as a gem and diamond trading spot.

Part of my salary—£25 a week before tax—was paid in luncheon vouchers, a book of tickets that could be exchanged for food at various accommodating cafes. My dietary aim being bulk and stodge-based carb-centric in those days, a voucher worth 15p would be enough for two cheese rolls and a bath bun. After getting all the lunches there were the toilets to clean and tools and gold to collect from the suppliers and smelters. Also the daily assay office run, I had to take the tatty Chancellor of the Exchequer-type briefcase to the assay office to drop off yesterday's pieces of almost completed jewellery so they could be tested for gold quality and subsequently hall-marked. As long as the assay master was satisfied that the gold quality was all it was cracked up to be, of course. If it wasn't he would simply crush it. The assaying of gold and precious metal in London has taken place in this same independent way for 700 years, making it the oldest form of quality control in the world.

On the way to and from the assay I had to pass through Smithfield meat market. By this time, I was a fully committed punk rocker, the condition of which was the ability to take the abuse that came with it. On the whole, this was verbal rather than physical—apart from one particularly nasty Christmas Eve attack on Gravesend High Street administered by some well watered, over age Teddy boys—but the young butchers of London's oldest meat market were not known for their tolerance of outsiders, certainly, those types who wore bondage pants. The Smithfield lads had white coats and hats covered in blood. They carried carving equipment and gruesome carcasses and ruddy, sinewy off-cuts. As soon as I entered the Victorian halls of Smithfield, one of them would spot me and the abuse would start. One white coat even threw a lamb shank at me once. Fortunately it missed.

After some months, the dream of a gilded future career started to wear off, partly due to the somewhat limited product range manufactured by my employers. Mostly, we were chain makers and no matter how complex a chain link is, a chain is still a chain. Repetition is the name of the chain game. Moreover, the other long-employed jewellers seemed to have lost enthusiasm for their craft, the general banter—constant put-downs and piss-takes—being no different to that in all types of workshops, foundries and factories across Britain. I was more than able to deliver and be on the receiving end of this badinage but I knew there had to be more glamour in the industry somewhere. I had been to art school after all. The other downside of the workplace was

Jackie and I in matching chains
and sunglasses, 1976

more basic: there was a distinct absence of women.

Now feeling that I had mastered all the skills required to make a chain, I asked my employees about going back to art school to further my jewellery education. Quickly, I was told, in no uncertain terms, that "day release" as it was termed, was not an option. From my very first day, when he'd interviewed me with a pipe in his mouth, I hadn't liked the foreman, Mr Pierce. I soon realised he did everything with a pipe in his mouth—all his teeth on the pipe side were ground down to stubs. Eventually, pleurisy got the better of him, but until his demise he was a miserable know-it-all who had reached his full potential and didn't want any of us achieving anything *above our station*.

There were men above miserable Mr Pierce, I just didn't have access to them, except for when they used the facilities—the same loos I had been cleaning for the previous two years. Luckily for me, even the big boss Tony Shepherd wasn't above going to the toilet, so one day I stopped him on the way in and asked if I could talk to him. Possibly compromised by his state of urgency, he very politely agreed. I pitched my request to be able to return to art school in order to improve my skills, in turn benefiting the company. He not only approved but was also hugely encouraging.

I was over the moon. My enthusiasm for becoming a jeweller was immediately reignited. Mr Pierce almost blew his pipe, furious that I had had the audacity to disturb Mr Tony—as we were told to address him, so as not to confuse him with his father, Mr Shepherd. Pierce really had it in for me from that moment on but I was untouchable! Every now and again, on a comfort break, Mr Tony would actually enquire as to how I was progressing with my classes. Over the years, long after I left S&S, Mr Tony and I remained in touch. He is quite rightly proud of the manufacturing business founded by his grandfather that he managed to retain despite massive changes in the industry and pressure to shift the type of work the company specialised in to the Far East.

Eventually, armed with my Advanced City & Guilds qualifications and a few years experience, I could no longer face making another inch of gold chain. In order to keep my hand in, I would make nine stone clusters and solitaire rings in my lunch break, except on Fridays when all the apprentices would go to the upstairs bar of the Rose pub on Hatton Garden where, bang on 1pm, a grubby looking stripper would take to the stage. The lunchbreak at S&S was 12.30–1pm so I thankfully only ever saw her fully clothed. It was time to move on.

By then I knew that there were different types of jeweller: the classic, the mass producer and, the most recent addition to the community, the designer jeweller. This latter group pursued a more modern approach—the same disciplines and most of the same precious materials but embraced a few non-precious additions. The difference was the design element. This being the late 1970s, there were lots of organic forms to the gold and gem work. Significantly, each designer had a design signature, something that was almost non-existent in the more traditional jewellery community.

One such designer, John Donald, had a small, modern store on London's Cheapside. Despite the bargain basement name this is an expensive *la-de-da* area near St Paul's Cathedral and the Goldsmiths' Hall. I knocked on the door and to my surprise the man himself answered. Donald was a good-looking cove who had been a model and a professional golfer before turning his hand to jewellery. I showed him my college work and he gave me a job. Better still, he doubled my wages.

A different type of jeweller staffed John Donald's subterranean workshop—young people who looked more like the older students at my art school. One of my old teachers also worked there. The pieces they made looked amazing, using techniques I recognised, but each piece like a mini sculpture. Oh, and there was a woman at the bench whom I ended up marrying, but that's another story.

John would give us all a work sheet, on the top of which would be an artist's impression of a piece of jewellery. The jewellers were trusted to interpret the pieces as they saw fit. This approach left a huge impression on me. The

The Brian Ferry years, c.1980

drawings were arty and loose, a marked contrast to the stiff more precise renditions that were—and often still are—the preferred style of the designer jeweller.

Within six months of my arrival at this creative hotbed, John's team of jewellers in his London workshop started to resign, mostly to start up their own businesses, leaving a staff of just three: the foreman, *the blonde* and me. I was still happy, confident and able to tackle, in my own way, every job that came along. Once, I made a brooch for Princess Margaret—a regular client, John moved in those racy circles—and had to deliver it to her husband, Lord Snowdon. When I rang the bell the aristo photographer answered the front door, but instead of taking the package from my outstretched hand, instructed me to go to the tradesman's entrance, where I belonged.

In order to complete my City & Guilds qualifications, I continued art school evening classes in specialised skills such as *chasing and engraving*. Despite the abundance of women at the college, plus the fact that I now owned a cheap but inarguably red sports car, the craft of chasing officially—but not exclusively—involved a hammer, some punches and a cast iron bowl of pitch. These were the tools required to *chase* deep relief patterns into sheets of metal, namely copper and silver. Sadly, chasing is now a dying art.

During this time *the blonde*, Kathy, became my girlfriend. Age 23, she was four years older than me, and had an art degree. I don't remember being old for my years or her being young for hers, but because my life experience at that point had been conducted in jewellery workshops, I was definitely the more experienced of the two of us, whilst at the jeweller's bench at least. As a rule, working alongside a person with whom one is in a relationship should be avoided, but before I knew it, I was living and working with my girlfriend. Despite the odds and numbers stacked against us, we pulled it off.

Soon after my 21st birthday and blind with ambition, it was time to cast off the security shackles of gainful employment and realise my full potential as an entrepreneur. I bought a cheap suit and an even cheaper briefcase, which I still own, and made an appointment to see my bank manager at the Midland bank, Chiswick Highroad branch. My only piece of security? A 12 year-old Triumph Spitfire. My income? Soon to be nothing. Nevertheless, the plan was to try and secure a small business loan for £1,500. Despite what can only have been considered as high risk, the manager was so impressed by my plan that he said "yes."

By this time I had already earmarked a tiny workspace in the Barley Mow workshops further down from the Midland Bank on Chiswick High Street. Every penny of the loan was used to buy timber and other building materials and I worked day and night to construct my 40-square foot working space. This included the business end of the operation—my bench. A bench, you see, is the heart of a jeweller's world. Nearly everything is done at or on, beside or adjacent to the bench. It's the jeweller's equivalent to the chef's kitchen counter and hob. Mine was a bench so solid and free of vibration that even though it has been subject to years of rigorous hammering, we were still employing it until fairly recently, finally letting go when its battle scars no longer suited the rest of the SW aesthetic. That same loyal and steadfast bench is now in semi-retirement, residing in a suburb of North Croydon, where it lives with Mike, my first employed jeweller, who earned the right of ownership having created so many wonderful things at it.

My toil and slog was worth it and within a year I had even paid off my loan. I'm sure that had I needed it and if I hadn't then decided to go and work somewhere cold and faraway, I could have gone back to the bank for more. I wouldn't try and pull the same suit and briefcase job in the bank manager's office these days. High street banks now have a distinct lack of balls and foresight when it comes to new business, preferring to err on the side of caution, rather than take a punt on a budding entrepreneur. That £1,500 was the first and only bank loan I ever managed to secure. I hope the manager at Midland, Chiswick got a gold watch. As things turned out, I could certainly have bought him a nice one myself a few years later.

Yet another ring, or possibly a bracelet? It's hard to tell from here, c.1980

Hands on a bespoke piece
for Christina, 2008

CHAPTER 3

THE GREAT JEWELLERY ILLUSION

The great precious metal price-fixing scam of the early 1980s—which ran in neat parallel with the great horse doping scandal of the same era—meant that I had no choice but to turn my now, highly-skilled hand to some of the worst paying and unsatisfying work the jewellery industry had to offer. This came in the form of *illusion setting*. To gain access to this work, I signed up to a low rent, mass production factory in Hatton Garden.

For those who will probably never stoop to the depths of illusion setting, let me explain. The illusion occurs when a diamond setter takes a very small, very poor quality diamond, places it in a small hole drilled into the top of a ring, which, under normal circumstances, would be considered disproportionately large for such a modest stone. This is where the wizardry of the illusion setter is engaged. Using a highly polished, razor sharp *setting tool*, the nine karat gold surrounding the stone is systematically cut away, each cut leaving a mirror finished facet in the metal. The illusionist, in what can only be described as a frenzied attack—because time is of the essence here—cuts scores of similarly polished facets until the demure diamond and the surrounding heavy metal appear to be one massive, blinging jewel.

Enhanced even further by the magus-esque smoke-and-mirrors lighting effects of the jeweller's window, it's quite understandable that the thrifty shopper will take one look and consider the finished product to be not just highly desirable but also an exceptionally good buy. The problem, of course, is that over a short period of time on the finger, the magic, literally, wears off and the true dimension of the original stone is revealed. Sadly, by then, the unsuspecting bride-to-be has an engagement ring with a small rock and has committed herself to a man, who even at this embryonic stage of their relationship, has proved that he is quite prepared to pull a fast one on her. At one time, illusion setting was cited as one of the main causes of early divorce in the UK—the technique being very much a British thing, the continentals would never entertain something as contemptible. The work may have been a little more palatable to the setter had it paid better, but at just 13p a stone the process represented a crime to everyone involved.

One particular morning, feeling poor and wanting to get a full day's work in, I recall making an early start, which, back then, was around 6.00am. This happened to be a Saturday. I liked working Saturdays because most of the other small workspaces in the Barley Mow studios and workshops located in Chiswick were empty. The Barley

Mow, so-called because next door was, you guessed it, an old pub called The Barley Mow. Legend has it that Oliver Cromwell, or at least some of his New Model Army stayed at this hostelry on their way to fight it out with the loyalists during the English civil war. The fable is most likely to be the beer talking, the vinous invention of the locals, but it is true that Chiswick was the first stop for the old Ironsides after a day's exhaustive marching out of London; which is a long hike. Chiswick, in case you weren't aware, is remote Zone Four on the tube map.

On this Saturday morning, I laid out all my tools, rings, dust bag and, of course, the stash of *barely there* diamonds and got cracking. Eight hours later and suffering with something akin to arc eye—aka "welder's flash"—due to the brilliance bouncing around my bench peg, I had illusion-set 60 stones and earned myself a grand total of £6.80. Less than £7.00 for an early start on a cold Saturday. Admittedly, things were different in 1980 but even Fagin was offering upwards of a tenner for basic scallywagging. It was time to rethink my career path; jewellery was fast losing its lustre.

CHAPTER 4

NORTHERN EXPOSURE

David J Thomas was a well-known, London-based jewellery designer who would occasionally give me some half-decent work for some half-decent pay. One such day, David called me into his studio in Old Church Street, Chelsea and told me of a job opportunity. From the outset the offer appeared reasonable and lucrative. Then he went and spoiled it all by throwing in a killer caveat "… but you will have to move to Canada."

I'd only been abroad twice, both times to Torremolinos on the Costa Del Sol. The first time when I was 14 and under the jurisdiction of my Auntie Peg, so I wasn't 100 per cent sure if I liked it or not. The second time, I was 18 and went with my girlfriend. This time my fears were confirmed: I didn't like *abroad*. It was hotter than hell. I acknowledged that some people enjoy that kind of climate but being boiled wasn't for me. What's more, everything else was just shit—the smell, the food, the hotel, the *discoteca* and worst of all, the other holiday makers who all seemed to be loud, northern and bright red. I would never have gone to places that attracted a crowd like that at home, so I definitely didn't want to hang out with them when I was on holiday either. The fact was, I was happy in London. The capital had it all—music, fashion, edge, damp and, best of all, great people, from diverse and interesting backgrounds. If *abroad* was so great, why did everyone come to live in London?

David Thomas persisted with his proposal. He had found a Canadian retailer through whom he could distribute his work. The problem was that Canada, in a bid to protect its own manufacturing output, imposed prohibitively high—35 per cent—import duty on things made abroad. For a country still featuring the Queen's head on its currency, this seemed to be rather bad form. David explained that as long as components were sent from abroad and Canadian labour was used to assemble the parts, then everyone was happy and the import duty fell to a more commercially viable 10 per cent. This was where the plan became cunning; he needed someone familiar with his work embedded in Canada.

At this point in the story, it's probably worth noting that the Cold War was still waging chilly political and military tension between the East and West and talk of placing people behind the lines in any capacity—even an artisan like me—was bound to be subject to scrutiny. As a consequence, much of what follows was carried out covertly—John Le Carre style. A third person entered the equation; let's call him "The Canadian." I had never met a Canadian before. From what I could surmise after meeting this mysterious type, they seemed to resemble British people, only with much better teeth and a stronger build, but sounded like Americans; who, without exception, they hated to be mistaken for. They used the term "A" (eh) a lot at the end of a sentence as though constantly looking for answers, so a conversation with a Canadian could be never ending. They also drank weak tea. It was all very confusing.

This particular Canadian had a small store and workshop in Western Canada. He was a gem collector or "rock hound" as they call them over there. He traded important mineral specimens, sourcing them himself by travelling to the world's most remote and dangerous places. He'd then bring the stones home and sell them to collectors and museums all over the world, but mainly to Americans.

As a rule, wherever valuable gem specimens are found, gem materials suitable for use in jewellery are also in abundance. The Canadian—or the "Quiet American" as I later referred to him—started buying up this gem material and had hired a German goldsmith, based in Canada, to fashion the gems into jewellery. Now tired by Wolfgang the German's creative repertoire, the Canadian—Mike Ridding was his name—had come to London to hire a jeweller from the more classical English school. Which is where I stepped in.

Kathy and I, new romantics,
Banff, Alberta, 1983

The offer on the table was a cool $30,000 a year—I'd never even heard of a salary with multiple noughts at the end of it! Being the unworldly lad that I was back then, I presumed a dollar was a dollar and had no idea that some dollars were worth more than others. Actually, the Canadian version was trading at approximately 20 per cent less than the almighty American dollar at the time and there were roughly three Canadian dollars to the pound. It turned out I was even greener than the famous American banknote.

Once I had mentally prepared myself to make the transatlantic leap, I managed to secure a position for my then long-term girlfriend—and future wife—Kathy. In the end, with still a lot to learn, we shook on the deal of a joint salary of $36,000, plus moving costs.

Before I actually committed to the move, Ridding had offered to fly me to Canada, to take a look at my potential new home. It was February. My Aunt Peg, who had once been on a cruise and had a man friend from Guernsey called Johnny Brigard—so had seen a bit of the world—alerted me to the fact that Canada has a harsh winter and insisted on buying me a winter coat. Like most young English people, I had never felt the need for a proper winter coat before. They were expensive and hardly a vital fashion item unless, of course, you count the mod parka with its rabbit fur merkin around the hood. I ignored my aunt's grave weather forecast, shopping for style first and insulation second. What sort of mad man actually dressed for warmth? Kitted out in a kind of New Romantic-does-après-ski get up, I made my way to Heathrow and a plane bound for Calgary.

We landed at night. Met by Ridding, we drove for two hours to his home in a snowy place called Banff, Alberta. I was aware that the terrain had changed from flat to hilly during our journey into town but nothing could have prepared me for the view from my window when I woke up the next morning. Everything was white. Deep, heavy-looking white. The heavy snowfall of '64 back in the UK had nothing on the scene outside. Bright white Rocky Mountains in every direction—just like the mural of the Swiss Alps in Hilda Ogden's *Coronation Street* parlour.

After breakfast we took a wander down Banff Main Street. I quickly learned that Main Street was the only street with shops. Banff was just a snow-covered, one horse town like the ones I'd seen in *The Magnificent Seven* or *Hang 'Em High*. All 100 yards long, we soon had Main Street covered.

The first building I remember was a bar called The King Eddy—part of the King Edward Hotel—which had swinging, saloon doors. After I moved into town, I tried to go in for a beer, only to be met by a drunken cowboy who took a long look at me and called me "a fucking fruitcake." The rest of Banff consisted of restaurants, fur and souvenir shops, ski hire shops, the Hudson Bay Company and a jewellers called Silverhorn, where I would be working. The workshop was in a shed in the Riddings' garden.

At the end of that first day, I saw a sign that should have set alarm bells going in my head. Something to the effect of "please place all unwanted food waste into the bear-proof bins provided." Bears? Where the fuck was I? Canada would eventually become a word that would make me shudder. Not just because of the face-numbing cold that greeted us that first day, or the bears, but for darker reasons.

That night the Riddings took me to a restaurant called "Caribou" next to the Rocky Mountain railroad. The Caribou was/is famous for its prime rib; a massive steak, served bloody with a big lump of juicy fat on one side for added flavour. A jacket potato was the recommended accompaniment. The steak was amazing—it could have fed my whole family and it melted in my mouth.

Next day we went cross country skiing on long skinny skis and in footwear that resembled Victorian workingmen's boots with a protruding square sole. Once I stopped going backwards and mastered the art of forward propulsion, I actually really enjoyed it. It was like winter running. The physical endurance was such that after some miles, despite it being minus 20, my faux winter coat had to be unzipped a little. I later found out that this could be one of the most dangerous things to do if you are out in the wilderness on your own. If you get really hot and sweaty and remove a layer, when you stop or slow down for any reason the sweat freezes and very quickly you're in big trouble. That day I had company, the Riddings plus a young woman goldsmith Margot and her partner Natasha. They were to become really great friends during my time in Banff.

As a kind of test, I spent the following five days in the *dry* shed, alongside Margot and the self-taught Wolfgang. I was given a Malaya garnet, which I had never heard of, which seemed a lot less abrasive than the only other garnet I knew of at the time: Alf Garnett, the ranting, working class Tory off the TV show *Till Death Us Do Part*. No one told me what to do with the exotic-looking stone, so both my jewellery-making skills and my talent as a designer were on trial. I dug deep into my creative reserves and came up with a kind of modernist version of a traditional cluster ring, which, of course, I could've probably made blindfolded. Under the scrutiny of Wolfgang and Ridding, both of whom stood close by, I hammered, stretched and soldered my Malaya garnet masterpiece with as much confidence as I could muster. After setting the centre stone, the diamonds and polishing the finished ring, the piece was whisked away and placed in the shop on Banff Avenue.

After my return to London and some sleepless nights evaluating my trip, I decided that I had to give it a shot. Kathy quit her job at John Donald and I gave notice on my studio in Barley Mow, Chiswick. We stored the few bits of Habitat furniture we owned in my parents' loft and carefully crated my precious hi-fi system and vinyl record collections, which, apart from clothes, were the only things we took with us to Alberta.

Skiing home, Lake Louise, Banff, Alberta, 1982

Back in Banff we hit the snow running. Our first accommodation was the basement of the Riddings' house. It was May, so very much still wintertime in the Rockies. I knew what to expect, but the cold was a huge shock to Kathy. She had always been a good sport and very supportive, but wasn't exactly charmed by the frozen mountain village we were now calling home.

The day after we arrived Ridding had me back in the shed. Kathy could do the settling in but I needed to get back to that bench to make up for lost time and the expense of two economy flights and the shipping by sea of my records and stereo. Luckily for him, I was a sleeves-rolled-up, nose-to-the-grindstone kind of a guy. Never a question asked, just get on with it. For the next three years I worked long after everyone else had gone home. Ridding was a gem adventurer, disappearing for weeks on end to places where gems came from: Brazil, Namibia, Afghanistan, Pakistan, Tanzania and Mozambique. For a chronic dyslexic like me the names of the countries he visited were bad enough but the gems he brought back with him were just impossible to pronounce: tsavorite, tourmaline, tanzanite, morganite and, always the crowd-pleaser, kunzite. But while I couldn't spell them, I could make a nice ring with them.

Returning from such trips, Ridding would empty another pile of juicy gems on my peg and give me *carte blanche* to make what I wanted. It really was all down to me. Ring after ring, piece after piece, always striving to be more and more original. No matter where Ridding had been on his Indiana Jones gem hunts—despite the more accommodating climates and exotic locations where gemstones are sourced, the actual mining areas can be quite grim—he would always say that it was "great to be back in Banff." "The most perfect place on earth to call home," he'd say. Of course, I knew this wasn't true. I had lived in London and he hadn't.

18k gold, peridot and citrine heraldic earrings, an example of my work for Silverhorn

My time in Banff was by no means perfect but I give full credit to the experience I gained through working alongside Mike Ridding. He introduced me to a new world of gems and the opportunity to express myself through my jewellery in a way that wouldn't have been possible had I stayed back in London. Still, I was working in a shed, with no running water or toilet, in a community so provincial it didn't even have the one horse small towns are supposed to have. I had cabin fever and it was no laughing matter.

Rather than admit defeat and move back to the UK, I stayed on in this frozen hell. Not wanting to let myself or Ridding down, I buried myself in gold and gems. Abnormal working hours became normal and I would work later and later into the night. What had started out as real enthusiasm gradually turned into grim obsession.

Looking back, yes, the town and the conditions were challenging but that's what living in a ski resort is like. People are there because they love to ski or hike or snowshoe or whatever else can be done at 7,000 feet. The town doctor was in Banff because he was a skiing injury specialist. The dentist and solicitor were big backcountry skiers also. In an effort to become the skiing jeweller, I did take up downhill skiing and in order to keep fit—and thin—I continued cross-country skiing and even tried racing. The endurance and solitude of this sport suited me and I discovered a sport similar to the long distance running I had enjoyed so much at school.

Once a week, mostly at the request of Kathy, we would escape the cabin and drive to the city of Calgary to do some shopping in stores that sold stuff that wasn't designed specifically for the great outdoors. The oil town of Calgary is located on the prairie with streets that howl with a wind chill factor even colder than bitterly cold Banff. *Wind chill* was a term we had never heard before moving to Canada. It's when something balmy like minus 25 degree Celsius can turn to a seriously nippy minus 45 degree Celsius. We were advised by the announcer on *Wild Rose Country*—the Alberta state radio station—to "wrap up warm" as that day the wind chill was going to take us to the despairing depths of minus 60 degrees Celsius.

Each morning after the news on the radio, full of trepidation, we would listen out for the gruesome forecast and exactly how long it would take to freeze exposed flesh. Sometimes this was just ten seconds. *Ten* fucking seconds. The locals thrived on it, urging every day to bring a new low, a colder temperature and a more viciously biting wind chill factor. Kathy and I hated it.

Every couple of months, to find relief from the big freeze, we'd get into our new convertible Triumph TR8—aka officially the worst car British Leyland ever cobbled together—on a Friday evening and drive right through the night—14 hours straight—across the Rocky Mountains. A British ragtop in the frozen Rocky Mountains of Canada. What was I thinking? During the night's long journey, the snow would gradually fall away revealing the ground below, something Banff would only see towards the end of May. By the time we hit Kamloops in British Columbia we even saw fruit trees and flowers. Colours! Not just white! We started to feel elated and alive. Arriving at English Bay, Vancouver at around 6am we would park up and stare at the sea I missed so much during my time in landlocked Banff.

After muffins and coffee at the English Bay Hotel, Vancouver would come alive. First thing was a visit to Trish from Liverpool for haircuts. In Alberta there were only two male hairstyles: mountain man or mountain man with mullet. Trish was only just behind the tonsorial curve with London trends—or at least we thought so at the time—and with the elaborately quiffed Spandau Ballet number one in the UK charts that week, her scissors got to work on my new, New Romantic style. The rest of the day was spent shopping for clothes, records and British food. I forgot to mention that Vancouver, back then, was more British than Yorkshire. With the exception of the largest Chinatown outside of China and San Francisco, the whole place was like a Great British pavilion and we loved every inch of red, white and blue bunting. Plus, the weather like the British beer they served in the bars, was mild—the most accommodating climate in Canada.

Back in the Banff shed, beavering away again, we started to develop a strong following for the bold and colourful designs that had become the Stephen Webster signature at Silverhorn. I was getting more confident about working with the big coloured gems, which were the starting point and heroes of all the pieces I designed and made.

No craftsman likes to be interrupted in the middle of

Crossing the line with the 118 boys,
Banff 10k race, c.1981

working on a piece, especially during the high intensity period of setting a valuable stone, but such trivial matters never prevented Ridding from frequently phoning the shed from the store to request that I come over to meet a client. This meant a ten-minute walk and wrapping up in multiple layers to prevent exposed flesh from freezing in ten seconds flat. Waiting at the store would be a couple of enthusiastic tourists who had been told that there was this crazy British master jeweller behind the scenes who liked nothing more than to design pieces of jewellery on the spot, right there in front of them. Said Brit would then retire back to his wooden shack.

Life had become all work and very little play. Not much skiing either. I didn't even have time to notice that I was changing. The happy-go-lucky youngster who'd once embraced life as it came and enjoyed pretty much all of it, was becoming less enthusiastic, less embracing, more angry inside and out. The things that I had loved, including being a jeweller, skiing and my girlfriend, became chores to be endured rather than enjoyed. Still working ridiculously long hours at the shed/bench, life started to close in, shrouded by a wintry gloom as heavy as the snowfall outside.

Almost a year after we had moved to Banff, my parents and brother came to visit us. It was the end of June 1982, officially Canadian summer time but, true to form, the day before the family arrived we'd had a huge dump of snow. The month of June had been unseasonably warm in England that year so, taking this into account, the family had packed almost no thermally appropriate clothing at all and certainly no fur. The family's transit to Canada ran smoothly until the last push through immigration where my brother Dave's appearance quickly alerted the authorities.

Since I had last seen him Dave had started sporting a wardrobe heavily inspired by the popular cross-dressing entertainer George O'Dowd, better known as Boy George. Amongst the fashionably-forward of 1980s London, a 6 ft 10 in guy—including the additional height achieved with a spiked, two-storey Barnet and rag extensions—wearing a dress, distressed jeans, 18-hole Dr. Martens, a sleeveless jerkin and the compulsory eye liner, may have gone unnoticed. Not so in Calgary, home of the world's largest rodeo.

So concerned were homeland security by my brother's look that they requested backup from the Royal Canadian Mounted Police. As if Dave's appearance alone wasn't enough to provoke a thorough strip search, upon opening his luggage the officers came across some intimate ladies' apparel. My brother was as surprised as they were having no idea that my mum, after maxing out her own baggage allowance, had packed a few extra pairs of knickers and bras into his. After almost two hours of the immigration officers' grilling, the Mounties escorted David into Canada along with a note that assured any police that might stop him—a highly likely occurrence—that he was no cause for concern to the God-fearing locals.

The reason why the Royal Canadian Mounted Police were so interested in my brother upon his entry into Calgary, 1981

opposite Watercolour and ink artwork of Wild Rose Thorn Cuff

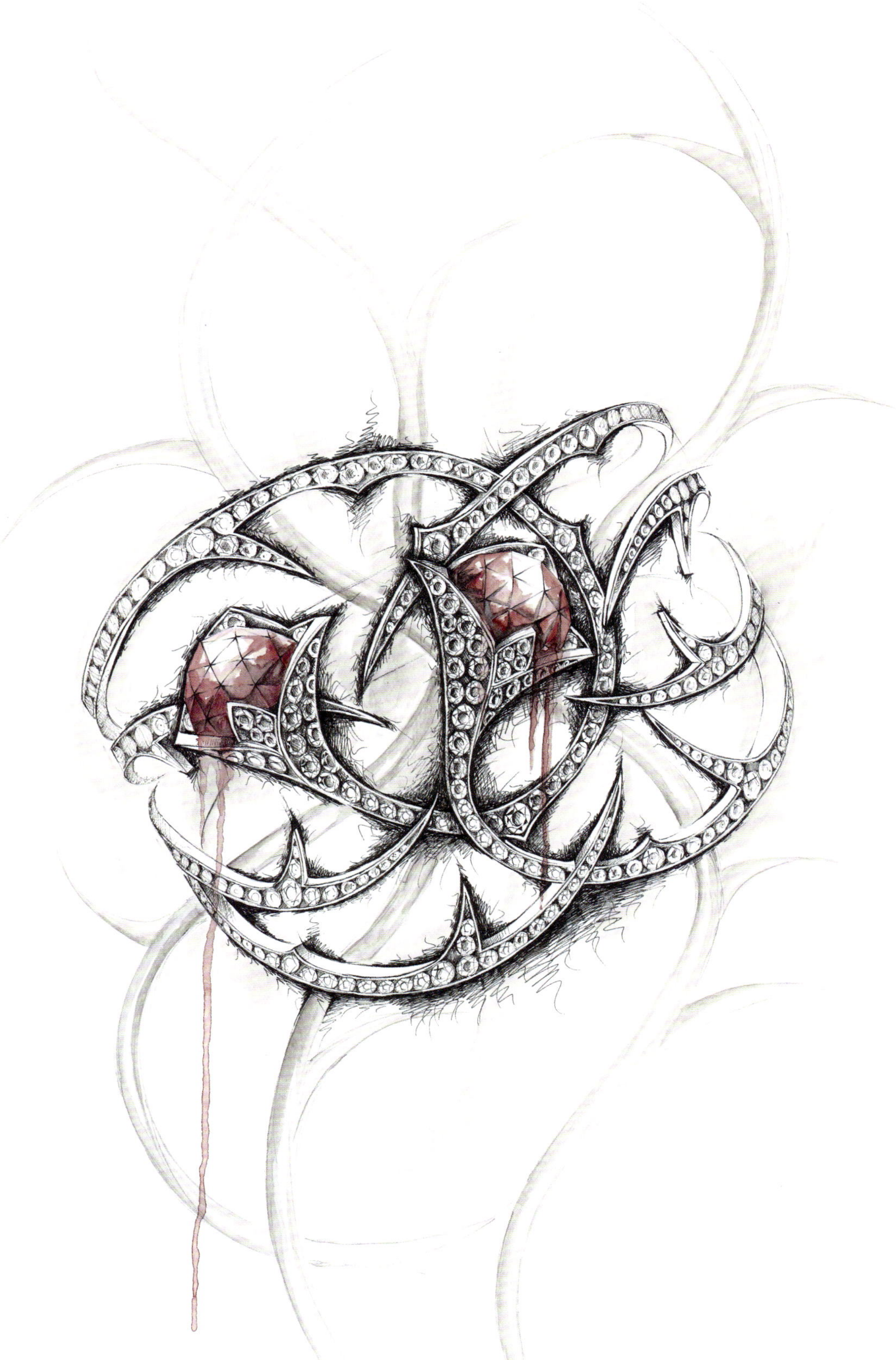

My first Harley Davidson, outside
my home in Santa Barbara

CHAPTER 5

CALIFORNIA DREAMING

After having lived in Banff for three years, someone called a gathering at the King Eddy. Those in attendance included my doctor, dentist, lawyer and some local bar staff, all of whom had become our closest Banff friends. However, I'd had enough of them and they'd had enough of me. There was no longer room for me in the mile high hamlet. I was being run out of town. Kathy and I packed up our—mostly thermal—clothing, my vinyl record collection, sold the furniture and the totally ridiculous convertible Triumph TR8 car—this purchase was a sure sign of just how much my judgement had been affected—and made our second transatlantic move, this time back home to London.

The journey to the UK was easy compared to the one back to good mental health. I had reached a really low point. Despite having received psychological counselling for the entire year prior to leaving, I was still clinically depressed and, to make things even worse, nurse, a certified anorexic.

I'd been seeing a Banff psychiatrist who only visited town for a day, once every three weeks, divvying up his attention to all the crazies in the village; which, from what I recall, included almost all of us. I'm not sure what the others were suffering from other than the obvious malaise of living in an isolated, freezing-cold town of 3,000 ski bums but most of the mobile shrink's treatment seemed to consist of a brief diagnostic consultation followed by an over-prescription of brand name drugs. These doses were at least enough to keep us sedated and generally out of trouble for the three-week stretch until his next visit. In my case the drugs definitely didn't work. They made my eyeballs shake which was a real challenge when trying to perform my role as a jeweller working with high value and delicate, precious materials. To make matters more miserable I also gave up drinking. I was that ill.

Back in London, our respective families were happy that we were home but the first few months weren't easy. We took up the generous offer of a room in a friend's house in Fulham. The owner Roy was renovating the house, so we made a deal: I would help with the heavy lifting, including converting the attic, and when it was finished I could use the room as my workshop. The teamwork definitely had a therapeutic effect on me; we even played squash together, a sport I had taken up in Banff.

I was now seriously anorexic and was barely eating at all. Despite being skeletal I would drive myself even harder on a subsistence diet of next to nothing. It didn't matter how little I ate, the next day I would try to eat even less. Having started the morning with an hour long run, the ultimate goal would be a totally food-free day. Every mealtime was a panic-stricken nightmare and the pressure on Kathy was unimaginable. Despite my destructive, best efforts she stood by me and—between meals at least—we had a reasonably normal existence, although for the life of me, I can't imagine how.

Once the attic workshop was complete I got stuck in and started making some individual pieces using a few beautiful gemstones I had bought from Mike Ridding before leaving Canada. I can only remember one piece from that particular period—a cocktail ring, the centre stone of which was a hot fuchsia pink tourmaline from Afghanistan. Yellow gold, diamonds and fuchsia pink. A gaudy, eye-catching combination. A conversation piece. Within a few weeks, I had mounted all the gems in my stash and began doing the rounds of jewellery retailers in London. I won a few compliments for my craftsmanship and unique designs but there was precious little to suggest that I might be able to pay the rent from any business generated on my own.

Reluctantly, I made a trunk call to Banff. Mike agreed to buy all the pieces I had made on the condition that I would return to Banff for a while, taking up my old position until the ski season was over. This was, of course, a loaded proposal because the ski season was never over—once, it had even snowed in Banff on my birthday, 13th August. Stupidly, I agreed. Kathy was very upset. She had taken a job working for Kutchinsky, a well-known Knightsbridge jeweller and could no longer just up and leave. I flew off with the promise that I would eat properly and come back in much better shape, physically and mentally. Of course, this didn't happen. After almost three months in Canada, Kathy came to meet me at Heathrow airport. My cheeks were hollow and my stomach dangerously concave. She burst into tears. Incapable of making good decisions around food, I had let us both down really badly.

There was one unexpected ray of light resulting in my return to the Canadian cold, however. The Riddings had decided to sell the business in Banff and move their operation to Santa Barbara, California. They asked if we would join them there and help establish a business similar to the one they had just unloaded. After a split second, we decided that California was an offer too good to turn down.

I flew out and started building a small workshop, adjacent to the property where the new, sunnier Silverhorn jewellery store was going to be. Once the benches and general carpentry work were complete, I made regular drives along the Pacific Coast Highway to Skid Row, the jewellery quarter of downtown LA, opening accounts with the tool stores and the diamond and bullion dealers. This was 1985. Skid Row was, and still is, downtown and since the 1960s, the largest display of human misery in the US. With a population of around 40,000 homeless, mentally ill, drug and alcohol addicted or just plain forgotten people, walking around that part of town with a pocket full of diamonds was risky. It was like entering an episode of my mum's favourite cop show, *Hill Street Blues*.

Eight weeks after landing, the workshop was up and running and I started making stock. The store, located on Coast Village Road, Montecito, the getaway of choice for Hollywood's royalty, opened soon after. Pretty soon we were part of the landscape. There are probably many great places to establish a modern jewellery store but being right in the heart of a ghetto for the rich, shallow and self-obsessed takes some beating.

Kathy quit her job in London and moved over. Our new home overlooked the Pacific Ocean and came complete with an avocado orchard. To go with my new home and my Los Angeles lifestyle, I bought my first Harley Davidson. Riding it 90 miles along the coast from the dealership in San Luis Obispo, with the SoCal wind in my hair, I thought I was Peter Fonda.

After establishing the business and recruiting a couple of local goldsmiths I began, for the first time, to develop *a look* with my designs. Prior to this, partly due to the way I had learned to work—mainly around individual stones—each piece was treated as a one-off. Now the enthusiasm for the work we were producing gave me more confidence to institute an aesthetic that I enjoyed rather than always trying to accommodate the clients' often-questionable input.

18k white and rose gold handmade rings from the *Cloth of Gold* collection; left: with green tourmaline; right: with chalcedony, sold to Elizabeth Taylor, 1984

I was also keen to employ as many jewellery techniques as possible. This meant that my contemporary style became very detailed with a vintage feel. The technique I used the most was hand engraving, inspired by a pocket watch my father gave me—Dad having been gifted it by his own father. With a silver outer case that was completely engraved, it had aged beautifully, giving a soft, embroidered effect. Not having any specialist affiliated craftsmen on hand, I had taught myself a variety of skills that I probably wouldn't have bothered with had I still lived in London where almost every skill was on tap within the jewellery district. I was impatient and never once doubting my ability to turn my hand to something new, I taught myself.

One of the threads that ran through my designs was a hand engraved rose and thorn vine pattern, which I first saw as an illustration in an old Japanese etching. It was old and modern at the same time. I still love it. One such group of rings was set with large, cabochon cut stones such as chalcedony, chrysoprase and amethyst—still one of my favourites, a lot of purple for the money. The chalcedony was a deep lilac, much deeper in colour than normal. I designed and made a big white gold ring and, just below the setting edge, next to the stone, I inlaid a strip of rose gold. On this I engraved the rose and thorn pattern and in the centre of each engraved rose I set a small, round diamond. All the pieces were for stock.

One day I received a call from the second store we'd opened in the famous Biltmore Hotel on the beach at Montecito. Elizabeth Taylor had just bought that ring! The actress was known to have vivid, lavender-coloured eyes and she thought the gem was a good match. I had never sold anything to a celebrity before. I needed to tell someone, so I phoned my Mum.

My Mum and I had always been close, never in a stifling way but she had always been there for me. When she thought I was gay, despite my protests to the contrary, she just wanted me to know that it was all right with her. When she thought I might be a drug addict—again, I wasn't—she wanted to know what she could do to help. When David and I were young, in the late '60s, mum would drink the water that she had boiled the cabbage in because she knew, quite rightly as it turned out, that all the goodness was left in the

My Mum and I, Santa Barbara harbour, 1986

pond-like water. Other mums didn't do that. Like many women of her generation, Mum had worked in an office straight after leaving school at just 15. Unfortunately, because she'd contracted TB and was bedridden for two years, she felt she had missed out on those vital years between 16 and 18 when girls really had some fun. She was absolutely beautiful, the spitting image of her idol—and my new client—Elizabeth Taylor. At her untimely funeral, Mum's sisters told David and me that there was a line-up of boys all ready to sit by the bed and talk to her during her convalescence post-TB. Eventually, my dad was the lucky fellow of that group.

About two years after moving to Santa Barbara my mum was diagnosed with breast cancer. It was horrible being so far away and the 6,000 miles between us might as well have been a million. Like everyone in the States I only had two weeks holiday a year and couldn't drop everything to be there for her longer. After weeks of treatment my mum and her fighting spirit pulled through—she seemed to have beaten it. As a treat, I insisted that she come to stay with us for a few weeks and was over the moon when she agreed. It was so brilliant to have her in California and show her what our life was like beyond the postcards and weekly telephone calls. To this day, I am so grateful that she made the trip because a few years later the cancer returned and this time she didn't stand a chance. Those days with mum were magical. We drove in our gold coloured sports car all the way to Reno, to the Sequoia National Park and up to San Francisco, the Napa Valley, Carmel and back along PCH1 to Malibu and Hollywood. She loved it and was happy for us but I could tell she knew we weren't happy in ourselves.

Life was definitely easy in Santa Barbara. I had the chance to develop my design style and I got to meet lots of interesting people. I took home a good salary, drove a metallic sports car with gold magnesium wheels and rode a bright red Harley. The only thing that tainted that gilded, shiny-hubbed existence was my ongoing battle with anorexia. After such a long struggle and so much therapy, I no longer knew what it would be like not to be thinking about food and how I could avoid it. Living where we did—image besotted California—only fed my phobia. After all, nothing else was feeding me. At meal times, not taking any notice of what the other guys were eating but watching the women push lettuce around their plates and then declaring themselves "full," I did the same. My unhealthy diet meant that I wasn't great to be around and Kathy threatened to leave me almost every day. The drab persistence of my condition had taken its toll. We didn't laugh much anymore.

Finally, after four years in California, Kathy gave me an ultimatum; either we go back to London together or she would go back on her own. I didn't want to go. I had everything I needed in America. London would be the same, only this time, because we were now fully *SoCal*, we would feel the damp even more. Still, I couldn't let Kathy go. She was the difference between me hanging in or, quite possibly, being hung out to dry.

I gave in. We returned in 1989, four years after pursuing our Californian dream and nine years after having originally emigrated to Canada. Now we were back where we started.

To familiarise ourselves with London again, we started looking for a flat in Chiswick, the exact same area that we had called home back in 1981. I even set up a workshop again in The Barley Mow studios, just as before. Very quickly, orders started to come in for my work from Silverhorn in Santa Barbara. Virtually all the designs had been my concepts and even though they now belonged to Silverhorn, the team out in California didn't have anyone

18k gold broach, graduated green enamel carved peridot angel fish, pavé diamonds, 1995 who could make them like I could. This made me nostalgic. With an ocean and a continent between us, I was now able to acknowledge that Silverhorn was a truly amazing store. Brand new to an area and completely unknown to anyone—unless they happened to have visited Banff—within three years of trading the pieces were flying off the shelves like hot, low-fat, gluten, dairy and sugar-free cakes—did I forget to mention that Santa Barbara was the food fad capital of the West?

In London I hired a young chap called Lee Buckingham. I had informed my old art school that I was back in town and the lecturers contacted me to say they had a new graduate who reminded them of me when I was his age. When we met I could see what they meant; it was his attitude, he seemed impatient. Lee wanted to live in the States so we made a deal that he would work for me for a year or so and I would then introduce him to my old boss. I don't remember exactly what I paid him but I do recall that it involved a lot of bacon sandwiches and probably not much else.

I was impressed by Lee's dedication. He was keen to study, had good ability and applied the skills he learned in the workshop very quickly. Significantly, Lee was my first employee and played an important role in the foundation of the business we have today. Sure enough, just as he'd planned, Lee moved to California after one year with us. I also hired the next recruit from my old art school. His name was Mike and 23 years later he is still with me.

The following few years were spent flitting between two studios: London, where I'd make one-off pieces and complete orders for Silverhorn on a freelance basis, and Santa Barbara. Our business ran like this: we would make a collection of pieces then I would secure the cheapest flight to Los Angeles to assume my position in the studio at Silverhorn. Back in Cali, I would sit with clients, go through the latest gem acquisitions Mike Ridding had made and then return home. I'd say "hello" to the wife on the way back to the London studio and then start the whole trans-Atlantic farrago all over again.

A few momentous things happened during those unsettled, peripatetic years. Our daughter Amy was born, my brother David left the security of his long-term employment to come and work with Mike and me, and American Airlines wrote to congratulate me on having flown a million miles with them. Taking these things in order of priority, Amy being born was, of course, the most amazing event. Fortunately, it coincided with me being in the country, too. Almost immediately, Amy's crib moved into my studio rig, along with the noise, flames, chemicals and bad language and she soon became one of the boys. Like a good drummer, I could perform almost any function required to make jewellery using my hands, at the same time maintaining the slow, steady rhythm required to rock her cradle with my foot, keeping baby sound asleep. It was bonding.

We moved out of the small studio in Chiswick to a comparatively plush workshop below the London shop of modern master jeweller David Thomas, the person responsible for fixing up my Banff job. Having made the move to the countryside, David no longer required the space. Kathy worked part time in the shop upstairs, little Amy preferring the atmosphere of the workshop. With my brother Dave now working with us it was a bonafide family affair; albeit a family where the father/husband figure would fly off to America for up to six weeks at a time. As selfish as this appears, it was the only way I knew how to provide a steady income stream for us.

I had become nomadic and I liked it. I even liked the flying, especially while smoking was still allowed in the back of the plane. The minute wheels were up, it was 11 hours of inhaling one's duty free haul, scrounging as many miniatures as the hostess and the flight time would allow. I will never forget receiving the million-mile notification from AA—that's American Airlines, by the way, not Alcoholics Anonymous, who didn't write until much later. I remembered learning at some point that the moon is only a third of a million miles away and thinking that I had flown three times that. I had turned the life of a jeweller, traditionally conducted at a bench no more than four feet square, into something more panoramic. Because I took the

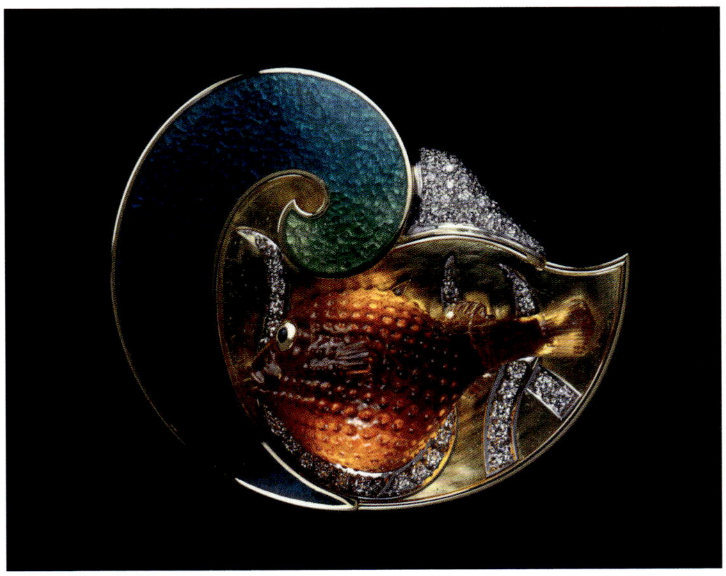

18k gold broach, graduated blue enamel carved citrine puffer fish, pavé diamonds, 1995

same route regularly, I became familiar with some of the air hostesses. When one of them proudly showed me a picture of her grandson, I knew the days of the Pan Am beauties and mile high club had now been firmly relegated, like Pan Am, to history. I blame the unions.

My brother Dave held things down back in London when I was away. Dave had started his career in jewellery two years after me, working for a retailer in Black Fen, a suburb of Bromley on the South Circular. Dave had applied too late in his year and missed his chance to take the same course I had completed at art school, so had settled for *Plan B*. Fortunately for him, on the first day of term, one of the students had a personal crisis and wasn't able to attend. So, as first reserve, Dave got the call. A week later he joined the dynamic duo of Brian and Brian to pursue a career as a bench jeweller.

When I returned from the US, the first person I asked to join me at Chiswick was Dave. His then, long-term life partner—or "girlfriend," as we used to say—wasn't sure about this arrangement. Probably correctly, she assumed that I would be off to America again at any moment, leaving him high and dry. After a couple of years, Dave and the life partner split up and he came to work with Mike and me. The three of us made a great team; hard-working, highly-skilled craftsmen.

Shortly after Dave joined, I received another call from my old art school. Did we have room for a graduate? This time the hopeful student had a different skill set: wax carving. All of us could carve wax to a fashion but this guy Arman was on another level—more a sculptor than a jeweller. Arman, originally from Turkey, worked for us part-time while he finished his degree. Later, I sponsored his permanent move to the UK. Arman's skills meant I could design more sculptural, figurative designs. Pooling our own and the talents of various out-workers in London, the pieces we were producing incorporated almost every technique that could be employed by a modern jeweller. We were maximalists, not minimalists.

This was the most exciting time for me. Whatever fanciful design I came up with on my sketchpad, we could make. Dave and Mike and I could persuade gold to do anything we wanted it to do, while Arman could carve it in the most intricate detail. Samantha Johnson, the gun engraver with whom we worked, could decorate a surface of metal so intensely that gunsmiths such as Purdey or Holland & Holland would commission her to engrave shotguns with pictorial decorations. These would sometimes take her months and cost tens of thousands of pounds to complete.

The enameller we used was Fred Rich, the best art enameller of his generation. Fred was so busy with his own commissions that he would normally refuse to enamel other designers' work but he made an exception for us, partly because I was so pushy but also because he liked what we were doing. One of the most successful collections we produced featuring Fred's work was called *Jungle Fever*, its pieces all replicating animal prints: snakeskin, leopard, tiger and zebra. There was nothing in fine jewellery quite like it.

I would also make regular trips to meet with the stonecutters and carvers of Idar-Oberstein in Germany. My favourite one-of-a-kind pieces, usually brooches, would sometimes require the skills of up to eight different specialists. Still, 90 per cent of the work was ending up in Santa Barbara—it was as though a big jewellery-eating monster was consuming it as fast as we could make it.

Back in the 1980s, jewellery shops in the UK were still places where men shopped for women, but in Santa Barbara the reverse was happening. In LA, female "jewellery junkies" were our regular customers and the pieces we made for the Californian store were bought, almost exclusively, by women, for their own pleasure. This meant that pieces were more bold and adventurous; women knew what they wanted, they knew their own style and what would work with their wardrobes—and boy, did they have wardrobes. Strange to think how a more conventional jewellery shop back in the UK would operate, predominantly selling things for women but staffed by men who really only knew how to serve other men. For this very reason alone our jewellery had no place in such a stuffy, outdated environment.

In fact, the retail jeweller's network appeared to have little or no place for a creative element from the industry.

Outside my studio with good clients Doctor and Mrs Grant, and one of my goldsmiths, Santa Barbara, 1986

18k gold graduated enamel python
head belt buckle, 1997

Back in the 1980s only two business models were allowed. High street jewellery shops like Ratner's catered to the masses with product lines so poor that the only thing precious about them would be the men behind the counter. Gerald Ratner's retail empire fell faster than Pompeii after he made a candid, after-dinner speech in 1991, admitting that a pair of his gold hoop earrings had no more value than a round of Marks & Spencer prawn sandwiches "but probably wouldn't last as long." At first I thought this was an expose of M&S' over-inflated prices but people were genuinely angry. They had been made fools of. Even though he'd actually given the same talk many times before, Ratner's words were considered cocky and controversial and hit the headlines big time. Soon after the story broke, the value of the Ratner group plummeted by around £500 million. Gerald Ratner was fired in 1992.

The other options included the county jewellers, actually more high and mighty than the high street retailers they sneered at. These rural or market town jewellers were usually independently owned businesses, often passed down from generation to generation, resulting in owners who were about as progressive as the flat earth society and whose single drive in life was made with a nine iron.

Top of the pile were the jewellers of London's West End. Here there was some potential, with the likes of Asprey and Garrard, and a few others stocking a little designer jewellery. Customers who frequented such establishments would include a few Brits but largely consisted of the influx of American, Middle Eastern and Asian visitors to the capital.

There was, we discovered, another opportunity for designer-makers to show off their wares: The Goldsmiths' Fair. Held annually, over one week, in the Livery Halls of the glorious—and what appeared to be solid gold—Goldsmiths' Company in the City of London, the fair was established to provide a showcase for small jewellers and silversmiths' businesses to connect directly with the public. Just what we needed. We applied to the selection committee and, amazingly, were selected first time around. The subsequent show in 1992 was an amazing success. From the opening day we received a hugely enthusiastic response to our work—the same work that we were selling in the States. And just as in the US, clients were mostly women, purchasing pieces for themselves. This was a massive boost to our confidence and my ego. It had always bugged me that my designs had never sold in my own country. To this day, over 20 years later, some of those first clients are still friends.

Later that same year, I received the honour of being granted "Freedom of the Mystery of the Worshipful Company of Goldsmiths" along with "The Freedom of the City of London." Now a qualified, working jeweller of some 15 years experience, much later I would be called to the livery and become a Liveryman. The aforementioned freedom is not automatically granted. The achievements of the individual are considered at the annual meeting of the membership committee, made up from members of the guild and the prime warden. It is a great honour. It goes without saying that my parents, who were invited to the ceremony at Goldsmiths' Hall and later at Guildhall, were very proud to have a son who, despite all the odds, seemed to have been accepted by the establishment.

I was thrilled, of course, not least by learning that amongst the list of privileges that came with my new-found city freedom was being allowed to take my sheep over London Bridge on a Sunday and being given the option of a silken rope should I ever find myself sentenced to death by hanging. Probably the only modern benefit is that I can now never be arrested for being drunk and disorderly within the City of London, a dispensation that, unfortunately for me, does not extend to the West End.

One of the other jewellers bestowed his freedom on that day was the MD of Garrard. Over a ceremonious cup of tea and a slice of cherry cake, Richard Jarvis and I introduced ourselves to one another—now this guy really was "establishment." Some months after the successful Goldsmiths' Fair—my proof that there were clients for my work on this side of the pond—and armed with a couple of my one-of a-kind brooches, I made contact with Richard.

I rode to the appointment on my imported Harley Davidson, a souvenir from my life in California; not really considering what would be appropriate attire for an

18k gold, tortoiseshell print enamel, citrine carbunkle and diamond suite, *Jungle Fever* collection, 1997

appointment with the MD of the Crown Jeweller, custodian of the Queen's official jewels. Richard was the nice guy I had chatted to at the freedom ceremony, he had been interested in what I did and me. He wouldn't care how I was dressed, would he?

Well, people who turn up at Garrard on a motorbike, no matter how fancy the machine, are directed to the tradesman's entrance along with the dispatch riders, couriers, suicide cycle jockeys and foot messengers. Generally, these people would not be asking to see the MD. Nona White, Richard's personal assistant came to see what all the fuss was about. I could tell by the look on her face that what she really wanted to say was "there has obviously been some terrible mistake. Thank you and goodbye." She asked for some ID. I broke out my motorcycle driver's licence. Thoroughly intimidated now, I followed Ms White and was shown to Richard's office. I later found out that on my arrival, Nona had told him that there was "a long haired man in leather waiting to see him, who appears to have an appointment... could it possibly be one of those awful strip-o-grams?" Now diverted to his stone buying expert Nabil, I removed from my pocket the brooches I had brought along to show. Nabil studied them, said they were very nice, "not really for Garrard," but to please keep in touch. A polite brush-off, I reckoned. I rode away on my bike.

A few months later I came back and did it all again. This time Richard saw me personally. I could tell he was really impressed. The pieces were "exquisite," he said; the craftsmanship outstanding and the designs really progressive, but he still didn't feel they were right for Garrard. I revved up and left but did as I was told and kept Richard in touch with what I was up to. Finally, a couple of years later, my persistence paid off.

I was a workaholic. My self-imposed regime was brutal. More often than not, I'd work six, ten to 12 hour days a week, with a 6am run beforehand. I had been running and racing long distances throughout my time in California and continued back in London. I had run my first marathon in 1987—the Portland Marathon—in two hours and 50 minutes. What's more, I'd enjoyed it. A few marathons later it was London, 1991, in two hours 47 minutes. I really enjoyed that one too. I was placed in the top 1,000 out of 25,000 runners. Running and jewellery were my life. I didn't have much room left for my family.

Kathy and I split up. We had been through so much together; some amazing travels and adventures, but so much of it under the shadow of my destructive psychological problems and ten-year battle with an eating disorder. Amy was now four and more than ever, I was determined that I was going to make time for her, even if it was too late for our marriage. Faced with the grim prospect of being yet another weekend dad, I wanted to be more of a present figure in my daughter's life. So, when an opportunity came up, I took it.

Amy's school had sent out a letter to parents asking if they could spare time to give specialist classes as volunteers. I signed up and every Tuesday, for two years, taught art to Amy and her friends. It was brilliant. I would roar up on my Harley after lunch break and get stuck in with 30 four to six year-olds. Later, Amy told me that she loved having her dad as the teacher but hadn't wanted to share me with her friends. I believe that extra time together was crucial and the foundation for the incredibly close relationship we have today. Now grown up, Amy has become a very creative and talented artist herself.

Amy and I, 1997

CHAPTER 6

THE CLOTH OF GOLD

By 1993 I had worked for Silverhorn, on and off, for 12 years. As much as this was a gravy train, I was now keen to broaden my horizons. I'd heard that a new, annual jewellery show had started up in Las Vegas and I told the Riddings that I planned to exhibit. Somewhat freaked out by the prospect of me going it alone in the US, they agreed to take part with me on board. Leading up to the show the Webster team went into overdrive. Between the three and a half of us, we made as many pieces as we could possibly produce—the *half* being Arman, who was still finishing his art school degree. The resulting collection comprised of one-of-a-kind brooches, the first *Crystal Haze* pieces, one-off cocktail rings and the Art Deco-inspired bracelets, earrings and pendants that had started to develop into another collection. After flying to Santa Barbara to make some last minute tweaks, organise our props and run through the checklist of essentials needed for setting up a booth at a show, we set off for Vegas in a rental truck.

The road from Santa Barbara to Vegas takes you through the eastern sprawl of Los Angeles toward the low desert and then across barren terrain. Somewhere around the halfway mark lies the truck stop and Borax mining town of Barstow, made famous in Sheryl Crow's song, "Leaving Las Vegas": "Used to be I could drive up to Barstow for the night, find some crossroad trucker to demonstrate his might. These days it seems that nowhere is far enough away. So I'm leaving Las Vegas today." Not being truckers or hookers—or indeed, Sheryl Crow—the bars and restaurants of Barstow weren't for us. To this day, it is the only time I have witnessed someone eating meat and potatoes with white gravy whilst smoking.

The next route highlight is the blink-and-you'll-miss-it town of Baker, "home to the world's tallest thermometer." As a rule, being the world record holding anything in America doesn't necessarily acknowledge the achievements of the rest of the planet. "The world" just means as far as the naked eye can see. That said, the thermometre in Baker is pretty tall, not high enough for the temperature to be any lower than it is on the ground, mind. I've never seen it below 95 degrees Fahrenheit, and it's often into the 100s. After t he Baker burner, it's the home stretch to Vegas.

During daylight, your first sight of Sin City can be disappointing. In the context of the massive landscape surrounding it, the fabled Vegas "strip" doesn't seem to be particularly long or impressive but by nightfall it's a different scenario; every twinkling bulb, fluorescent neon and dazzling

David threatening a large 18k gold cuff, *Cloth of Gold* collection, 1998

laser beckoning you to misbehave. I was rather innocent back then.

We stayed at a resort, more like a motel than a hotel, it was also a non-gambling establishment, favoured by the Hasidic members of the jewellery community. Most importantly it was cheap. Over the years the resort—it still exists—has let itself go a little. When one of my staff members stayed there seven or so years back, halfway through the first night he was rushed to ER and was treated for severe bed bug bites. I remember walking the strip at night on that first trip, lapping up the spectacle. All-you-could-eat global buffets for $9! Start in Italy and work your way through to China, maybe stopping off for a taco and a steak inbetween. Drinks were free of charge if you played the slots, which we did, and the line to get into any nightclub looked like a cast call for a porno film. I loved it.

Our booth at the trade show was 10 × 10 ft. Manned by the four of us, it felt crowded even before anyone else attempted to enter. We were one of 3,000 other exhibitors. How would we ever be noticed? If you are exhibiting at a show and you have something different, word spreads and people start to notice. Our problem wasn't the product but the pricing; our pieces had been made in England, shipped to California and then doubled in price.

Walking around the show I started to get an idea of the massive size and diversity of the US industry. We won praise from other designers, who all wanted to know who our designer was. Ever cautious, I still didn't feel ready to make the break however. Even though that first year was a commercial disaster, our lack of success in Vegas made no difference to me because Silverhorn bought all the pieces that we had shown.

One of the things I noticed about other designers, especially Alex Sepkus who most inspired me, was that they had a defined, signature *look* that flowed across their collections. My only signature was colour, which, because it changed so much and styles wildly varied, wasn't really a signature at all. Until that point, I'd prided myself on the fact that I could be all things to all customers: organic, geometric, detailed, metallic—you name it. The common element in my work was gems, which were all different colours and qualities and my Deco grouping was the only collection with any sort of recognisable signature at all. Furthermore, I had no idea about *merchandising* or how a buyer needs to see some cohesive theme in a designer's work in order to define his style. My signature, I decided, had to be achieved via the choice and finish of the metals, which on the whole stayed the same, rather than the choice of gemstones, which were so diverse.

top One of a kind engraved 18k gold necklace, with buff top amethyst, pavé diamonds and a huge South Sea pearl, *Cloth of Gold* collection, 1998

bottom 18k gold, purple enamel brooch, set with intaglio carved green beryl and pavé diamonds, *Thorn* collection, 1999

I'd always loved hand engraving and was convinced that reviving this traditional technique could become my signature. I designed a brand new collection using diamonds and gold, with no coloured stones at all. The collection was full of big volume pieces, very organic in style. I kept Samantha the gun engraver busy for months, scratching out elegant patterns like those she applied to Purdeys side-by-side shotguns. The entire surfaces of the gold items were detailed with intricate patterns, some floral, some regal, some Paisley. The look was beautiful, like a rich, golden tapestry. We were excited—it seemed we had found a signature in metal.

The next thing we needed was a name. Rather than spoil it by coming up with something myself, I went to my friend David Sinclair, a super smart, long-lunching, professional advertising copywriter; a latter day Mad Man, no less. Having noted from my brief that the engraved gold pieces were reminiscent of a golden tapestry, David came up with an inspired name for the collection: *Cloth of Gold*. He'd swiped it from a historically factual meeting of monarchs, which had ended up being a lavish display of cock-waving between the King of France, Francis I and Henry VIII, in a field near Calais some time in 1520. This was a three-week bonanza so lavish that it nearly bankrupted both treasuries and consequently became know as "The Field of Cloth of Gold," which sounded a good party to me.

We now had a signature collection with an appropriate name, steeped in history and with a story to tell. The *Cloth of Gold* collection was launched at the Vegas show the following year and the response was fantastic. Gold was very much *en vogue* so people loved the detail, the effects of the engraving, the diamonds and the pearls. Later on, unable to resist the temptation, I introduced some coloured gemstones and even more colour via the old jewellery technique of enamelling.

Once again, we drove to Vegas for the show. The collections received a great reaction. Our dazzling, signature *Cloth of Gold* pieces were the perfect addition to the more individual gemstone pieces and the more provocative

Polishing. The grubby side of the jewellery business

Crystal Haze collection. More and more, people were coming by just to see what was going on at the quirky Silverhorn booth. Eventually, a direct and confident chap came by with several lackeys in tow. He was in a hurry, but slowed down long enough to let us know he was from Neiman Marcus and would we contact him in Dallas after the show? I was beside myself. This was the big time. Neiman Marcus' founder Stanley Marcus had written the book on retailing and his stores across the US defined the concept of luxury shopping.

Despite the positive reaction but again due to the inflated prices—we sold very little. Once again the paucity of orders made no difference to me as Silverhorn bought all my pieces.

CHAPTER 7

ANASTASIA

The red in my bed

One of the perks of being a Freeman of the Worshipful Company of Goldsmiths was the Freeman lunches at the Goldsmiths' Hall. I took my dad and my brother David along as guests to my first one. It was an older crowd, a reflection of the ageing population of the august institution, but across the sea of grey hair and grey flannel I spotted a beautiful, young woman. I don't remember if we made a tactical manoeuvre of the dining placement but, rather miraculously, we found ourselves at the same table. Her name was Anastasia—"call me Assia"—and her luncheon partner for the day was her colleague at Spink, the medals and precious metals arm of Christie's auction house. Having learned to speak English in Manhattan, Anastasia sounded like a New Yorker but was actually a Russian. None of the Webster boys round the table had ever met a Russian before. We were intrigued, especially yours truly.

For years I had been an avid reader of all things connected to the Cold War. This was probably due to a combination of punk propaganda and my cousin Carole's Trotskyite friends, a politically charged group of actors that included Julie Covington and Gary Oldman. This seductively subversive bunch was a big influence on me—especially after a few joints and some cheap plonk,Trotsky red, of course. Open to their ideas, I'd developed fashionable left wing leanings and a romanticised view of the Communist state, despite having read of the drab, tragic demises of infamous fifth column traitors such as Kim Philby, Donald Maclean, Guy Burgess and Anthony Blunt. After this group's widely publicised defections to the East—with the exception of Blunt who decided to come home rather than see out his days deprived of cricket, Gentlemen's Relish and *The Telegraph* crossword—I was fascinated by the revolution and the plight of the Russian working class. Heavy conversation topics for a Tuesday lunchtime with a bunch of poncey jewellers, perhaps, but there you go.

Anastasia from Leningrad—soon to be returned to its pre-revolutionary name of St Petersburg—was an exotic, intelligent and clearly well educated creature, more than happy to talk to my father about the war. Her granddad, it transpired, was a heavily decorated war hero. I pushed her on spies, defectors and life behind the Iron Curtain. My brother tucked into his lunch.

By the time the pudding arrived, I was smitten. It was love at first sight. The only hurdle in the way of our romance being the fact that Assia was married to a Wall Street risk analysis expert who had relocated from New York to

London. She told me her story. Armed with an art history degree from NYU, Assia had secured a job in London as Special Projects Manager—part of which was to organise the first ever art sale held by Christie's in Moscow—but she hated London because she thought everyone was so unfriendly. Really, all Assia wanted to do was to move back to New York where she had been living for the previous five years since scaling the wall in 1990.

Assia didn't strike me as a Communist but then again she could have easily been a spy. She told us that she spoke five languages and her American English was free of any trace of the Russian accents made familiar to us via villainous Bond girls. She had a few Bond baddie traits but this Anastasia sounded a bit more Disney than sexy Soviet.

After lunch we exchanged numbers. Assia was planning a trip to California to visit her parents who had recently moved to Loma Linda from Leningrad. Her father had been recruited as a medical physicist, bringing with him his experience and knowledge in developing the cutting-edge cancer procedure known as proton dosimetry treatment. Guess what? I was also planning a trip to Los Angeles as well! True, because I was forever planning trips to LA. I said I would call when I arrived to see if she had time for dinner.

Now I couldn't stop thinking about her and as soon as I landed, I called. We arranged to meet in Santa Monica and boldly I booked a hotel room. Assia turned up for our tryst with a male chaperone. We had a nice dinner and went to some club but it wasn't quite the intimate dinner date I'd had in mind. Back in London, Assia and I saw each other a few times. One day she called me to say she was leaving her husband. I didn't know it then but when Assia says something, she means it. The next day she walked out on her miserable life in London and returned to New York alone. I didn't think I would see her again but kept in touch by sending her a postcard every week; always the same card, an image of Fragonard's *The Swing*, a cheeky Rococo painting, the original of which hangs in the Wallace collection, housed opposite my old Stephen Webster shop on Manchester Square.

Eventually I flew over to see her; and to help decorate her new apartment, buy her a bed and hang up her new curtains. Unfortunately for me, I didn't get to draw the curtains or sleep in the bed. She made me stay in a hotel. In total, I visited her in New York on three separate occasions, each time hoping to get lucky. Maybe this Assia character was an old fashioned kind of a girl? In fact, she had a boyfriend.

A year later, still obsessed with her, I asked Assia to join

top A startled looking Assia sporting two crystal haze cocktail rings, and a diamond-set Borneo Collar, c.1998

bottom Deep undercover, Assia and I outside the Hermitage, 1997

me in Las Vegas where I was going to show my work at a show as part of the Silverhorn collection. She agreed and I later found out she had also finished with the boyfriend. What happens in Vegas, stays in Vegas, they say. We were no exception to that rule.

The next few weeks were spent agonising over our next move. Certainly, I couldn't really go and live in New York because I had a business and a daughter to consider but could Assia possibly give London another shot? After all, in New York she didn't have a career to speak of and was reduced to cold calling businesses, trying to sell art by the yard. She sold nothing. This was our dilemma; either she would move back to the UK or we would write off Vegas as a one-off fling. She chose London, moving over to live with me in my tiny loft off the Holloway Road. The previous plush and spacious London flat Assia had shared with her former husband had been in Kensington—she reminded me of this regularly—and she made no attempt to disguise her shock upon seeing her new neighbourhood for the first time.

Those first few months were really difficult. Assia wasn't working and being stuck in gloomy Holloway was driving her crazy. In the end, using all my contacts, I managed to get her an interview at Garrard, which was just starting to encounter the first round of rich Russians visiting its store. Although Assia's gift for languages was considered useful, the position didn't work out for her. The head of the department became very threatened by this smart, Russian beauty and moved her over to the watch department at Asprey, Garrard's sister company at the time. Assia hated it but it got her out the house.

Recovering from mental illness of any kind takes time and a lot of therapy. By the mid-1990s I'd had about 12 years worth, keeping up the psychiatry sessions long after having moved back to London. I was no longer depressed, more just a functioning anorexic. The people closest to me had got bored of trying to change me so when it was becoming obvious that I wasn't going to completely fade away they simply turned their attentions to more pressing matters.

My deep-seated fear of food remained—some people have a battle with the bottle, mine was with the BBQ, all that outdoor man-cooking with fire being the meal I dreaded the most—but for the first time in over a decade, I'd noticed that I had actually started to feel hungry every now and again. Still, I couldn't shake off that last semblance of control and indulge myself. Until I fell in love with Assia, that is.

People who grew up in the Soviet Union, I quickly learned, tended to not be fussy with food—the concept of a vegetarian, for instance, was beyond Assia's comprehension. Obviously, I kept quiet about being not only a veggie but also someone with profound food issues. The first dinner Assia cooked for me was beef stroganoff and when it was put on a plate in front of me I knew that there was no turning back. I tucked in to the first meat I had eaten for 14 years and it tasted great. The trouble was, my system wasn't used to digesting anything more robust than a pulse and extreme cramps were the price I paid for dinner. The transition to healthy eating definitely didn't happen overnight but that hearty, Russian stroganoff was the first step toward turning a food nightmare into something a lot more nourishing.

A popping jay and an ex-communist at the launch of Stephen Webster for Hamilton Inches, Beauchamp Place, 2000

My name in lights at The Hard Rock Casino and Hotel, Las Vegas, 2003

CHAPTER 8

SURFING SOLO IN THE USA

Having exhibited at the Vegas jewellery show for several years I had made friends with quite a few of the other designers. The one I became closest to—and for whom I had the most respect—was New York-based Alex Sepkus. Alex's business partner Jeff is pretty much my best friend. Alex and his wife Dange originate from Lithuania, which means they both speak Russian. From the minute they met Assia, at the first show she attended, they adopted her as one of their own.

The three of them—Alex, Dange and Assia—having seen how unhappy I had become exhibiting under someone else's name, encouraged me to cut the cord and go it alone. Apparently, everyone now knew that Stephen Webster was a designer of skill, imagination and repute but only had access to me through Silverhorn. Having to buy through another retailer didn't work for the majority of retailers who were well aware that this convoluted way of selling added a substantial mark up. Insecure as ever, I was nervous to make the break, after all, Silverhorn was my only guaranteed income stream. I had an ex-wife to consider and a small child to feed. Assia was having none of it. We would be fine.

I made the call to break the bad news to the Riddings, owners of Silverhorn. Sadly, after 17 years of giving it my all—in Canada, in Santa Barbara and working as a freelancer for many years after that—that call was pretty much the last time Mike Ridding and I spoke, until we met in an elevator in 2015!

Things began to move fast. We applied for and secured a booth in the design centre of the JCK jewellery show in Las Vegas. There was also another smaller, more select, boutique show starting up. Billed "Couture" it was to become a rival to JCK, taking place in Phoenix, the week before Vegas. I really wanted to be a part of Couture's debut but it was full.

As it happened, there was a guy called Craig who worked for the UK Department of Trade and Industry. Somehow Craig, in his capacity as the man from the DTI, was responsible for progressing and assisting the needs of British jewellery industry talent and had put together a group of four jewellers who were looking to export. I wasn't one of the selected four. Then somehow—and I can't for the life of me remember how—I was.

Craig was aware of the oversubscribed Couture show but as well as being a government official, he was also a politician, a smooth operator with a brilliantine finish and slid us all in to the Couture show under the guise of a trade mission. We were "Brand Britain," heading for Phoenix

and then onto Vegas. With two US shows ahead of us, as well as the prestigious Baselworld show in Switzerland, Stephen Webster was suddenly going global. Then, with approximately seven months to go before we launched, Assia broke the news that she was pregnant.

I don't know what panicked me more: the financial implications or the inevitability of sleepless nights ahead. The ever-resourceful Assia had already thought the latter through; we would get a Russian-speaking nanny and we weren't to worry about the expense. She would source us a live in nanny who would cost very little. I wasn't convinced but I agreed. What else could I do?

By this time, Assia was working full time for SW between Duke Street, Mayfair and our new concession in Harrods. We did hire another stern looking woman to work in the world's most famous department store but because it was open for trade seven days a week, manning the concession was clearly a two-person job. The aforementioned woman possessed a unique Victorian dental arrangement, not so much teeth as a combination of mixed nuts, mostly peanuts but also a few cashews and Brazils. Despite her colouration being very close to the shade of the famous Harrodian green, she was never a comfortable fit in the newly refurbished, fine jewellery room. Finally, the poor woman quit, leaving us to muck in on the shifts. Eventually, after having to cover on Boxing Day whilst suffering chronic food poisoning from a bad batch of Christmas Day oysters, I could take it no more and threw in the towel. Some years later we returned to Harrods better prepared, efficiently staffed and with a more aesthetically pleasing set up.

Coming to terms with the prospect of becoming a father once again, I calculated the arrival date—it fell smack bang in the middle of our debut at the Vegas show. No worries, I said. After all, how many babies arrive on the exact day they are meant to?

At this point, Assia was still very much a Russian passport holder, most definitely not the most useful travel document and always guaranteed to cause a long and drawn out experience at US immigration. So, in the December of that year, when my divorce finally came through, we decided to get married. Documents in hand and three months pregnant, Assia and I legged it to Marylebone registry office and our shotgun wedding was planned and executed within a week.

Choosing to tie the knot in vibrant red—a less than subtle nod to her communist roots—Assia looked every inch the radiant, pregnant bride. Our immediate family and two close friends celebrated the union with a suckling pig feast at Peg's Club in Covent Garden—the same meal that Assia's parents Stan and Tatiana had enjoyed at their wedding in Leningrad many years previous. It was meant to bring good luck to the marriage I was told!

We honeymooned in Brazil and while walking around Rio, looking for inspiration, I bought a few specialist tattoo magazines. Then, back at the hotel, I started drawing jewellery pieces inspired by some of the beautiful work I'd seen over the magazines' pages. Pretty soon, with Assia busy sunbathing, I became obsessed by the complex, thorn tattoo-inspired armband I was designing. It was going to be diamond set and the edgiest piece of jewellery ever. I was perfecting the way the thorns would weave together when Assia demanded that I down pens and join her outside. Unable to stop thinking about the pattern, I started drawing on her tight, round belly, its delicately stretched skin providing the perfect canvas for my intricate design. As soon as the holiday was over I was back in the workshop, all of us working on our first *Tattoo Thorn* collection.

Leading up to Vegas, I shed any creative inhibitions I may have harboured. We would be premiering our *Thorn* and *Rock Star* novelties along with the expanded *Cloth of Gold* and *Crystal Haze* collections along with some more, one-of-a-kind pieces. The centrepiece was to be a Tahitian pearl necklace, its design a diamond-set thorn motif. Inspired by the dark pearls and gothic feel, I called the piece *Thorn Noir*. A few days before flying off to the shows our baby still hadn't arrived. We even went to St. Mary's hospital in Paddington for an induction. Still nothing. Finally, after two days the nurse advised us to go home and sit it out.

Shotgun wedding at Marylebone Registry Office, 1998

I can't say that it wasn't a little strange flying off to Vegas in the knowledge that I would probably be absent for the birth of my child. Assia was, of course, bitterly disappointed that she hadn't been able to give birth before I left but was totally cool with me going; she had her mum and her best friend for company.

First stop was Couture Phoenix. Held in a beautiful resort hotel, the event was intimate and intense. Buyers were pre-screened and asked to attend on an invitation-only basis, weeding out the riff-raff, window shoppers and tyre kickers. Whilst all the other exhibitors had nicely designed, enclosed booths, the *British Pavilion* consisted of four small coffee tables, one per designer; none of which mattered, we were just thrilled to be there.

Having decided that there was no way I was going to blend with the bland attire favoured by the bulk of the industry, I had been to see my tailors prior to the shows. You could say I stood out. Even with the meagre support of just a simple, round, three-foot diameter coffee table, when a man in a purple Ozwald Boateng suit peddles jewellery like ours, people start talking. First it was the journalists, followed by the retailers. I was mobbed. "Who the hell are you?" was the most commonly asked question. "Have you seen the English guy in the purple suit?" was the word around the corridors.

At the end of the week, even though I hadn't taken any major orders, I had still sold more than in the collective shows I had done with Silverhorn. Better still, the people from Neiman Marcus, who I had flown to Dallas to meet after the previous year's show, wrote a follow-up order of $25,000—our biggest order to date. Over the following years Neimans became our biggest and most important client in the US. The then Fine Jewellery buyer Tim Braun and all of the senior members of staff showed incredible support and enthusiasm for our work and us. We are now fondly known as a *house brand* and part of the family and the furniture. The show culminated with a black tie gala and the Couture Design Awards. To my shock, we won the "Editor's Choice" gong, this being awarded to the designer considered by all of the magazine editors to be responsible for the standout work of the show. If they didn't know me four days before, everyone knew who Stephen Webster was that night. It was amazing.

Clutching my trophy, I drove to Vegas to meet my brother who was joining me in our booth at the JCK show. The response was, again, overwhelming. We were being called "the rock stars of the industry" and it seemed like everyone in Vegas wanted a backstage pass. Dave and I never stopped writing orders. Half way through selling yet another tattoo-inspired, diamond jewellery set, the phone rang: "You have a daughter," said the woman's voice, "mother and child doing well. Congratulations."

I think I may have alarmed the people in the booth because I shouted out the good news for everyone to hear. All the other exhibitors knew my wife was due so it seemed as though the whole show was cheering. Better still, in all the excitement, the person half way through her order doubled it. I'm not an emotional man but the doubling of an order was enough to make me shed a little tear.

Those memorable shows changed our lives. Jeff, from Alex Sepkus, had predicted we would write $600,000 worth of orders and this had seemed like a fanciful, telephone number figure prior to the show, but when we did the math, he was right. I went home to a new member of my family. Dave recruited five new jewellers.

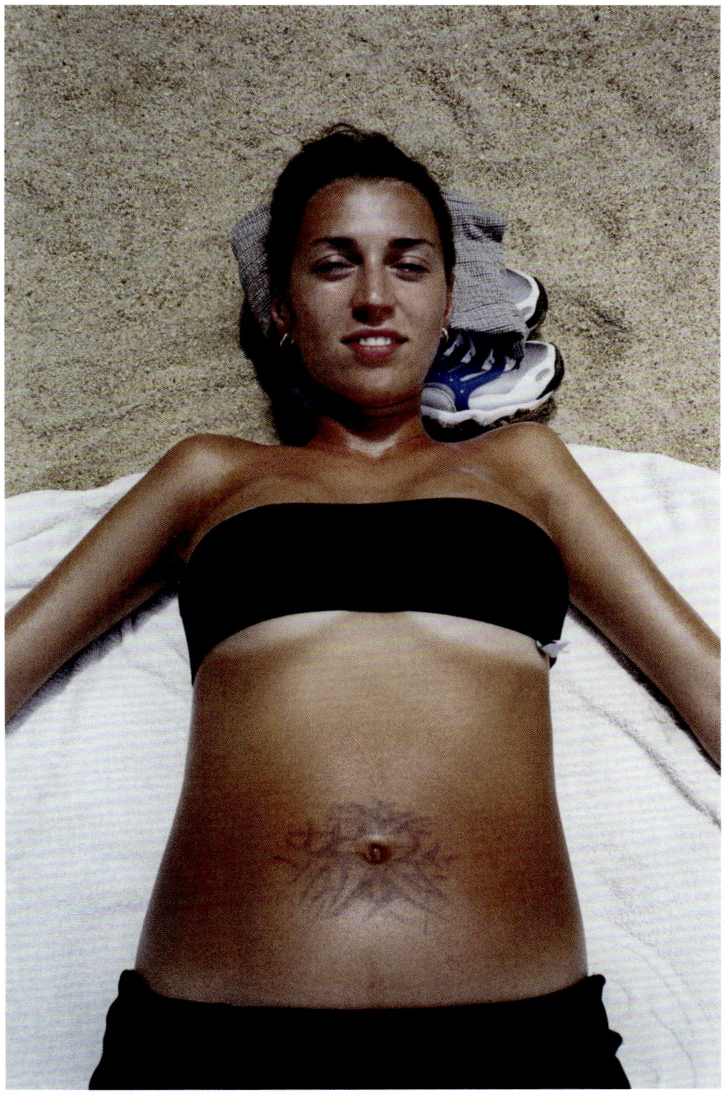

Assia baking Nika, whilst being tattooed by myself on the beach in Brazil, 1999

Stephen Webster

CHAPTER 9

THE CROWN JEWELLER

Exhibiting at the Vegas show had really pushed us to develop our product. I was also very careful with money and pretty much everything went back into making more stock. That said, back on the home front, we were still very much under the radar. The shop on Duke Street was selling pieces to the odd American tourist along with a few of the people we had met or sold to at the Goldsmiths' fair but local custom was very thin on the ground.

I maintained my periodical visits to Richard Jarvis, MD of Garrard. Even his PA Nona had become less frosty. One day, Richard contacted me—instead of the other way around—asking me to bring in a selection of our work. This time, he took me to lunch. At the next table sat his teenage daughter Kate accompanied by Nona. With some apprehension, I sat down. Richard asked me to show Kate and Nona some of my pieces, so I unrolled my velvet jeweller's roll revealing 15 cocktail rings—*Crystal Haze* with a smattering of *Cloth of Gold*. He asked the ladies what they thought. As I found out later, when she came to work for me, Kate thought rather a lot. She is one of the most direct and brutally honest people I know—she loved them. So did Nona. Richard concurred. There and then he told me that Garrard was going to give me a solo show. I almost fell face-first into my lobster bisque—it was that kind of restaurant. This was off the charts; the establishment had accepted the upstart.

Putting this into context, Garrard, established 1734, was as proper as it got. Since Queen Victoria bestowed the purveyor of fine jewellery watches and silverware the title of "Crown Jeweller," no one other than they were allowed to touch the Crown Jewels, housed in the Tower of London. Monarchs and rock 'n' roll stars shopped there.

With a stomach full of butterflies and fishy broth, I had to get back to the workshop to tell the team and phone my mum and dad. The next six months was the longest, single stretch of time I had spent in London for many years. This time we were busy making things for our show in my hometown. Corrina Pike, who was to curate the show, visited us regularly. She liked the atmosphere of our little shop on Duke Street and decided to recreate it within the palatial Garrard shop on Regent Street, commandeering all our furniture including the purple and gilded chaise longue with its matching puff cushions. We worked and worked, often into the small hours to prepare for the opening night. We were also visited by a phenomenon new to me; a public relations person. This particular PR was the widow of Sir Richard Burton, who had, on several occasions, been

Our very first shop, 1a Duke Street, London, W1, 1996

married to Elizabeth Taylor, my first celebrity client. Sally Burton was great, commissioning me to design and make for her two bespoke cocktail rings incorporating a carved crest and stone from rings Richard had worn.

Just two days before the opening party, I finished the final brooch I had been making; a carved aquamarine angelfish, swimming in an 18k gold, graduated blue enamel and diamond set sea. We were done.

Now I needed a suit. But I couldn't have just any suit—this had to be special. I was finally in show business and I wanted to dress appropriately. After hours scouring the West End I came across a small men's boutique; William Hunt. From the moment I was inside I knew this was the right tailor for me. Willy Hunt was a proper, working class Mancunian and had the side I dressed on correctly sussed as soon as we met. Eccentric but stylish, referencing everything British, Willy was continuing a tailoring tradition started by the likes of Tommy Nutter and Lord John in the 1960s and '70s. I left with a bottle green velvet two-piece with a black velvet collar and exaggerated cuffs.

On the day of the opening, a big black and white portrait had been erected outside the entrance announcing the upcoming show of the work of "designer's designer and jeweller's jeweller Stephen Webster." It was a proud moment. The party was a great success with over 200 people packed into the store, all seeing our work for the first time and approving of the little Webster world that Corrina Pike had created using our furniture and other bits and bobs. The installation lasted a month but my relationship with the Crown Jeweller lasted a lot longer.

Designs and finished ring for Sally Burton, incorporating the engraved crest belonging to her late husband, Sir Richard Burton, 1996

opposite 18k gold carved Thorn-Tattoo Choker, buff top amethyst, coloured freshwater pearls and white diamonds, 2000

Two more very fruity cocktail rings in 18k gold, featuring enamel, pavé diamonds, intaglio carved amethyst and carbunkle garnet, 1999

CHAPTER 10

BASEL

I think it was Chaucer who once wrote something very condescending about the Swiss city of Basel. I couldn't find the exact quote but have it on good authority that it involved something about a mean spirit and a higher than expected population of bishops and whores. With the exception of the bishops, I'm not sure that much has changed during the 400-odd years since Chaucer scribed his disdain for the place.

Basel, as most people know, is an exhibition town, conveniently located on the borders of both France and Germany. Art Basel, its big art fair and global brand, now extends to the far more accommodating cities of Miami and Hong Kong but Baselworld is going nowhere. Originally the showcase for the Swiss wristwatch industry, Baselworld is now the most prestigious international watch and jewellery fair in the world. As such, its organisers, with typical Swiss hospitality, have pushed and pushed the prices to exhibit so stratospherically high that only those with numbered Swiss bank accounts now need apply. It wasn't always that way or we certainly wouldn't have been able to afford to exhibit back in 1998.

That first Baselworld year I shared a 10 × 10 ft booth with a London based outfit called D.A. Soley whose boss told me that no one would buy my jewellery because it was too "out there" to be considered "fine," and Basel was all about "fine." The same man ate his words some years later when he finally realised how out of touch he was with a changing world. Having blagged the use of a sofa for the show's eight-day duration—thanks to a client, Jain Castiau, who worked for a bank in the Swiss city—I did my first Basel on a very tight budget.

The first couple of years were somewhat light on orders. In fact, that first year I don't remember selling anything at all. The second year I sold something to a retailer, Moodys of Crewe, who was so hungover that I truly believe he thought he was actually on the part of the stand belonging to Soley, with whom he had been trading since the days when his father ran his shop. Adding insult to injury, when we sent this order to Moodys of Crewe, it was returned with a letter from his mother, Mrs A Moody, advising us that we must have sent the package to them by mistake. Eventually her son, the man with the sallow complexion and the morning-after headache, convinced his mother that things were changing and that Stephen Webster was the face of the new breed.

I desperately wanted our own booth but there was a long waiting list for the entry-level 10 × 10 ft spaces and no real indication as to when one might become available. Prior to the show on our second year, I was asked to join the panel of judges for Baselworld's "Designer of the Year" prize given to graduates from jewellery schools across the globe. The panel consisted of heavy hitting members of the industry. And me.

Having decided on a winner, the Baselworld marketing people wanted to have one of us talk a little about how we'd come to our unanimous decision when the winner was declared at the show's opening gala later that night. For some reason the rest of the panel pointed to me. Without thinking about the responsibility too much, I agreed.

I'd never attended the opening gala before so had no idea that it attracted a crowd of over 3,000 people from across the industry. It was a massive and comically choreographed event. Before I was to do my turn on stage—surrounded by models draped in the work of the finalists—Sir Peter Ustinov—aka the world's greatest raconteur—was going to give a talk about the sterling work of UNICEF. Quite an act to follow. Despite some reassuring, encouraging words from Sir Peter backstage, I was petrified. With no turning back I did my bit and realised that I quite liked the limelight. Afterwards, the Basel marketeers were very happy and asked if there was anything they could do to help us. I asked for our own booth and lo and behold, I got one.

Experience has shown us what it's like to be the new kid on the block at a big trade show and the kid who thinks he can change things. The truth is, in the cautious, slow moving jewellery business, you have to be very, very patient. It took over four years before retailers, some of them actually sober, started to venture onto our stand. Over those four years we were constantly being written about, not just in trade publications but also in the fashion glossies and, as soon as we made Madonna and Guy Ritchie's wedding rings, in the newspapers and colour supplements also. There was a new buzz around jewellery and we were most definitely at the centre of it.

Until that point, our sales force numbered just one person: me. So, as we became busier at both the Basel and Las Vegas shows, we quickly outgrew our starter booths and I needed to employ some sales people to cope with our newfound attention. The first person to assist was Assia, who, despite her failure to sell even a single square inch of canvas during the six months she had spent on the New York commercial art scene, had proven she had what it takes to sell Stephen Webster goods. She took over our boutique on Duke Street and started running it properly. Slowly but surely, buyers came from all over the world. After opening our first boutique in Moscow, things really ramped up. From zero to hero, our booth became the meeting point for visitors from the ex-Soviet Union. As a result, we kept moving into bigger and bigger spaces until we became the largest British jewellery brand exhibiting at the show.

Since those early years, our collective fondness for Basel hasn't changed all that much. It's still the show we love to hate but we can't deny that Baselworld attracts a better quality of buyers, all in the business of luxury; which, in turn, is all about status and something the Swiss know more about than most, money.

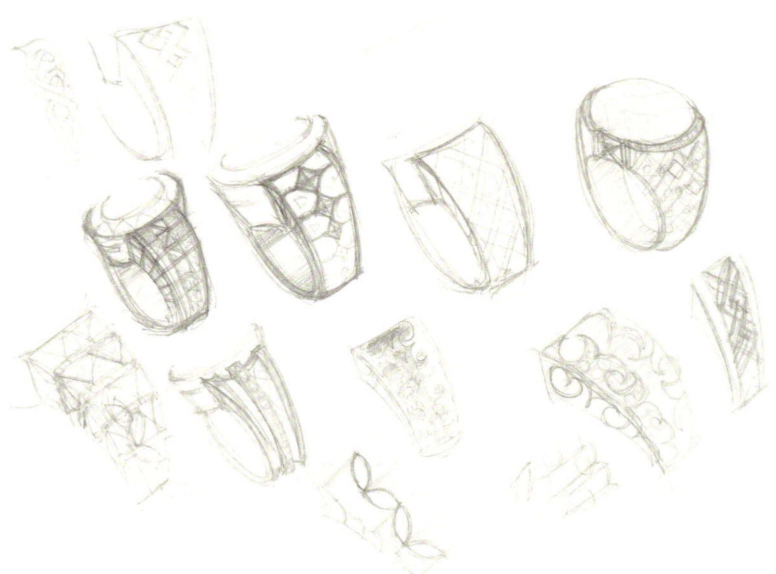

Checkerboard cut amethyst and TV screen cut topaz, 18k white gold, diamond-set cocktail rings, 2000

Working sketches for various cocktail rings

Working sketches for bespoke gold and gem-set Cloth of Gold Necklace, 1997

RUSSIAN
ROULE

CHAPTER II

STEPHEN WEBSTER IN RUSSIA

(or "Carry On Up the Urals")

The deal that took the Stephen Webster brand into Russia was brokered one Saturday lunchtime in 2002 at a Zizzi pizza parlour behind Selfridges. We met up with Galina and her husband Andre, two Russian friends of Assia's from Leningrad, now living in London after a spell in New York. Acutely aware of the opportunities on offer back in their Russian motherland, they made us a proposal, there and then, over an American Hot and a thin crust Diablo. With the help of their business partner Nastia, a well connected and very well off *it girl* resident in Russia, they wanted to open a Stephen Webster shop in Moscow—the first independent designer jewellery boutique in the country. In between mouthfuls of pizza, we said "yes" and with that our great Russian adventure began in earnest.

Just a few months later, accompanied by an entourage of 25 or so of our London friends, we flew to Moscow for the store's grand opening. The location couldn't have been better—right next to an insanely expensive sushi restaurant in the brand new, five-star Ararat Park Hyatt hotel, a hang out for newly-rich Novi Ruskis who would smoke, drink Chernobyl-strength coffee and push bits of yellow tail around their plates at all hours of the day and night.

The opening party was incredible; Moscow's most glamorous women all politely lining up to get into the bijoux boutique. Each had two ursine, Boris-type bodyguards waiting in the lobby—having just one at your side was, apparently, a declaration of poverty—all dressed in black leather jackets and those special pointed shoes that Russian men seemed to love so much, smoking and being silently menacing. All in all, very much like a service in a Russian Orthodox Church on any given Sunday morning. With the shop opening done, the London crew was escorted out and taken to the VIP tables of one of the new and very shiny nightclubs in the city for a protracted, vodka-fuelled session. This definitely wasn't a trip for anyone with a fragile constitution.

A couple of hours later, our partners Galina and Nastia joined us at the club with an announcement—we had sold one third of the entire boutique's stock at the opening party. "No!!" we cried in disbelief. "What did we expect?" the girls shrugged, "This is the store's opening party. People want to show their support." We raised a glass of vodka to Novi Ruski generosity and Muscovite manners.

Word about the Stephen Webster name spread across the ex-Soviet Union and very soon we were gaining clients from places I had never even heard of. Not just the Eurovision

Watercolour and ink artwork of Russian Roulette Ring

Song Contest nations of Azerbaijan and Kazakhstan, but also Kazan, Krasnodar and, far away in the Ural mountains between Russia and Siberia, the city of Yekaterinburg ('Ekaterinburg'.) Over the next few years, we would visit them all.

First we went to St Petersburg, my wife's home city, where a second SW boutique was to open. It was mid June—*Belíye Nochí* ('white nights') season when the sun never drops low enough below the horizon for the sky to darken. Despite the potential romance surrounding this annual phenomenon, the constant daylight soon became a problem. It's hard enough to coerce our friends into their duvets on big occasions at the best of times, but when it's sunlight 24/7 and the World Cup finals are in full swing, the task of playing the responsible dad role at the party becomes completely futile.

One day, quite without warning or respecting the niceties normally associated with room service, security walked into our hotel suites and removed the entire contents of our mini bars. Even Assia, speaking to these unsmiling men in frank but reasonable Russian, couldn't dissuade them from their coldly efficient party-pooping mission. While most guests, perhaps fearing a stretch in a freezing gulag, handed over their alcoholic booty without much of a struggle, our friend Tracey Emin, on particularly feisty form that day, quite rightly refused to give up her stash without something of a verbal exchange. As you can well imagine, Ivan vs. Emin was a ding-dong of a fight. As much as we had enjoyed bringing an entourage of friends along with us for our inaugural Russian boutique openings, the trips had also proved quite exhausting. So, when we opened our boutique in the Ural Mountains, the great dividing line between Russia and Siberia, we decided to go it alone.

With partners Vladimir and Vladislav standing alongside a special stretch Hummer, complete with two wood burning stoves, provided as transport while at the opening of the SW boutique in Yekaterinburg

By 2008, thrilled to find that things were moving at a very fast pace for us across the ex-Soviet Union, we never questioned the motives of the hairy, motorbiking jewellery entrepreneurs who proposed opening a Stephen Webster store in their home town of Yekaterinburg. Again, we said "yes" and booked our plane tickets. The only two passengers in Ural Air's business class—"gin tonic with a slice of juicy yellow lemon" it said on the in-flight cocktail menu—we arrived in Yekaterinburg to find our new partners waiting with flowers and a stretch Hummer to take us to a late night feast.

Due to the permafrost in Russia's north, the Ural region's streets are mostly packed dirt and quite narrow, rendering the long and ostentatious Hummer totally impractical. But in the wild, wild East, no one cares about such minor details. Especially when the vehicle in question is fitted with a pair of fully functioning wood-burning stoves, one at each end of the entertainingly over-adequate interior.

The next day, we had a quick tour—which included visiting the wall where the Romanovs were lined up and executed after the revolution—and then drove through Yekaterinburg to our new boutique, nicely situated between Cartier and Van Cleef & Arpels. To my delight, the streets were festooned with banners welcoming SW to the city. In Russia, we soon learned, it's always useful to have the mayor's office on your team.

We had no marketing department or corporate guidelines in those days, so the Yekaterinburg store's design was an approximated interpretation of how an official SW shop should have looked. Somewhat naively, we figured that as long as the colour scheme could be described as purple, the logo matched ours and the pervading gothic style was generally similar, we accepted. Our somewhat lax and freewheeling attitude towards corporate identity was highly unlikely to do us too much lasting damage, right?

As was becoming customary for our opening parties, this event would be pitched as the highlight of the week. Guests included some very glamorous women and a lot of quite frightening men but nothing that Anna—one of our business partners—and Assia couldn't handle. True to form, it was quite a party. The mayor bought our most expensive necklace for his lady mayoress, while Vladimir, our main local partner, skipped the champagneski and hit the vodka hard. We later found out that this great Siberian bear of a man, still only in his early 30s, had suffered more than his fair share of real tragedy, and he was dealing with it his own way, the Russian way. The following morning, a remorseful Vlad met us at the store with 100 long-stem roses. He was

top A Webster duet, Yekaterinburg, 2009

bottom Our beautiful, glamorous, partners since the beginning in Russia. Me with the Bond girls, Anastasia and Galina

the sort of guy you just wanted to hug.

The rest of the day was spent doing interviews for print, radio and TV, in between performing 15 point turns in the wood-burning Hummer. In the evening we had dinner with a local personality—a Johnny Hallyday-ish, old rock star type, all snake hips and rhinestones. He owned a lot of property in town, including Yekaterinburg's *hottest nightclub*. He also had the cheek of looking at me and commenting, somewhat disparagingly, that he thought I was "supposed to be rock 'n' roll." If his version of rock 'n' roll was anything to go by, I was happy to be a square.

The grand finale of our whirlwind tour was to spend the night in his nightclub and get filmed by Russian MTV. This is when things started to get somewhat surreal. After a few similarly bacchanalian nights across the vast region, I was getting to know the score: I would take to the stage and say something that no one understood, while a woman wearing something tight and shimmery would either talk a lot or sometimes—God only knows why—sing to me. This time, as a nod to my partners and my motorbiking background, we shared the stage with some bikini-clad beauties, writhing over a parked up Harley. All filmed and broadcast in real time by a TV crew. There followed a breathtaking moment when the bike, nowhere near adequately secured for the enthusiastic gyrations of the girls, crashed over. All live on MTV.

With no one hurt, the show went on. But just when I thought my duties were over, I was called back to the stage where an elaborate throne had now been placed. Refusal to play the visiting royal dignitary would have been insulting. So, lead to the chair by yet another Siberian beauty, I sat down in front of 700 or so complete strangers while a topless girl performed a lap dance on me to the *James Bond* theme tune. The crowd cheered while Assia, looking on in horror and amusement from the wings, instructed my dancer—in rather forthright Russian—to keep her knickers on. It was quite possibly the longest rendition of that famous tune that I had ever endured and the sort of thing that could leave a man scarred for life. Apparently, this had been my gift from our gracious hosts.

On the morning of our departure Vladimir showed up to say his goodbyes. He wasn't alone. Over his shoulder was an enormous bear—a seven-foot bear, its head alone of leonine proportions. Vlad had read that I collected taxidermy so had spent the latter part of the previous night scouring trappers' posts until he found what looked like Big Foot. There was no way our Russian friends would see me off without my new friend in tow. At the airport, despite my best protests, the guys had him wrapped with industrial cling film that people use to protect their luggage. We ended up checking in two bags and a huge, organic shape. All very well at the Russian customs and excise end but a different story at Heathrow, I reckoned. As a token of validation, Vladimir handed Assia a certificate decorated with myriad Soviet-style embossments, declaring that the beast had been legally slayed. That should satisfy even the sternest of customs officers, Vlad assured us. During the flight home, all I could think about was the oversized package in the hold and how I was going to explain it to British airport officials.

Heathrow's Terminal Five was, at the time, the most expensive building project in Europe, but had opened to computer glitch-generated luggage chaos. On arrival, a terminal piled high with bags met us. Surely, I was going to be in real trouble when a bear-shaped package with my name on it appeared on the luggage belt? Especially seeing as I had signed a "nothing to declare form." But miracles do happen. An announcement made over the Terminal Five tannoy advised us that bags from Moscow would be arriving at carousel five. Amongst the chaos and against all my instincts, out came our bags and the massive bear-shaped thing with them. Coolly, I loaded up two trolleys, avoided eye contact and went through the *nothing to declare* channel.

For the last seven years, my souvenir from party-loving Siberia has taken pride of place in our front room, along with a certificate declaring he was shot legally, should anyone ever ask.

Watercolour and ink artwork of
Seven Deadly Sins Wrath Ring

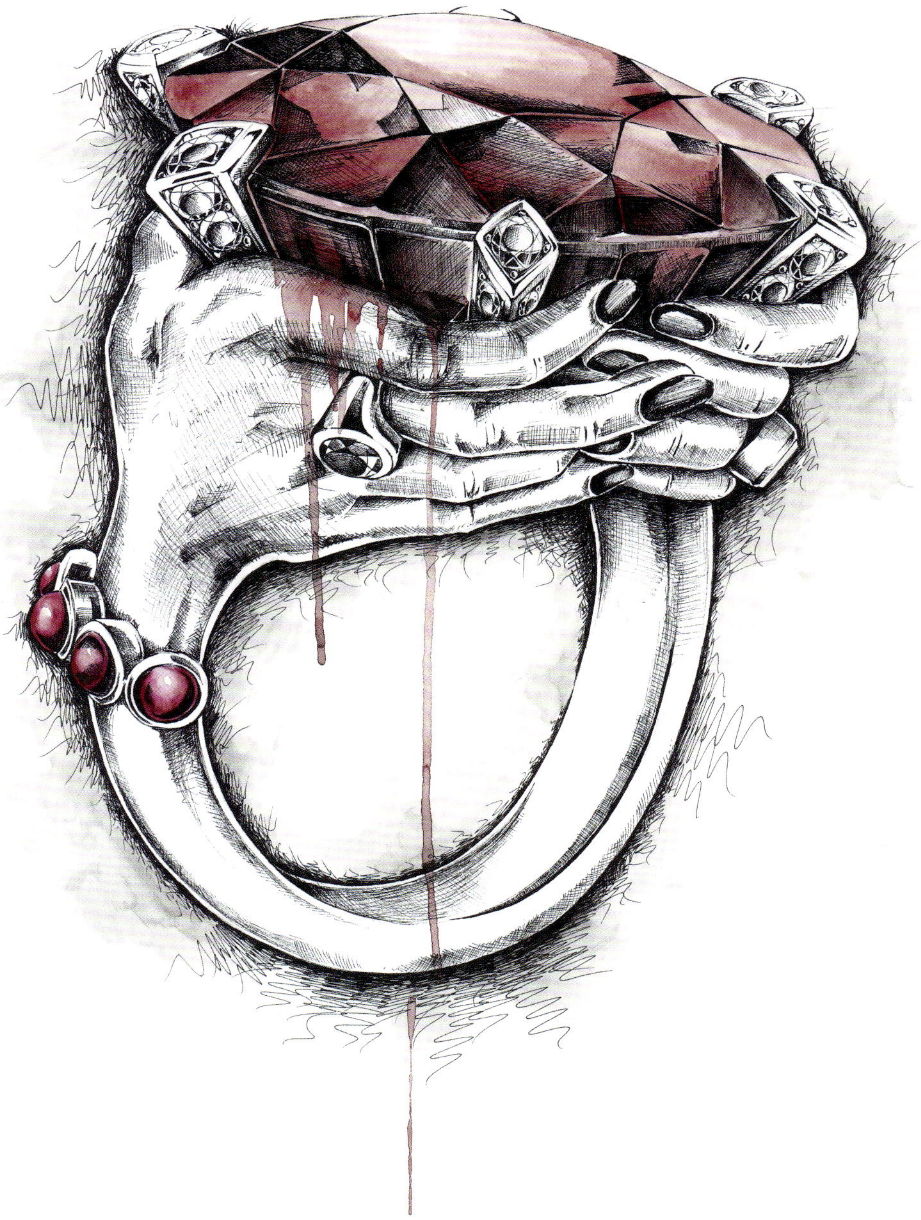

CHAPTER 12

THE ROCK STAR RING

The Chateau Marmont, West Hollywood, Los Angeles. Assia and I were having dinner at this low key establishment with our friend Michael Stipe, the iconoclastic lead singer of the band R.E.M. Michael was telling us about the vintage Hermes picnic set he had just bought from his favourite store, Maxfield on Melrose Avenue. Somewhat incredulous on learning that we had never heard of Maxfield and, indeed, that we had no idea that Hermes made such frivolous accoutrements as picnic sets, Michael told us that we must go there and show our work to Tommy, the store's proprietor.

So, the next day, on our way to the airport, we stopped off at Maxfield. We weren't disappointed. The big, modern, concrete monolith of a store didn't look like the kind of place where we might shop for anything, except perhaps, DIY materials, and the security guard at the front door was hardly welcoming but once inside... wow. A sensorial overload of black clothes, gothic jewellery, bizarre taxidermy, vintage watches and, of course, vintage Hermes picnic sets. The showstopper was the large cabinet of phallic curiosities. If it was dick-shaped it was in there.

Tommy, Maxfield's owner, *wasn't available*. We were told to open our jewellery rolls on the floor of a changing room. Sarah, the manager came to take a look and quickly went off. She came back with Tommy who appeared like a mix of Roger Daltrey and Max Wall, as styled by Keith Richards, with a million dollars worth of skull and bone themed jewellery hanging off him like Dickens' Jacob Marley. He moved like a man burdened by the weight of his wealth.

Tommy loved what he saw and was particularly taken with my *Rock Star* ring, a five-pointed knuckle-duster that was so angular, bulky and uncomfortable that if you greeted someone with a handshake anything more rigorous than *limp* it was like delivering an electric shock. I'd only ever considered this ring for show but Tommy, as we soon found out, had other plans. I looked at my watch; we'd missed our plane home—a minor inconvenience that would pay considerable dividends. How come? Well, pretty quickly we learned that Hollywood's A-list shopped at Maxfield or at least their stylists did—on the way out of the store Bruce Willis was coming in. He was much shorter than he appeared in the movies.

True to reputation, sometime after we had made our first delivery, Tommy called me in London with a Hollywood-sized enquiry: "You know that *Rock Star* ring you make?" he growled, "Well, I want one in yellow gold with the star cut from a massive ruby and surrounded by diamonds." "That

The original Rock Star Ring.
18k gold and star shaped
buff top cut citrine

would be crazy," I replied. "The people who shop in my store are crazy!" Tommy shot back. "Can you do it or not?" Of course I could but I needed to work out a price and make it very clear that if we made such a thing, it would have to be a non-refundable order because it was so crazy.

My brother David contacted one of our German stonecutters, who confirmed that we were, indeed, "crazy." Finally, I got back to Tommy and gave him the news. This was going to be a six-digit figure *Rock Star* ring. Tommy didn't flinch. "I want it," he said. Respecting the policy of client confidentiality, I didn't ask for whom it was intended. Fast-forward a year and I happened to pick up a copy of *Entertainment Weekly* magazine. On the front cover was the wild man of rock himself, Ozzy Osbourne, his arms around wife Sharon, and his kids Jack and Kelly. The cover line read: "Living With The Osbournes," and there, on the legendarily crazy, rock star's finger was my crazy ruby and diamond *Rock Star* ring.

Make no mistake; this was a culturally significant moment. Not just an old rocker making a comeback with a tour or a new album, but the beginning of a reality show that would change TV forever—without the Osbournes there would be no Kardashians to keep up with. The world fell in love with the mumbling, shambolic, family-loving Dad and husband, moaning and bickering in a broad Brummie accent in his sunny California home. It was a big moment for SW also.

Somehow, in ways that only journalists can do, we were tracked down as Ozzy's jeweller-of-choice. A *New York Times* writer had been commissioned to write a piece about Stephen Webster, who, he had heard, lived a life similar to that of his rock star clients. The writer wanted to join us for a night out in London and turn the experience into a story for the paper. Game but slightly panicked, I agreed and immediately turned to my social secretary, Assia, and asked her to make the arrangements. I chose my best tangerine Ozwald Boateng suit for the occasion—it was the same year that I painted my downstairs toilet pillar-box red and purple.

First stop was at an art gallery opening on Cork Street. This would have been a very sober affair had it not been for the fact that the artist was Stalin's grandson, an acquaintance of my wife's and a bit of a poser. The accompanying photographer took a few snaps and we moved on. Next stop was somewhere unmemorable: we were in danger of our night out becoming an early one. Out of the blue, Assia's phone rang. It was Michael Stipe wanting to know if we could possibly squeeze his good friend Macaulay Culkin into our nocturnal schedule. We obliged. Apparently "Ma" was in London rehearsing for a play and didn't have too many friends in town. Squeezing him in would be easy as everyone knows he's only small. OK, so the star of the *Home Alone* movies might not have been the rock 'n' roll company of our fantasies, but he was irrefutably Hollywood and good colour for the story. To my surprise, Macaulay had, well, grown up quite a lot since I had last seen him in *Home Alone 2*.

The evening went like gangbusters from that moment on. The young American hack retired to his hotel in the small hours fully refreshed and entertained. A couple of weeks later *The New York Times Style* section hit the stands: "A Night Out With Rock Star Jeweller Stephen Webster" screamed the cover. An accompanying photo featured me, tangoed in tangerine and finding something hilarious… probably the slightly preposterous notion of being written about within the pages of an American media institution by way of Michael Stipe, Ozzy Osbourne, *Entertainment Weekly* magazine, Stalin's grandson, Macaulay Culkin and a vintage Hermes picnic set. Crazy.

First outing for the Ozzy Osbourne bespoke Rock Star Ring

The New York Times

SUNDAY, JULY 30, 2000

A NIGHT OUT WITH

Stephen Webster

Jeweler's Daily Regimen

By JAMES COLLARD

LONDON, July 28 — "What are *you* doing here?" Stephen Webster demanded in gravelly tones as he arrived at the opening party on a recent Tuesday for One Fine Thing, a new boutique in St. John Street, in Clerkenwell. He was greeting an old friend — not the store owner, but the doorman, Danny Moore, an elderly gent of military bearing, apparently moonlighting from his day job at Goldsmith's Hall, home of the Worshipful Company of Goldsmiths.

Mr. Webster is one of London's most innovative jewelers, a favorite of clients like Madonna and Kate Winslet, but as a member of the Goldsmiths, an ancient London guild, he is honored by his more traditional peers. In a city where parking spaces are more valued than any celebrity clientele, Mr. Moore is the man who lets Mr. Webster park his motorbike in one of the Goldsmiths' four coveted parking spaces.

Mr. Webster, 40, goes to openings and parties several nights a week after working long days in his workshop, making bold, big, one-of-a-kind designs that have made him a darling of accessories editors at fashion magazines on both sides of the Atlantic. "It's part of the job, really," he explained of his day-into-evening schedule. "It's like a game, isn't it?"

His first port of call had been the opening of a Georgian art show at a gallery in Cork Street, Mayfair. There, he and his Russian-born wife, Anastasia, found themselves greeting one old acquaintance, Count Andrei Tolstoy (an offshoot of the writer's family) and making a new one, Jacob Dzhugashvili, an artist and great-grandson of Joseph Stalin. Nash Tavkhelidze, godson of the former Russian Prime Minister Yevgeny M. Primakov, was also on hand — he's the lead singer of Blast, the first Russian band to be signed to a British label.

"What a bizarre party," Mr. Webster said, laughing, to a friend, Neil Cunningham, a couturier. In the sultry weather, the party had moved onto the sidewalk, where the Websters mingled with scions of White and Red Russia, Georgia and the fashionable London art crowd.

"Count Tolstoy's a wonderful guy," Mr. Webster said, as Ms. Webster fluttered from guest to guest in a feather-fringed dress like some exotic, especially sociable little bird, one moment speaking Russian, the next Italian or English. The count organizes London's War and Peace Ball ("I'd go, only they do all that old-school dancing and you've got to have lessons," Mr. Webster said), which helped finance the building of the rather grand Russian Orthodox church, blue onion domes and all, that is currently astounding visitors on the road from Heathrow. "He got hold of two kilos of caviar — at an amazingly good price — for our wedding, and a band of balalaika players," Mr. Webster said.

After a flurry of good-bye kisses, the Websters and Mr. Cunningham squeezed into a car to head across town to the boutique. Soon it was time to head farther east to a cousin's party in a loft apartment in newly fashionable Shoreditch.

Along the way, Mr. Webster explained something of his life story: apprenticeship in London, long stays in Canada and Santa Barbara, Calif., before returning to London, and opening his store in Duke Street in 1996. His reputation is spreading well beyond this prestigious Mayfair address; Mr. Webster's workshop is working flat out to fill orders from Bergdorf Goodman in New York.

At the party, after a quick climb to the roof to survey this lively corner of the old East End, Mr. Webster suggested they go dancing. Ms. Webster's answer was a gentle but convincing no. It was getting late, and there was work to do in the morning.

Jonathan Player for The New York Times

The jewelry designer Stephen Webster attending party No. 1.

A framed page from *The New York Times*' Sunday paper that hangs in my office, detailing "A Night Out With" SW, following publicity surrounding the making of a unique Rock Star Ring for Ozzy Osbourne in 2000

Rotten Hill Gang featuring Mick Jones of the Clash, performing at the SW *London Calling* collection launch at Wilton's Music Hall in London

CHAPTER 13

I FOUGHT THE LAW AND QPR LOST

I first encountered Mick Jones along with several thousand of his closest friends when The Clash played a Rock Against Racism concert in Victoria Park, Hackney in 1978.

Back in the late '70s this now fashionable and rapidly gentrifying area was just another poor, neglected East London borough where anything bad could happen... and usually did. Our Hackney house was a stone's throw from the park and despite having little of value other than our clothes and a few pot plants, would get broken into almost weekly. On one memorable occasion I remember someone getting shot in the pub at the end of our road. The gunman struck early in the evening when the bar was packed so it was rather remarkable that only the intended victim took the slug and the rest of us, busy enjoying pints of light and bitter and those crisps that had a blue paper twist of salt in the packet—the fun was to locate the wrap and shake in the salt—emerged unscathed.

Like many inner city neighbourhoods, Hackney was a mixed race community with a strong West African and West Indian population that made it very colourful compared to the grey drabness of life in other working class parts of Britain. In celebration of the Queen's Silver Jubilee in 1977 our street party had reggae bands at either end of the stretch—the Rastafarian spectrum of red, gold and green strung from the lampposts alongside patriotic Union Flag bunting.

There was also, just as there is today, an irrefutable undercurrent of racial tension in the area, largely brought about by the new found and loudly voiced might of the right wing fascist thugs who rallied under the political banner of the National Front party. Following an on-stage outburst by a drunk Eric Clapton encouraging support for the anti-immigration politician Enoch Powell, younger, more left wing musicians reacted to the rising tide of hate by aligning themselves with the Anti-Nazi League. A huge rally was planned; a meeting at Trafalgar Square and a march through London towards Hackney where the anti-Nazis felt they would be more welcome and free to enjoy themselves.

The demonstration was to culminate with the Rock Against Racism festival in Victoria Park with a line-up that included the cream of cutting edge, 1970s punk and reggae: X-Ray Spex, The Ruts, Sham 69, Generation X, Buzzcocks, The Tom Robinson Band, Steel Pulse, Misty In Roots and the headline act of the day, The Clash. The event was set to become legendary.

Only problem was my Dad didn't want me to go. Due to

Invite for the SW *London Calling* party, created by the SW design team

the inevitable violent clashes that had already surrounded any marches or protests that went against the National Front Party's meat-headed ideology, the well-publicised Rock Against Racism rally was all but guaranteed to attract violence, either *en route* or at its parkland climax and my Dad, bless him, didn't want his son to get beaten up by some fat, drunken skinheads, *Sieg Heiling* as they put the boot in.

Still, motivated by militant politics and the golden opportunity to see a load of my favourite bands for free, I went along. I'd be fine, I told my Dad. After all, amongst the buttons and patches pinned and sewed on to the black leather biker jacket I wore that day was a badge depicting a carrot and the slogan "Vegetarians Against Racism." If that provocative, rabbit food-munching statement didn't cause any members of the National Front I might encounter to blow a high cholesterol blood vessel, then I didn't know what would.

As soon as we arrived at the park it was obvious that the concert organisers had vastly underestimated the attendance. The capability of the PA system, which had been prepared for an anticipated crowd of 20,000, was lost somewhere between the tenth and twelfth rows of the 80,000 or so people who had made the pilgrimage on the day. Some of the more melodic acts and the gentler reggae bands weren't particularly compromised by the lack of audio muscle but The Clash was the kind of band that needed a big system to deliver the full force of their message.

I was already a fan, of course. The Clash were a rebel military outfit dressed like rock 'n' roll outlaws. Topper Headon's drums clattered out rat-a-tat rhythms like an AK47, Paul Simonon wore his bass low and swung it like a weapon. Front man Joe Strummer—white jeans, white brothel creepers, knee pumping like a piston against the mic stand—delivered songs like "Janie Jones" and "White Riot" with passion, velocity and attack as if spoiling for a fight. Mick Jones on guitar, his hair grown out to Keith Richards mop by now, was airborne most of the time. Unfortunately, because the sound from the underpowered PA was so feeble, as far as most of the crowd was concerned the band may as well have been miming. Johnny Green, The Clash's uncompromising and straight-talking road manager was probably the loudest thing in the park that afternoon.

Despite seeing The Clash play again in Calgary, Canada a few years later, I never actually got to meet Mick until 25 years after the Rock Against Racism gig. Our paths finally crossed in the decidedly un-punk rock venue of Hakkasan, the Michelin starred, Cantonese restaurant in Mayfair, London—culturally, politically and geographically speaking, a long way from Anti-Nazi League rallying Hackney, needless to say.

It's always exciting to meet one's musical heroes, it can also be a major disappointment, but Mick was easy going, warm and engaging. An all-round good egg—which was appropriate because, as I later found out from Paul Simonon, there had been times on the road that Mick would survive on an eggs-only diet. We hit it off there and then. Like me, he's also a Queens Park Rangers fan.

Even though I couldn't claim the lifelong affiliation to the West London football team that Mick had, I'd adopted them as my own, partly because they were local—I was living in Paddington—and partly because of their compromised position in the, then First Division—soon to be elevated to the newly conceived Championship league—it was easy to just rock up to the ground and get a ticket on the day.

So, in a somewhat masochistic move, the following season after Mick and I had met, we bought season tickets, which we still renew every year. Our seats are behind the directors' box and include lunch and also cost far more than the inconsistent performance of the team could ever warrant. The reality is the 90 minutes of actual play is only a small part of the reason why we keep going. QPR fans are long suffering and have subsequently developed a rose-tinted memory of the past and a wry sense of humour that fans of more successful clubs could only wish for.

One evening, Mick, his then partner Miranda, and two other friends, interior designer Kelly Hoppen and her boyfriend, Arsenal and England defender, Sol Campbell, came to our house for dinner. After several large gins, Mick and I sang a duet of the QPR terrace song:

Chim, chimney
Chim, chimney
Chim, chim, cher-oo
Who needs Sol Campbell, when we've got Shittu?

The ditty, of course, referenced QPR's star defender at the time, Danny Shittu. Thankfully, Sol was amused.

Over the years I have often turned to music as inspiration for my jewellery, our *Rock Star* ring being perhaps, the most blatant reference. Noticing that the artist Banksy had used The Clash's *I Fought the Law* as the title of one of his street pieces, I felt another musical inspiration coming on. With Mick's blessing, I borrowed the title of The Clash's anthemic, rabble-rouser *London Calling*—also, a QPR theme tune down at Loftus Road—as the starting point for a London-inspired collection for men.

The resulting collection was launched in the UK with a spectacular party. The theme was "Victorian Punk," the venue, Wilton's Music Hall by Tower Bridge with entertainment provided by fashion designer-turned-DJ Pam Hogg and a live set by The Rotten Hill Gang. Mick Jones and Spandau Ballet's Gary Kemp made special guest appearances. Everyone came appropriately attired in Dickensian punk clobber... including my Dad and, perhaps more surprisingly, the manager of both my own and the Queen's bank—Coutts of the Strand—donning, amongst other things, a spiked dog collar.

The UK wasn't alone in its enthusiasm for the *London Calling* collection. It also went down a storm in the US and Japan—a market that has always lapped up Western rock 'n' roll references. The Japanese also love all things small, so in response we created the same collection only a quarter of the size and called it *Tokyo Calling*. It sold out immediately.

Inspired by punk music, the collection had plenty of Dickensian London references—textures mimicking the marks left on pavements and brickwork; the contact of hoof, heel, wheel and hand upon the lanes, thoroughfares and buildings, many of which are still evident today around the East End and other old parts of the city.

In the same way that Dickens depicted the human fabric of the capital at the time through his characters, such as Uriah Heep, the Artful Dodger, Mr Pickwick and Fagin, Mick Jones via his contribution, influence and passion for his home town, is—to me at least—a latter day Dickensian; inextricable from the popular culture of a generation, a London *character ambassador* the likes of which they just don't make anymore. He also gave me my favourite piece of clothing: a vintage Victorian-inspired, Vivienne Westwood frock coat. It's a little threadbare now, but like Olde London itself, it still functions admirably and looks utterly magnificent.

A sterling silver and onyx inlay men's band ring from the *London Calling* collection

CHAPTER 14

THE HISTORY OF CRYSTAL HAZE

Some 20 years ago now, I first played with the concept of layering gems, a technique introduced 100 years prior to my experiments as an attempt to increase the appearance of the size of valuable black opals. This is how it's done: a gem cutter takes a slice of the stone, carves a high dome carbuncle or cabochon out of a piece of quartz, then cuts a thin layer of onyx similar to the slice of opal and then bonds them all together. On the top is the clear quartz, on the bottom, the slice of onyx and in the middle, creating an opal sandwich—everyone knows I love sandwiches—is the business layer: the meat, the cheese, the marmite, so to speak. Once fashioned into a piece of jewellery, making sure that all visible seams are hidden, the effect is of a large, alluringly, deeply orchidaceous, blacker-than-black opal. It's a terrific trick.

This, by the way, is not an expose of the skullduggerous practices of the unscrupulous gem dealer, more an explanation of a technique intended for one purpose at the bottom of the gem food chain and the story of how I successfully hijacked, modernised and turned a similar process into something altogether different.

By the mid-1980s, in the more fashionable jewellery circles of the US, where I was living at the time, big, semi-precious gems—we don't call them that anymore, it's degrading—were all the rage. If your jewellery wardrobe was void of unconventional sounding and looking rocks, then it wasn't worth wearing. These were exciting times; the jeweller's palette was no longer restricted to the red, royal blue, green and white of the four precious stones. Customers were getting hip to the new colours too and once a girl had gone *exotic* there was no turning back. I had been at the forefront of this movement. At a tender age, during my education and apprenticeship, I had become aware of the exaggerated proportions that were possible when using less expensive materials. Accordingly, my designs were big, bold and colourful. I explored every inch of the gemstone spectrum. For me, the future wasn't just orange; it was purple, peach, grey-green and salmon. In other words, I'd gone totally tonal.

Then the rest of the industry caught on. The skilled, keenly discerning eyes of the German stone cutters, once known to just a few of the jewellery cognoscenti, soon became suppliers of choice to the masses. But by this time there was no returning to more traditional materials—I just didn't see that as progress and, after all, I was a rather progressive fellow.

Watercolour and ink artwork
of Crystal Haze Classic Ring

A common practice applied in gem cutting, predominantly when working with sapphires—is to find a crystal that has a tonal intensity in one area but little or no colour throughout the rest of it. If the gem cut from such a crystal retains even a small amount of the colour on its underside, or *culet* as it is known, this colour will diffuse throughout the whole gem. It's a similar principle to the aforementioned opal doublet or *sandwich*, as you and I might call it. I always found this phenomenon amazing. Just one of the ingenious illusions played out in the jeweller's atelier over the centuries—the concept that increasing a gem by the smallest amount would add exponentially to its beauty and desirability.

Armed with this knowledge, I started to pester the cutters I knew to work with me using clear quartz and opaque gems, trying to mimic the effect of the sapphire with colour in only the base and in the pumped-up opal. At first there was huge reluctance: "How can a fine jeweller employ such techniques to such low value material and then sell it as fine jewellery?" To be honest, they had a point, but never one to let sound advice stand in my way—I would be an unemployed dockworker if I had—I ignored them.

Of course, as a designer, I intended to make this thing my own; the piece of rock crystal or quartz was to be cut in a high dome as before, but this time faceted in the style I had applied to solid, semi-precious stones. Under the clear facet cap was to be set a slice of either turquoise, blue lapis or silver obsidian. The rough material for this technique was relatively inexpensive, and needed to be, as the initial failure and breakage rate was 100 per cent. This sounds silly but it was true. I was making rings but instead of cutting the coloured material in flat slices I wanted the stones to be cut in curves, which would wrap around the top half of the finger. Employing unconventional materials and methods, I wanted to create a mystery... an illusion.

In the end, most of the cutters got fed up with me—and trust me, you only want to push a German stonecutter so far. They work with heavy equipment and tend to live in isolation. Armed with a few crystal tops and a few more of the carved thin layers of coloured rocks, I worked on my own, spending hours and hours, months and months, grinding with diamond compound to achieve the perfect fit between the two surfaces. Once the seam was as tight as a Scotsman's wallet, I would mix up my epoxy, apply it, clamp the two together and retire, hopefully. Inevitably, what appeared as slightly mucky, potentially dazzling perfection the previous night, would have developed thousands of tiny air bubbles by morning. It was soul destroying. But being

In my ultimate man cave,
a subterranean rock cellar,
Idar-Oberstein, 2013

First picture taken of the original
18k gold and diamond Crystal Haze
Ring, created by bonding Blue
Agate and faceted rock crystal

stubborn—a quality I can thank my father for—I would not give up. I could see that if teething problems could be overcome then the finished effect would be truly amazing... and my fortune in the bag.

The final key to my perfecting this revolutionary method lay not so much in the cutting but in the gluing process. While the two halves of the stones—perfectly curved slices and beautiful faceted crystal tops—were always textbook examples of the skill of the great gem cutters' art they just wouldn't stick together and over the weeks would be reduced to a pile of useless broken bits. After a year or so of such trial, error and disappointment, someone told me about an epoxy that had been developed specially for use by a group of specialist glass sculptors, located on the north west coast of the US, lead by the famous glass artist Dale Chihuly.

After some intense detective work, I found the secret mixture required—and I mean very secret, if I told you the formula, I'd have to kill you—which we still use in abundance in our studio today. It consists of two solutions—both with coded names to protect their identities—so thin in consistency that they appear like water. A very small amount is dribbled over the surfaces to be bonded, most of it surplus and running out to waste but, magically, with the liquid excess, the potential air bubbles run away also. Three days later, the two have become one and the complete stone is set so strong it would have to be smashed to tear it apart.

That glue changed everything and my *Crystal Haze* technique is now probably the most copied in the jewellery trade. The secret process has allowed me to introduce many, many more materials to my designs, cutting each stone individually in Idar-Oberstein, the small German town that became the centre of the European stone-cutting industry 100 years ago. As a renowned retail jeweller in the US once said to me: "Stephen, only you could make pebbles look so damned glamorous." That said, at first, most of the business dismissed me as a sort of jewellery hooligan but once they realised that almost every celebrity worth their salt was sporting a Stephen Webster *Crystal Haze* cocktail ring, things changed.

The volume of stones required was such that some of our German friends started farming out their cutting jobs to Thailand. In principal I had no problem with this, as the quality remained the same. Then I had an idea. I boarded a plane to Bangkok, visited the Thai cutters myself and cut out the scheming middlemen from the Rhineland-Palatinate. SW now has almost 100 people permanently employed in cutting the hundreds and hundreds of gem sandwich patterns that we have since developed.

The most recent trip was particularly fruitful; we were able to reintroduce an old favourite—Matrix Ruby—to the mix. Apart from having a name like some kind of corundum superhero, this type of ruby, mostly found in Tanzania and other East African locations, has a wonderful, semi-opaque raspberry hue making it perfect as a base colour for our *Crystal Haze*. Other new colours include deep London blue topaz over mother of pearl and pale blue topaz over hematite.

Even though the industry now feels that mimicking our original technique is fair game, no one else has yet shown that they can cut the complex, curved designs that I spent so long developing, or has the creativity to experiment with the same profoundly complicated mix and variety of materials. Imitation, as they say, is the sincerest form of flattery.

Fuelled by Cali-gas, at the end of another successful fishing trip on Romney Marsh, 1968

CHAPTER 15

FISHING

Luring a jeweller

My father was a keen angler and coarse fisherman, his quarry the river, his game freshwater species of roach, rudd and tench, his equipment the cane rod and fly. I can't recall any recreational time of my childhood when I wasn't fishing or digging for bait. Some weekends I would get everyone up at five AM in order to get to the seaside, a couple of hours and a car picnic away, just so we could catch the tide and fish for 12 or so hours. My brother was similarly fanatical about fishing, but well aware of my fiercely competitive and volatile personality, he dreaded a situation where he might make the first catch of the day. So much so, in fact, that he would even consider throwing back a quick biting fish just to keep the peace.

I don't remember whether I actually liked eating fish, especially those disgusting eels we'd hook sometimes, but my Mum and Dad seemed to consume everything so it didn't matter. Like most fishermen, however, I loved the tackle; reels, weights, feathers, scales and the pretty, shiny lures that you could never have too many of. Lures could be anything, mostly some interpretation or another of a fish or crab or squid. They were always detailed and creative, some realistically painted and accessorised, but all with one thing in common: a nasty three-pronged, medieval-looking hook or multiple hooks hanging from the rear. It still makes me shudder to think of the potential pain inflicted by such beautiful things. Lures have a lot more in common with expensive jewellery than you might think.

My love of fishing ran alongside a fascination with anything that lived below the surface of the water. Most young lads show some interest in pond life but almost all of my youth was spent up to my knees in water. For seven consecutive years we took our holiday the first two weeks in June—God knows why, it meant asking for time off school—in the same tiny caravan equipped with gas filament lighting and a two ring stove, positioned adjacent to Pett Level Beach, East Sussex. To the right was Hastings, providing Victorian amusements and a pier for fishing, to the left was Rye, with a pottery, which would eventually, rather conveniently, provide a wife for my brother—Dave is now married to the granddaughter of the owners of the unique Rye Pottery whose distinct 1960s glazed mugs and coffee pots were collected by our parents, two mugs at a time, until they had a complete set. Behind was the expanse of dykes and fields known as Romney Marsh—some of the best coarse and eel fishing in the south east, and home to thousands of frogs. Out front and under the waves sat a seabed, which, way back in the Jurassic period, was a prehistoric forest. Not only were these rock pools alive with crustacea and jellyfish, but also molluscs and fossils.

My Dad made us a massive shrimp net—it seemed massive when I was seven and David five. The handle was lifted from an old grass mower; the agitator, a five-foot plank of four by two; its net, five foot by three foot of bright orange gauze. Some days, as the tide went out, we would wade in and catch up to seven pints of brown shrimps. At the same time my Mum would be filling her bucket with mussels. When the water came in again and the sea reclaimed the Jurassic forest, the real fishing would start. Depending on the time of day or the weather, the catch could consist of Mackerel—this was before sushi had been invented and the plentiful fish was still considered cat food—Pollock, Pouting, Bass or 'orrible eels.

My family will never forget the night when I was sitting on the beach watching my dad fish when he got what appeared to be the most humongous bite. With my usual enthusiasm, I dashed back to the caravan to tell my mum to put the saucepan on—Dad had a fish! By the time I ran back to Dad he was fighting with what I could only recognise as a sea serpent, its head popping out of the waves to reveal a mouthful of gnashing teeth. It turned out to be just that; a serpent tying itself in knots, covered in slime—a six-foot conger eel. A Loch Ness monster of a catch. With firm boot control, Dad finally managed to get the writhing beast far enough from the sea to begin the complicated task of putting it out of its misery. One thing was pretty clear—Mum's saucepan was the wrong utensil for boiling this deep-sea behemoth. Our family ended up feasting on conger steaks for a week.

On holiday, we would alternate between the sea and the dykes of Romney Marsh with its newts, frogs and slow worms—all the nasty, slimy things that little boys are made of, and all the things that made Pett Level the perfect place for a holiday. We were so lucky that we couldn't afford the new trend for holidaying on the Costa Brava and the melanoma inducing, mind-numbingly boring beaches of Torremolinos and Lloret de Mar.

My enthusiasm for all things sub aqua didn't stop with my recreational pursuits either. My reading material and the inspirations for my art classes was also aquatically themed. Recently, in my dad's attic, we found some of my old school books, amongst them an art project from when I was just 12 years old: "Studies of British Sea Fish." Even though I say so myself, my drawing of a cod was pretty fair likeness.

At school I made a fishing rod from scratch; then, a fibreglass canoe. My rod wasn't bad, it worked, I caught fish on it, it just wasn't my best rod. That was the one I got from my Auntie Peg. At the time, Peg was married to a jeweller called Fred—it was by complete coincidence that David and I later became jewellers ourselves. As an all round *bad 'un* Fred didn't leave much impression on us but he was a rather colourful character. After he'd left Auntie Peg, in a bid to keep his second wife in the style she demanded, he got himself in a pickle and faked his own mugging, telling the Gravesend cops that his attackers had got away with some valuable jewellery. Unfortunately for Fred, he'd cracked under interrogation and spilled the beans on his scam. I believe he even did a stretch for it.

So, single Auntie Peg treated Dave and I like her own. She was a cook in the Prince of Orange pub and couldn't have earned much, but all of the coupons she'd racked up from her 40 Guards a day cigarette habit were gifted to us. This was like winning the lottery. There were some things in the Guards' coupon catalogue that even the most enthusiastic, deeply inhaling chain smoker couldn't possibly hope to save up for during their curtailed lifetime—a Ford Escort car being one. Other booty represented a challenge but if Peg really put both lungs into her habit, it could be ours. Toward the back of the catalogue, amongst the high tar awards, was a fishing rod. The photo made it look like the best fishing rod in the world. Every Sunday when we visited Peg we would make a beeline for the coupon jar on the kitchen shelf, counting and recounting the vouchers and calculating just how many packets Peg was shy of the beautiful fishing rod. Eventually I got the rod and almost immediately, Peg gave up smoking.

The Cod, drawn aged 11 or 12. Inspiration for a million pieces of jewellery

Watercolour and ink artwork of Jewels Verne Diamond Collar

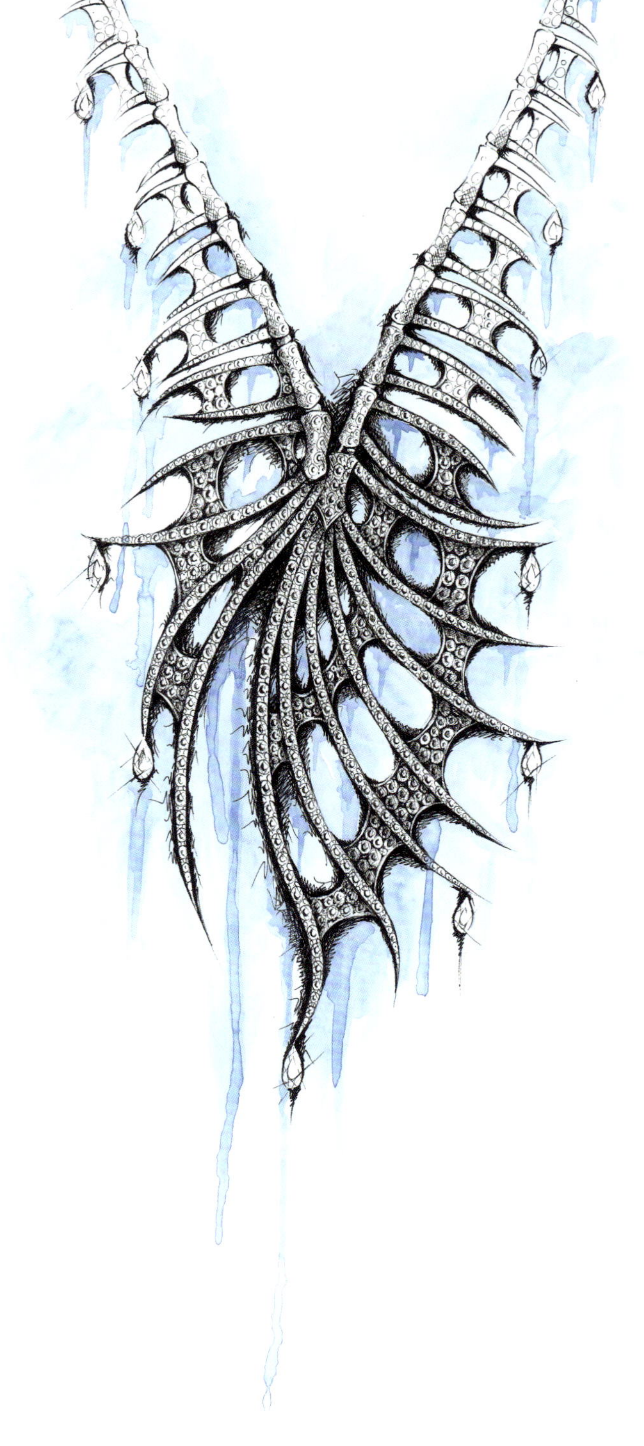

Needless to say, as I entered my teens, fishing got sidelined in favour of clothes, girls, music and motorbikes—the usual distractions. Throughout those formative years I had no idea what a huge influence the sea, and what it had to offer, would prove to be on my work later on in life. In the words of Jules Verne: "the sea is a living infinity." These days, I am very lucky to live in a house that looks out over the sea. Perched on top of the iconic White Cliffs of Dover, it's not actually Dover, but on the same stretch of coastline next to a castle and a lighthouse. From the house is an uninterrupted view across the English Channel at exactly the narrowest point between England and France. Mainland Europe is so close that turning into our road is marked by a "Welcome to France" message from French Telecom flashing up on one's smartphone screen. Not only do phones ring with the single tone that implies that the recipient is offshore, but the device's atomic clock also jumps forward an hour. Terrestrial TV and radio channels are also French. We make a point of only offering guests tea, toast and Marmite for breakfast, as a pain au chocolat or baguette would be throwing in the towel completely.

Waking up to a sea view is something I will never get bored of. No two days are the same—light, colour and conditions are always so much more dramatic in close proximity to open water. The channel is busy but never hectic. Apart from the odd speedboat, most large vessels travel by, their rhythms and corridors dictated by the sea's drag. At night the illuminated decks of the constant Dover to Calais ferries can look like glamorous cruise ships returning from exotic destinations.

At least two of the three years I spent in landlocked Alberta, Canada were the unhappiest of my life. There must be a condition similar to SAD (Seasonal Affective Disorder) that preys on those of us who need to live on the edges. Over the years the sea, sea life and life at sea, have probably been the most reoccurring influences on the jewellery my studio designs. The ongoing and hugely successful *Jewels Verne* collection, for instance, being inspired by a precious book from my childhood that I still own and treasure: Jules Verne's *Twenty Thousand Leagues Under the Sea*.

All of our collections start with an inspiration that leads to a moodboard of ideas and references. From these we start creating individual pieces of jewellery. Even though we only use the original inspiration as a guide, every now and again it helps to refer to the moodboard so that the collection remains focussed; which is important to me because, to be honest, staying focussed is not one of my strong points. I tend to get excited by the elements that come to light during the creative process and I get carried away. This is all part of being creative and in so many ways my talent for distraction got me to where I am today. *Jewels Verne*, the jewellery collection, was actually inspired by a kind of wildly imagined seafood buffet, some pieces almost anatomically correct, others total fantasy.

During the collection's design stage, my head designer Claire handed me a sketch loosely based on twisted, stylised shrimps mixed with different coloured gems. For some reason I immediately thought of "the girl with the prawn earring"—our creative process for a collection coinciding with the release of the movie *Girl With A Pearl Earring* starring Scarlett Johansson, based on the story behind the famous Vermeer painting of the same name. I decided there and then to make a film. Unlike the aforementioned, oil painting-inspired drama—which was, quite literally, like watching paint dry—my movie was going to be a short, sharp clip about a girl who wore shrimps as jewellery.

I wrote up a script and recruited my friend, BAFTA

Poster for the short film, *Girl with a Prawn Earring*, introducing Amy Webster, 2009

winning director Heidi Greensmith, to direct. The talent ended up being my 18 year-old daughter, Amy. The final component, and most fun auditioning for, was the voice over. I looked to Hollywood and found a brilliant voice-over actor who specialised in the clichéd introduction of the blockbuster trailer: "In a world, where one woman who had nothing, still dreamt of making a difference" etc. Shot on location at the home of interior designer Kelly Hoppen, we made *The Girl with the Prawn Earring*, a heartwarming tearjerker about a girl, who despite all the odds, ends up realising her dreams of having dendrobranchiata hanging off her shell-likes. Pitched as an art-house thriller and from the same studio that brought you the *The Silence of the Clams* and *There's Something Fishy about Mary*, we like to think that, if in competition, it may well have won a Golden Lobe.

Continuing our undersea theme, the *Jewels Verne* collection was followed by a new collection, *In Deep*, the most successful piece from this collection being, rather surprisingly, a cocktail ring in the shape of a crab; a crab cocktail, if you will. The first year we featured this £10,000 ring in our advertising campaign, modelled by the fair hand of our brand ambassador Christina Aguilera, we sold three or four. The following year we sold 50. Had the world gone crustacean crazy? As usual, it was the Russians that started it. They couldn't seem to get enough of them. For the following few years the crab cocktail was our biggest selling ring, all over the world. On something of a crustacean high, I had a brainwave; people like crab but they love lobster. So we created a long fingered lobster ring, a *fish finger*: the "longoustine." Believe it or not some people have both—crab and lobster—*fruits de mer* you can wear.

Telling tales with David on a riverbank somewhere in England

CHAPTER 16

GRIMSBY AND CAMERON DIAZ

I chose Grimsby over Cameron Diaz—the salty social life of a faded Lincolnshire fishing port over the celebrity razzle-dazzle of a Hollywood A-lister. This is how it happened.

Due to pressing artistic commitments abroad, my friend Tracey Emin, then a columnist for *The Independent* newspaper, invited some of her friends to guest write her weekly missive whilst she was away. I can't recall who stood in first but I vividly recall being followed by Sir Peter Blake—so, decent company. Prior to this lofty commission from a proper newspaper—a broadsheet, no less—I had only written a few pieces for trade rags. I wanted to get this just right. Frankly, I didn't really know where to start; after all, my specialist field was making jewellery. Tracey stepped in with some classic advice: "Write about what you know," she said—both of us having been raised in the same home county—"Why not contribute a column about being from Kent?" So I did.

Inspired by my hometown of Gravesend and a wedding I had recently attended in Cape Fear, North Carolina, I penned a few hundred words about the bleak outlook of people from towns with a condemned name. After extensive research on damned place names, I discovered that the top of the blacklist wasn't doomy sounding Gravesend at all, but the industrial fish-processing port of Grimsby; the "grim" in Grimsby sealing its fate, apparently. Maybe I am drawn to these communities with unpromising, misfortunate monikers, but I actually happened to like Grimsby. I'd made the pilgrimage to the rainy Lincolnshire coast many times, to Grimsby and occasionally on to its more glamorous seaside neighbour, Cleethorpes; not for my research as Tracey's stand-in columnist but because I had successfully sold my jewels to the locals, who were, as one might expect, mainly attracted to the dark side of my work, that and the fish-themed pieces, of course.

The year 2014 marked the ten year anniversary of selling our collections through G. Hewett & Son—a jeweller on Grimsby High Street—who, like most retailers that bought from us, enjoyed launching new collections with a party for clients. After several visits I was beginning to become something of a familiar face around town—I know, get me!—and perhaps more accepted amongst the locals than just the "poncey designer up from London" that they had, no doubt, dismissed me as on first sight.

I also got a bit of a perverse kick from my Grimsby connection. In my game, no one ever questions the worth of regular sojourns to places such as Las Vegas, Dallas, Los Angeles, Moscow and Dubai... but Grimsby is different.

An incredible montage of a shark and SW jewellery, created and photographed by Tzu Chen Chen. This was commissioned and given to me by the SW staff to mark my first 30 years as a jeweller in 2006

Grimsby has a cachet, a special allure all of its own, an elusive quality to which my friends and family could never quite relate. "Grimsby? What the hell are you doing in Grimsby?" they would ask incredulously whenever I announced that I would be returning, yet again. Locals are known as "Grimbarians" or "codheads," I would tell them enthusiastically. Sacha Baron Cohen has made a film called *Grimsby* and Elton John even wrote a song about the place, "Grimsby," off his 1974 *Caribou* album: "No *Cordon Bleu* can match the beauty of your pies and peas. I want to ride your fairground. Take air along the quay." I like to think that my annual visits were my way of giving back, a simple and gracious *thank you* to my customers and retailer, a demonstration of the democracy that runs through the SW brand like a stick of Cleethorpes seaside rock.

My annual Grimsby jaunts were pretty good for business too. The first trip was fun and commercially more successful than the glitzy Grimbarians and I would ever have thought possible. So, the next year Mr Hewett asked me to come back and, never one to say no to a party, I did. After seven or eight trips north, my wife was beginning to suspect that I had been courting the attentions of widowed fishwives in the area, of whom there are many due to the well-documented hazards of a life at sea. Almost a decade later, with the novelty—the unfathomable, esoteric magic of Grimsby, if you will—having worn off somewhat, I decided to show my face on the south side of the Humber estuary one last time.

The Cameron Diaz moment occurred on a Saturday evening: 5th November 2005, Guy Fawkes night. Due to the otherwise packed and riotous nature of the Grimsby social schedule G. Hewett's clients and beautiful people were only available for parties on Sundays so the best way to arrive for the noon kick-off the next day was to leave on Saturday afternoon. I'd stay overnight in a local boutique hostelry and head to downtown Grimsby after a leisurely breakfast.

I was about five miles away from the big smoke, making for the ribbon of the M1. It was raining, the heavy grey sky damply illuminated only periodically by the starburst of a firework in the distance. My mobile phone rang: "Hi darling," said my wife, "I just heard from Cameron Diaz's people. She is in town. She's been wearing our jewellery and wants to know if you would like to meet her. Where are you now? Can you turn back?" Cameron Diaz? Or the good people of Grimsby? My loyal North East Lincolnshire clientele or the gorgeous blonde who danced in her underpants in *that* scene in the *Charlie's Angels* movie? No contest. I hung up, focussed on the road ahead and put my foot down. Then I checked into the only respectable hotel in Grimsby, made myself a cup of tea and watched the *X Factor*.

The following day we had a good show. I told no one about my cancelled date with one of Hollywood's royalty. On the upside, John, the owner and grandson of the founder G. Hewett, gifted me three kilos of smoked haddock, the gold standard of English fish. On the drive out of Grimsby that evening, somewhere on the A180 just between Stallingborough and Croxton, the idea that I had passed up a date with sun-kissed Cameron Diaz in favour of a white polystyrene box of the North Sea's finest made me smile.

CHAPTER 17

JOHN COOPER CLARKE

I fell in love with poetry not by studying TS Eliot at school or reading Wordsworth at Oxford but at an Elvis Costello concert back in 1978. I'd arrived at the gig unintentionally early, in time to catch what I presumed to be a mediocre support act. Then John Cooper Clarke, aka the "punk poet," appeared on stage; garden hose thin, hair like Struwwelpeter and cursed with a Salford accent so thick it could descale a kettle with just a few, caustically drawn-out vowels. No guitars. No drums. Just this skinny, mod-suited Manc and a microphone. In an era when the statutory requirement for a rock 'n' roll show was a three or four-piece beat combo, being a soloist was eccentric enough, but to appear on stage denuded of all instrumentation and perform acapella was really pushing it.

Accompanied only by a plastic shopping bag, John pulled out a can of lager and yanked its ring pull. Much shuffling of loose leaves of paper from an A4 legal pad followed this manoeuvre. Finally, in a voice that came from the wrong side of Coronation Street, he spoke: "What's this?" he asked standing with his legs and feet together, arms out to the sides, his bantamweight body shifting in a waving motion: "Jesus on a rubber cross," he told us. He was chewing gum. He glanced at the top sheet of paper, the gum chewing became a kind of rhythm section and he launched into the first poem: "A romantic number."

I Married a Monster from Outer Space

I fell in love with an alien being
Whose skin was jelly, whose teeth were green
She had the big bog eyes
The Death ray glare
Feet like water wings
Purple hair
I was over the moon I asked her back to my place
Then I married the monster from outer space

I was hooked. With the Jack Sprat frame of the chronically undernourished, the Bard of Salford looked as though the slightest breeze from an open door would send him flying stage left, but John Cooper Clarke was certainly no lightweight when it came to performing. With punk's predominantly male and perpetually gobbing, glass-throwing crowd considered the norm at an evening's entertainment, standing out on that stage, on his own, to deliver the spoken word suggested that there was something powerful driving him. He definitely wasn't in it for the money.

The rest of the set was made up of poetry numbers that were soon to become classics and still requested at JCC gigs almost four decades later: "Health Fanatic," "Psycho Sluts," "Salome Maloney" and "(I've Got a Brand New) Track Suit."

John Cooper Clarke pretending
he needed to read his poems at my
50th birthday party in 2009

I loved every word, every rhyme and stanza. Instantly, I was a fan. I learned the lyrics and copied the Manc delivery. I bought the recordings and the books and could recite many of the poems off by heart. I went to more gigs. Then, approximately a quarter of a century after that first concert, I finally met him in person.

Standing in the VIP area at the closing concert of the iconic Hammersmith Palais who should I see? John had been the compare that night, dressed magnificently in Lurex and Terylene, he had hypnotised me. Never one to approach a hero and announce myself as "a big fan," I was happy to just be in his vicinity. My friend Hamish McAlpine had other ideas, taking it on himself to tell John that I had long been an admirer. Forced to acknowledge me now, John and I shook hands and exchanged small talk. But just as the small talk was heading nowhere, I remembered reading on a flyer that he was soon to perform in Whitstable, Kent. To my surprise, John said, "give me your number and I'll put you on the door." To be honest, I felt pretty certain that an ex-heroin addicted poet probably wasn't going to remember to put my wife and I on the guest list of a gig a few weeks down the line, but it was nice of him to offer. "I'll be on at 9pm," he said.

A couple of weeks later, leaving plenty of time to arrive for the nine o'clock show, we set off for Whitstable. On route, the phone rang: "Hi, is that Stephen? Johnny Clarke here. I made a mistake. It's not nine, it's eight. I'm so sorry. Where are you?" We were still half an hour away, I told him. "Well I'll try to hold the crowd." I put my foot down. We entered the small auditorium as quietly as we could, but John, already on stage by now, had heard us coming in: "Is that Stephen?" he said, loud and clear into the mic. With that, all the attention was on us: "Yes, John. We're here." "This is my friend, Stephen," continued John to the crowd. "He is an amazing jeweller, and he makes jewellery for Michael Stipe and everyone." Why he chose to name check Michael Stipe is still a mystery to me.

After the gig we went for dinner—surprisingly, for a man so thin, John eats like a horse. He wanted Chinese but in Whitstable, after ten at night, you get what you're given. So it was Indian. Since that concert and curry John and his wife Eveline have become close friends of ours.

On one such memorable occasion, I co-hosted an evening at a Notting Hill jewellers, inviting my friend and writer Olivia Cole to read a poem from her newly-published book and John to headline with one or two of his compositions. Because I didn't want to be left out of any part of this poetry and jewellery evening, I also wrote a poem—a semi-autobiographical piece called "Jeweller Boy."

The store was packed full of Notting Hill yummy mummies, there for the champagne and the jewellery, needless to say, rather than the poetry. First up was Olivia, followed by me with my first, and to be honest, rather weak attempt at the genre. "Jewellery Boy" was more of a limerick really but a crowd-pleaser amongst the wealthy, Stairmastered, lunching ladies of W11. Now it was time for the headline act. As the polite applause faded away, John Cooper Clarke came on stage. To this day, I've never had a proper explanation for his chosen opening gambit. This was a tighter space and a smaller crowd than he was used to, but nothing could have prepared the intimate gathering for the provocative nature of what came next: "I said to a friend of mine the other day that I wasn't sure if my wife has Alzheimer's or AIDS," he said, playing the brash Northern comedian in this polite West London enclave. "His advice was; take her to a place she's very familiar with and if she finds her way home don't fuck her." I learned that night that poets can be unpredictable and that John is no exception. If you book him, you can't censor him.

Over the last few years John has performed at a number of SW events, including both mine and my brother Dave's fiftieth birthday bash, and we have become rather close. Due to a few factors, not least that one of his masterpieces "Chicken Town" was used on the final episode of *The Sopranos*, and artists such as Plan B and The Arctic Monkeys using his lyrics in their songs, John has finally achieved the recognition and audience his genius deserves. On that night back in 1978, I knew I was witnessing something very special but I would never have predicted that almost 40 years later the same skinny punk poet would be headlining at the London Palladium and the Royal Festival Hall; and at my birthday party.

Behind the scenes at a Rankin
shoot for the SW 2015 campaign

CHAPTER 18

FASHIONING FINE JEWELLERY

And the inauguration of Rock Vault

Famously, Queen Victoria's extended period of grief following the death of her beloved Prince Albert, lead to a fashion for wearing "mourning jewellery." Jewellers from all over Britain turned their hands to the jet black, fossilised wood found almost exclusively around the north-eastern coastal town of Whitby, coincidentally the port by which the Prince of Darkness, Count Dracula, entered our shores. Over the years, trends in fine jewellery have kept pace with the changing times. Pearls have been in fashion, as have coloured exotics such as turquoise, coral or amethyst, mostly mixed with yellow gold. The vogue during the 1920s and 1930s was for white gold and platinum.

In the mid '70s when I started in the industry there had been a movement toward more arty pieces and visionary jewellers such as Andrew Greamer, Gerder Flockinger and John Donald had been deconstructing the tight symmetrical styles commonly associated with fine, gem-set jewellery. Their pieces were more organic and although made of the same precious materials, felt less formal. This approach lead to more design-driven pieces and collections in the following decades.

Living and working as a jeweller during the second half of the 1980s, I embraced an enthusiasm for big, bold, coloured exotics. This time around it was the turn of relative newcomers such as fuchsia pink and deep green tourmaline, purple/blue tanzanite, beryls and, my personal favourite, hot pink kunzite. The use of these materials was also championed on the main stage by brands such as Bulgari and Tiffany. This kind of jewellery suited the garish styles of the times, but fine jewellery was still not considered an essential part of a young and fashionable look. In fact, the all-powerful fashion magazines and fashion journalists wouldn't give fine jewellery the time of day. It wasn't just about the price, more that fine jewellery just wasn't "cool." All that was about to change.

We felt the effect sometime around the mid-to-late 1990s—the same time that I had sold one of my *Crystal Haze* cocktail rings to Madonna, in itself a big deal for me, of course. But when the first photos of her wearing the ring on her index finger, whilst holding a flute of Champagne and flanked by new boyfriend Guy Ritchie were published, things really took off. American *Vogue* cited me as the person who reinvented the cocktail ring and everything else seemed to follow—the New York fashionistas, including a young Tory Burch, all wanted one. Bergdorf Goodman came to London and took half my stock.

For myself and a few other design-driven jewellers, this was the time that our pieces became integral parts of the

The complete Rock Vault—
all designers in front of the SW
flagship boutique, Beverly Hills,
in 2015

look. The very same fashion magazines and papers that had ignored us before begun dedicating editorial coverage to new jewellery design. From zero to hero, fine jewellery was now in fashion.

Along with this newfound interest came an interest in the designers themselves: Who are the new jewellers? What are they like? Are they little old men in brown lab coats? I remember journalist Lydia Slater coming to my postage stamp-sized shop on Manchester Square, London. She had been commissioned by *The Daily Telegraph* to write a piece on my work and what made me tick, but I could tell from the first look she gave me that whoever she was expecting to meet, it wasn't me.

Today there are so many known young designer jewellers. There are also so many more retail and e-tail platforms on which to showcase and sell contemporary fine jewellery. Alongside the new wave of jewellery stores are concept stores, high fashion stores and online retailers. This has had an amazing effect on the progression not only of jewellery design, but also the way in which people wear jewellery. Customers and stylists are creative too. A few years ago, I'm not sure I could have imagined all the possible ways in which a ring could be worn—it's anywhere but the ring finger these days. There are long finger rings, double finger rings, rings that are worn above the first knuckle of the finger, four finger knuckle dusters, rings worn all over the hand connected by fine chains. The list goes on and on. Today's designers no longer bring versions of the same set pieces of jewellery to the party; the approach is more likely to be how their jewellery is worn. A stud earring stopped being just a stud a long time ago and is now much more likely to work its way all the way up the ear, probably taking in a cuff or two on its journey north.

Three years ago Caroline Rush, CEO of the British Fashion Council, gave me the great honour of curating Rock Vault, a new initiative for emerging jewellery talent. Recently, we watched our first Rock Vault graduates triumph from the initiative. Fernando Jorge and Melanie Georgacopolous are now two of the hottest new jewellery designers in the international marketplace. Fernando's use of coloured stones, sourced mainly from his home country of Brazil, is so beautifully creative, feminine and contemporary that every woman can find a piece or more to suit her wardrobe in his collections. Melanie has made pearls contemporary and her elegantly theatrical pieces are a showstopper. Amongst the next designers who will graduate soon is Tomasz Donocik who won the Diamond category design award and Best New Designer award at the Vegas show in our first year of showcasing Rock Vault in Vegas. Tomasz's collections are strong for both men and women, often incorporating creative use of leather with diamonds and precious metals.

This is a very exciting time to be a young designer jeweller. So many of the formerly emerging markets have now well and truly surfaced, introducing more and more young buyers, all of whom seem to love fine jewellery. Young, fashionable women from cultures to whom fine jewellery has always been important are now amongst the largest buyers of the most contemporary designs. The men's market is booming too.

Last year, after three years of development, SW introduced a ceramic link, which is inexpensive to make and can be created in many colours. We used the link to make a bracelet and a necklace; the intrinsic value belonging to the variety of clasps that we offer in a range of golds and detailed in gemstones. The idea is that the clasp can be removed completely allowing a different coloured ceramic link bracelet to be worn with it. This design became a huge hit for us. This year we introduced several new links, including three for men. My retailers consider this piece as key in the progression of the exciting men's jewellery category. What was once a backward looking industry, moving at a sloth-like pace now makes leaps and bounds into the future.

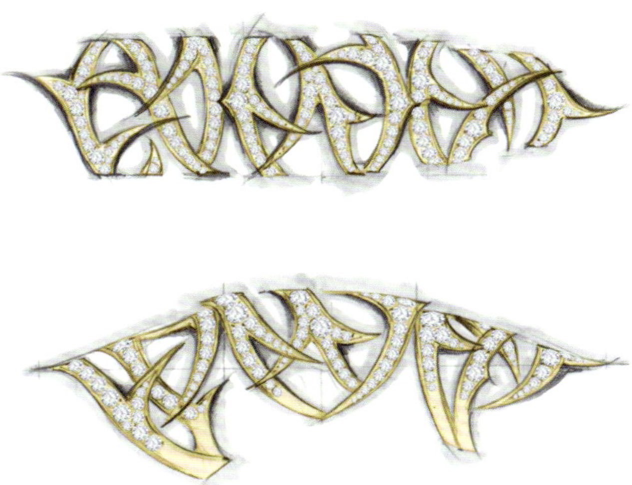

Design for Thorn Long Finger Ring, 2013

Squatting high in the mining area
of Peru, 2011

CHAPTER 19

THE SLOW GOLD RUSH

A few years ago, during the Basel show, I was approached by a couple of guys from Holland, asking if I would be interested in working with guaranteed, responsibly sourced gold. This was not the first time we had been approached with the same proposal—the first time had not quite worked out, the guy in question that time wasn't Dutch, but as it turned out, an out of work actor. Never one to turn down something responsible, we said yes. The next time we saw him was six months later. In his rucksack he had a small golden nugget—that being our allocation from the slightly larger nugget he had panned for over the duration of his trip to South America. Obviously we needed more of a flow than the trickle he was offering. With this in mind I cautiously said yes again to the latest offer.

Soon it became apparent that these two represented an NGO that was funded to offer a viable alternative to the thousands of poverty stricken families who toil in hazardous, artisanal mines across South America. The people involved in this massive unregulated corrupt form of gold mining sign a death warrant from the day they start. Not only are the mines unsafe and prone to collapse but also the extraction process involves the handling of huge quantities of mercury. Despite the metre being one of the most valuable things money can buy, the miners earn no more than $1 a day.

Like the out of work actor, we didn't see the two Dutch de Golders for over six months, the difference being that when they did turn up they had joined forces with Fairtrade, the most recognised name in responsibly sourced products—it's hard to find a banana these days with out the yin and yang symbol of Fairtrade. Over the next two years—we had no idea it would take that long when we signed up—we followed all the instruction required by the sticklers at Fairtrade/Fairmined, so that once the metal was made available, we would qualify for one of the first ever Fairtrade licences for responsibly sourced gold. We would be able to promote this fact at our point of sale.

Finally our business passed the stringent tests and all we needed was the precious metal. At this point my enquiring mind took over. I made my own proposal that David and I, and a one-woman film crew in the form of my friend Heidi, make a trip to the few villages in Peru who, through the help and education offered by firstly the NGO Solidaridad, and eventually Fairtrade, had been able to vastly improve their lot and income. For some reason the Fairtrade folk were surprised but also delighted that we offered ourselves up for what was inevitably going to be an adventure.

A month later we were bound for the unregulated mines of Peru. Lima was hot and sultry, just as we had hoped. The

man waiting for us at the airport might have been there all night had David not deciphered what was written on his plaque: "SPEPHAN WEBFPER"; so close, yet so far! Wanting to hit the town before heading to the mountains the next morning, we followed the instruction of the concierge toward what we asked for—Lima's hot spots. We never actually found Lima's hot spot but did find the hot fast food spot—the concierge later admitted he misunderstood our request—which was a bit like a steamy Shepherds Bush.

The next day we met our hosts and Heidi all ready for the trip. Aware that coffee in South America is considered to be top shelf, I ordered a cup with my breakfast. The locals all opted for tea. I soon found out why. The thick liquorice brew I was served should have come with a health warning—even after I emptied the contents of the milk jug into my cup, the coffee seemed to absorb it and remained black. The mouth puckering bitterness and instant palpitations lead me to believe it had been spiked. My new Peruvian friends laughed at my reaction and advised me to take the tea in future.

Despite the chronic and inevitable health hazards surrounding the handling of mercury in any capacity, these open pits have to be the absolute worst. As is always the case, this deadly form of extraction is also the cheapest. Men and women manually haul rocks blasted from mines deep in the ground to the open pits in which lies a murky mix of muddy water and mercury. In the middle of each pit stands a stone rig straight from *The Flintstones*, on which two men perch—balanced by holding a crossbar above their heads and transferring their weight from side to side—rocking the huge stone mass in a seesaw fashion and crushing the boulders being continuously fed into the pit, around which play tiny children. Apart from the odd truck or ratty motorbike, the scene could be from the Old Testament; unfortunately a depiction of the true price of gold.

We finally reached our destination, the Aurelsa mine, one of the first in the area to have stopped using mercury in the extraction process. Four years prior to our visit, Gonzalo and the Solidaridad boys visited the community who mine

My brother and I, with absolutely no regrets about travelling to Peru and going down a two kilometre deep hole in the ground

Aurelsa. Many have migrated there over the past 25 years from all over Peru, with nothing more than the allure of gold in the hills and the chance to strike lucky, but they sadly join the many others prospecting for precious little. Having seen far too many of their number retire to early graves, the village elders were keen to listen to what the visitors had to say.

Juan, who we were to meet, had lived in the village for 25 years, having arrived there as a 15 year-old. He and the other long-term residents had built, with their own hands, a school and other facilities, forming what is now a proper community. Having raised a family there, Juan and the others were desperate to provide better or, perhaps I should say, *some* prospects for their children. Through education and felicitation provided by the organisation, and of course a strong determination by the villagers, the Aurelsa mine is now free of mercury; the only evidence being the dry red scars where the toxic pits were being worked not so long ago. The current processing, which is almost organic in comparison, is carried out inside Canadian-made equipment, purchased by themselves, using funds raised by the massively more efficient mining and extraction techniques employed since being taught and guided as part of the Solidaridad package, in return for working toward becoming Fairtrade compliant and ultimately lifting themselves out of poverty. It must be working, because Juan and others have managed to buy small houses in Lima where their kids go to college—I'm sure with very little intention of following in their father's footsteps!

As I have now become accustomed, a trip to a mining area has to include at least one trip down a mine. Before we went down, we continued up and up an unexpected hell-raising journey of switchbacks and hairpin bends on a loose gravel mountain pass. Our driver, who must have stood no more than four foot five in his stocking feet, could only reach the peddles on tip toes—despite having the seat rammed up against the steering wheel. Against all odds we arrived at the mouth of the Aurelsa mine. We were each handed canaries and torch mounted hard hats, and putting all thoughts of the Chilean miners tragedy to the back of our minds, we entered. Determined to show us the full extent of his good mining practices, Juan intended for us to go in deep; just how deep *deep* was, we had no idea, because, beyond the illumination provided by our hats, the way ahead was just a black hole.

Then it happened, our worst nightmare; immediately in front of us a load of rock fell. Collectively the hearts of the non-miners amongst us stopped. Instead of guiding us to the nearest exit, Juan started shouting in Spanish; a light shone down from what was by then a hole in the ceiling, followed by more shouting. Apparently a miner carrying out some exploratory work above had miscalculated and had found himself following the same seam. Despite the danger passing, Heidi and Dave decided they had experienced enough and wanted to live to tell the tale. I, on the other hand, felt obliged to accept Juan's hospitality and continue into the abyss. After a kilometre or so we could hear deep thumping sounds at regular intervals. This could only mean one of two things; either the return of the 50 Foot Woman, or rock was being dynamited somewhere ahead—neither option was very comforting. We pressed on until we reached the business end of the mine, the *coalface,* so to speak. The dozen or so miners stopped drilling the bedrock and literally hammering in the sticks of explosive and gathered around Juan and I. I can honestly say I rarely stand tall but for that moment among those Peruvian miners I felt like a giant. In the confines of an artisanal gold mine, height is of no advantage.

The miners wanted to know what this stranger was doing at the bottom of their mine? Juan explained that we were to be amongst the first jewellers to be working using the gold they were extracting. It was a very emotional scene, and I realised why it had been so important to complete our journey in that place. All mining is a nasty business, whether it be a large scale open faced operation or an artisanal hole in the ground that one man can squeeze into. The difference being whether people are paid fairly for their day's work or, in the case of so much unregulated gold mining around the

Juan and I, two kilometres into the Aurelsa gold mine

world, people are subject to appalling conditions and a below subsistence wage, through a complete lack of choice in life.

We completed our trip by visiting other mines all in their transitional stages, but all determined to reach Fairtrade status and a better, safer, longer life. When we returned we became unofficial spokespeople for the process. Almost one year later we were invited to be at the Valentine's Day announcement and unveiling of the first large gold ingots to be brought to the UK from some of the mines we had visited, delivered by three female miners. The reception was of course an incredibly emotional and symbolic moment for the women. We were so happy for them and couldn't help but join in the emotions a bit, despite being British. We were also amongst the first 20 companies to be granted Fairtrade/Fairmined gold licenses.

The move to responsible sourcing of all materials is a slow one. Fortunately, nowadays, more companies in the luxury sector are making it part of their business to offer transparency into the sourcing and production of the expensive goods they sell. Very recently I had a consultation with one of the world's leading authorities on responsible business practice. I was advised that nothing that is continuously extracted from the ground can be considered responsible. Even though I see the point and completely agree, I still feel a responsibility to support the communities who, despite the odds, are starting to live better lives and offer alternatives to the next generations, just like Juan and the other miners we met.

CHAPTER 20

TANZANITE

The beginning of an African adventure

The first time I ever saw or even heard of the gem known as tanzanite was back in 1981. I was in Banff, Canada; half a world away from the planet's one and only source of the mineral, the Merelani Hills, Tanzania, just a gemstone's throw from the foothills of Mount Kilimanjaro.

Manuel de Souza, a tailor and part-time gold prospector, first discovered tanzanite in 1967. The first jewellers to work with the gem—then known by its mineral name of "blue zoisite"—was Tiffany, who promptly renamed it "tanzanite," believing that the name "zoisite," sounded too much like "suicide" and might limit its commercial potential. Despite its newness, rarity and extremely attractive hue of blue/purple, with occasional flashes of red, tanzanite quickly found itself elevated to the elite and exclusive company of the world's most exotic and valuable gemstones.

Not even 50 years into the known existence of the gem, the one and only 14 kilometre-long Merelani Hills seam has been mined by many people, mainly in the usual haphazard and consequently hazardous way that is the norm within the highly unregulated world of gem mining. In 1990, due to its elevated value, the Tanzania government became interested in the stone and imposed all kinds of regulations around its mining process. Much later, in 2005, a sophisticated outfit known as Tanzanite One—listed on the London stock exchange, no less—paid $40 million for the rights to a large *block* of the mining.

Proud of their achievements at the mine and facilities they'd provided for the community of mining families, Tanzanite One, via its promotional arm the Tanzanite Foundation, began inviting a few select jewellery designers and journalists to visit their *model mine*. Never one to turn down a jolly, I accepted the offer and set off for the Serengeti and my first African adventure.

After landing in Nairobi we took a cramped and rickety plane to Arusha. The flight was very early on a clear-skied morning and as we approached our destination we flew past the majestic, snow capped icon of Kilimanjaro.

After being greeted by the Tanzanite One top brass, our first stop was visiting the school and other facilities within the community including a rare and much needed health centre providing care for those living with HIV.

The school visit was just amazing. When we arrived at break time a pretty serious game of football was in full swing. The ball was just a bunch of rags bound together with string but it didn't seem to compromise the dribbling skills of the attack. This was a spirited lot. At first, these four to

12 year-olds didn't show much interest in the visiting white folk, but pretty soon the pushing, shoving and consequent giggling started. That was when I opened the bags of booty I'd brought along and dished out coloured felt pens, pencils, paint brushes, paint, pads and footballs. The headmaster, obviously well versed in how to handle mass child hysteria, quickly returned things to a twitchy calm. All bounty was reluctantly handed in. Teacher later explained that because the kids had nothing other than bits of chalk and a small square of wood with which to conduct all their class work, exotic products as precious as coloured pencils and felt tips have to be distributed in a planned and orderly fashion.

The children were meant to sleep at the school in dorms, on raised wooden bunks, but there was a shortfall of 70 cribs meaning that many kids had just a blanket on the bare concrete. Apart from the obvious discomfort, sleeping on the floor gave no protection from the odd snake, giant spider or scorpion also sharing the hard floor. We didn't need to be told that the younger ones got very scared at this prospect, so finding out that the raised wooden bunks cost no more than $10 each, my wife and I raised the funds to make up for the missing furniture.

After a very boisterous game of football and a drawing demonstration, we were aware that we had caused more than our fair share of disruption to the curriculum and reluctantly left the school. Each and every one of the students sang us out with the school song—it's impossible not to feel emotional when I recall that moment.

The next morning wasn't looking like so much fun—we'd be descending into the abyss of the mine. As a card-carrying member of the self-preservation society and club claustrophobia, to say I was petrified at the prospect of this now unavoidable activity would be the understatement of the century, but now was no time for my cowardly stalling techniques... I was going down. The fear in my eyes became apparent when I saw a photo taken of myself descending into the shaft. Decked out in the latest gem mining clobber, complete with hard hat, Davy lamp and caged canary, I'd turned "a whiter shade of pale" than even Procol Harum had thought possible; a pallid tone highlighted by the almost blue/black skin of the miners accompanying me in that skip to hell. The only good thing about being one and a half kilometres below the surface in a hot confined space with the constant oomph of dynamite being detonated somewhere along the tunnel, is the thought of coming back up to civilisation. The subterranean experience had been hellish but almost worth it for the total euphoria I felt upon surfacing.

The rest of the day was spent following the journey of the excavated rock through the crushing, washing and eventual separating of the good from the bad and the ugly. After this edit, the piles of rough tanzanite crystals are then ready for the cutters and dealers, mostly based in Arusha, who, in turn, sell the polished gems to jewellers like me.

That first proper African journey was one that I will never forget—in no small part due to that amazing experience with the kids and going down the mine. Six years later I returned to the same place, only this time, instead of going down, I was going up to the roof of Africa: the summit of Kilimanjaro.

My friend Anton Bilton supports a small charity based in Tanzania called Standing Voice, the beneficiaries of which are Tanzanian people born with albinism. Due to a geographic twist of genetics the number of victims in the country are abnormally high. Most societies faced with the difficulties resulting from such a pigment disorder, which often includes partial or total blindness, would care for the victims as best as possible. Sadly, this is not the case in Tanzania. Through fear and ignorance, sometimes spread by a few misguided witch doctors, the affliction is considered

top They only wanted me for my football... A high school in the Tanzanite mining area, Tanzania, 2006

bottom In Deep! 1.5km down a Tanzanite mine shaft, 2006

A spectacular Tanzanite specimen
from the Tanzanite One mine, set in
a one of a kind Lady Macbeth Ring

a curse. Babies born with albinism are often killed, mutilated or at the very least, along with their mothers, ostracised from their communities. With little or no shelter in a country where the climate could not be more hostile toward a skin lacking pigmentation, the prospects for survival of any kind are bleak. For the few that manage to struggle through infancy, there is then the question of education. In excess of 32,000 people are affected by albinism in Tanzania, but there is little help on offer from a government that would rather pretend it doesn't exist.

Some time ago, in the luxury of the Bulgari Hotel, London, Anton and his wife Lisa screened a short film called *Under The Burning Sun*, documenting the lives of people living with this condition. The film followed a remarkable man who suffered albinism and survived, and through a fierce determination and exceptional intelligence, also devoted his life to educating and helping people in Tanzania with the condition. Everyone who saw the film that particular evening was touched by the man's desperation and triumphs, and how the local Tanzanian people could learn to nurture their poor fellow tribespeople rather than condemn them to a death sentence.

One year, while visiting some of the atrocious camps that children living with albinism call home, alongside members of the Standing Voice charity, Anton's plane home flew past Kilimanjaro. It struck him that in 2014 he would be completing his first half century and what better way to mark the occasion than to climb the tallest freestanding mountain in the world, whilst raising money for Standing Voice.

A group of 18 of Anton's friends signed up for the trip and on 3rd September 2014, fully kitted out in this season's high altitude chic, we left London aboard a BA flight bound for Nairobi—the first leg of our big African adventure. After an overnight stay in Nairobi, we took the short flight into Tanzania and Kilimanjaro airport, where we caught a magnificent view of the mountain that we were about to scale. It was formidable.

On the first day's trekking we had torrential rain, and even more on the second day. Thankfully, the dense vegetation of the jungle leg provided some natural shelter but our camp was pitched on a waterlogged red mud bath and was soaking wet. Boots, caked and heavy, were removed as the rain played a tattoo on our tent roofs.

One of the rules of mountain climbing is to remain hydrated—five litres a day, minimum. I'd never been a big water quaffer, but some of the swots in the team had managed to down two litres before I had time to brush my teeth. The trouble is, if you don't down a couple of bottles early on you have to catch up later, which leads to so much night peeing that one could almost class your role in the camp as a decorative water feature—I'm talking up to three litres passed a night. Oh, and I didn't mention all the complications associated with sleeping at altitude, the snoring or the insomnia. Eventually, as we rose above the clouds, the rain and the trees cleared. Even though we were continuously ascending, the glacier-capped summit of Kilimanjaro ahead loomed tall. The way a trek like this works is that different groups pick different routes up, some longer than others, some just for an alternative type of adventure. Eventually all groups merge at *high camp*, the last place to pitch before the big summit push.

Considering Kili is pitched as one of the seven wonders of Africa and generates a small industry of guides, porters, Sherpas etc., the high base camp is pretty rank. Overcrowding is one thing, but as the result of absolute minimum basic facilities, the whole place has the stench and ambience of a refugee camp—a malodorous blot on an otherwise awesome landscape.

For some reason, apparently rooted in cruelty and tradition, the summit push begins at midnight when it's very dark and very, very cold; as fucking freezing as Banff, in fact. Some say this is so climbers, already dealing with the extreme effects of altitude, don't add to their already considerable burden by also being able to clock just how far they are away from the peak. Others put a light-hearted spin on the scheduling, claiming that the midnight start is timed to coincide with daylight bursting forth as climbers tip over the summit. Either way, the final 1,300 metres of ascent, an eight-kilometre distance travelled over a period of six hours, at a maximum pace of 1.5 kilometres an hour due to the impossible lack of air is about as challenging as it gets.

We were a pretty fit bunch; I've run a few marathons, some of our team had tried out with triathlons and one had even completed an Iron Man. An ex-army chap had actually completed a double marathon, in one day, while sporting a military uniform and carrying a fully loaded Bergen. But every one of us agreed that the *summit push* was the hardest physical task we had ever undertaken.

A day and a half, 3,500 metres of descent and a nice hot shower later, pain had disappeared and euphoria taken hold. We had conquered the highest mountain in Africa. We had experienced, first-hand, the effects of high altitude and had certificates to confirm that we were all mountaineers. Better still, we'd managed to raise almost £300,000, every penny of which was committed to the coffers of Standing Voice. Quite a high!

Taking Queens Park Rangers to the highest place in their history: 5,895m above sea level, Africa, 2014

CHAPTER 21

WHAT FIRST ATTRACTED ME TO THE BILLIONAIRE RON BURKLE?

We were in Phoenix, Arizona setting up for our third Couture show. The phone rang: "Hi, I'm Trish Summerville," said the woman's voice on the other end. "I just bought two of your skull rings from Bergdorf Goodman. I'm styling a video—a remake of LaBelle's "Lady Marmalade," with Christina, Pink, Mia and Lil' Kim. I want to use your jewellery on all the girls. Can you get me some pieces delivered to Los Angeles... in two days?"

By this time, we had already loaned quite a bit of jewellery for shoots, premieres, red carpet events etc. It was a great way to spread the word about our jewellery but we were in Phoenix, just about to start our most important trade show and we needed all our stock. To get the requested pieces to Los Angeles meant seriously depleting our display. Plus, one of us would have to get on a flight to Los Angeles the next day, be there for the shoot and miss the crucial first two days of trade. In the end we made an executive decision and Assia boarded the plane for California with enough jewellery to dress the girls but leaving me with sufficient pieces for the start of the show. As things panned out, that one, hastily made decision started three long and meaningful relationships that would make a major impact on the future of our business.

Who is Trish Summerville? By the time she got in touch with us Trish was already a top celebrity stylist, dressing, advising and travelling with some of the biggest names in entertainment: Madonna, J-Lo, Ricky Martin, Brad Pitt and so on. She went on to become one of the most successful movie stylists in Hollywood, costuming blockbuster movies such as *The Girl with the Dragon Tattoo*, *Gone Girl*, *The Hunger Games* and many more. Trish's job was irrefutably glamorous but more complicated than it sounds because, as we all know, celebrities can be fickle, unpredictable or just plain impossible—whichever takes their fancy. They also need you to be around for them 24/7. This can even mean sharing a bed, not for fun but simply for company because they *just can't be alone*. As the person responsible for someone's complete visual identity, the bond becomes very strong indeed.

Soon we were part of the girls' schedule and every time Trish's two clients Christina and Pink came to London, Assia and I were always called upon to hang out with them. Great fun but also a chance to experience what it was like to live under the constant scrutiny of the paparazzi. Christina in particular seemed to attract attention wherever she went. The minute she left a building—sometimes with me in tow—the circus would begin. Years later, after I had

Looking far too casual with my muse, Christina Aguilera, 2006

designed the engagement and wedding rings for both girls and their respective husbands, Christina and Jordan—her then husband—came over to our flat for a drink before dinner. As always, Christina was accompanied by Big Bob, a man so large he could scoop up the pint-size pop star with one hand and put her under his arm when the melee outside the club or in the hotel lobby became too threatening.

When it was time to finish our drinks and leave I was the first to the front door, opening it to a scrum of 30 to 40 paps jostling for lens room on the steps and pavement. Reminiscent of that scene in *Notting Hill* when Rhys Ifans goes to fetch the milk in his scuzzy grey Y-fronts and gets accosted by a braying pack of baying Nikons? Well this time they were on my doorstep. I quickly closed the door. "What are we going to do?" The usual solution, we were advised, was to leave by the back door. There was no back door. Unfazed, Jordan called Big Bob who leapt out of the armoured truck parked near the flat and swatted enough photographers out the way until the rest of the throng got the message and backed off a bit. What a nightmare for that sort of scene to be the norm in your everyday schedule!

By this time, we had become very close with both Christina and Pink. We were invited to their weddings, one in Costa Rica and the other in Napa Valley, California. The girls also had a soft spot for our jewels, both building up very impressive collections. Of the two, Christina most definitely had the more substantial hoard. Once, when she was presenting and singing at the MTV awards she made ten outfit changes and, from her own collection, had enough SW bling for ten jewellery changes also. So, a few years into our friendship, towards the end of a very late night I suggested to Christina that she become the face of my brand—after all, she was pretty much doing the job already, so why not formalise the arrangement? To my surprise she agreed. We shook on it and I made a swift exit before she had a chance to remove her wine goggles and change her mind. The next day Christina was still up for it. Husband Jordan, who is a bit of a businessman—one of us needed to be—suggested that we started raising the necessary funds to take full advantage of having a global star as our brand's face and muse. Easier said than done, I suspected. Jordan and Christina were more confident.

Some months later, I received a call from Jordan. Christina had been booked to sing the American national anthem at the first game of the season for the Pittsburg Penguins, the ice hockey team of her hometown. Flamboyant, multi-billionaire investor Ron Burkle who was promising to elevate this currently moribund, but once great, ice hockey team to its former, stellar status had recently purchased the team. Christina had agreed to sing *The Star Spangled Banner* so long as Ron Burkle looked at a business proposal she had. Ron acquiesced. The anthem was sung, with not a fat lady in sight, and sure enough, within a week, two Harvard MBA business types came to see me. Within another seven days we had an offer—they hadn't even done due diligence!

Meanwhile, I'd heard through the grapevine that London's Garrard, the oldest jewellery house in the world, had found itself in a financial pickle and had been bought by an American billionaire called, wait for it, "Ron." Crestfallen, I called Jordan who in turn, called Ron's office. The rumour was true but Ron was still interested in the SW/Christina collaboration. Who the heck was this Ron Burkle fella?

At first we didn't know too much about Ronald Wayne

With Trish Summerville at the party to launch her stylists' window for the SW Beverly Hills boutique

Burkle other than he was American, extremely successful, a great friend of the Clintons and a diehard Democrat. He'd come from nothing, turning a single Yucaipa, California grocery store owned by his Dad into a huge, 35-brand group of supermarkets—Fred Meyer and Ralphs etc.—and earning him a reputation as one of the leading grocers of America along the way. A little like Mr J Sainsbury had done in the UK but without having to work at it for a tiresome century.

Ron Burkle founded a private equity fund called Yucaipa, a nod to his small, hometown roots, because that's where it all started, and because the folksy company name kept him grounded—vital when your office, lounge bed, bath and beyond are all on-board one's own Boeing 757.

Over the years, Ron and Yucaipa have continued to invest in very diverse types of businesses including sport, fashion, hotels and digital hospitality because even Ron sometimes needs a place to stay. Also, the businesses of celebrity, health, movies and TV. Not finished yet. There's also nightclubs and members' clubs—the most recent being the Soho House group—and actually, there's jewellery, because Ron knows what a girl wants.

Over the next few weeks Ron's people, my people and Christina's people managed to reach an agreement so labyrinthine and complicated that I needed to seek even more legal advice. After much negotiation, it was decided that SW would end up owning a piece of Garrard, the very store that gave me my first solo show 12 years ago, while Christina would get a piece of SW also. Billionaire Ron would have his stake in SW and Garrard and I was to be creative director of both brands, which seemed only fair and proper to us.

After we'd finished celebrating I realised that our task was now monumental. Up until this moment our decision making process and our business plan had been largely maverick and spontaneous, mostly relying on gut instinct, while marketing had been one of the many hats that Assia wore. Now we had the funds to design and create new collections larger than ever, structure a team, start advertising campaigns—featuring our new celebrity face, Christina—using the best agencies and fashion photographers available. As if that wasn't daunting enough, I had a new job, not just the creative director of the SW brand but also heading up Garrard—a company that was unquestionably "the establishment."

For the following few years our brand received a huge boost—it's amazing what money can do. Christina took on her role very seriously and from the moment we made the announcement of her ambassadorship the PR machine never stopped turning; Christina Aguilera and the Stephen Webster brand became inextricably linked. As well as being photographed for our campaigns, Christina would use any opportunity she could to talk about SW in magazines and newspapers, on TV and even in her film *Burlesque*.

Our Russian clients loved the celebrity association and would buy all the pieces Christina wore in our ads. At one point we travelled to Kiev to host an afterparty for Christina's concert and every billboard in town—we stopped counting at 50—seemed to be occupied by SW adverts featuring our new star. Perhaps the ultimate galvanisation of her commitment to our brand was when Christina offered to perform, along with her full band, for us and a group of our special guests at the Pure nightclub in Las Vegas. Choosing a Saturday in the middle of the Couture jewellery show, we transformed the venue into an SW club—our latest campaign and branding everywhere. We invited our retailers and friends only, trying our best to keep the gig as intimate

Myself and Ron Burkle, No Regrets Lounge, Stephen Webster Boutique, Beverly Hills, 2014

as possible. Once the word got out, everyone wanted to be invited to what was the town's hottest ticket. Grown men and their wives were suddenly huge Christina Aguilera fans. We found ourselves in the enviable position of being able to announce that the gig was for SW account holders only and to become one of those you simply had to make an opening order of $30,000. In ticketing terms this is, of course, extortion, an offence that possibly carries a custodial sentence. Actually, it didn't matter because most of our customers had placed an opening order much higher than $30,000 without us having to throw in a couple of concert tickets anyway.

The long and eventful relationship between Christina and SW impacted on our business immeasurably; despite some ridicule from—mostly jealous—folk that a pop star was not a good brand match for us, we didn't care. After all, it was an authentic, synergetic relationship; Christina was a great client, instrumental in our idea becoming reality, a global singing star and, most importantly, our friend.

Ron Burkle? He is still our investor and also a friend. We have grown our business together largely because of his enthusiasm for us and what we do. Vital elements for a good relationship between financial backer and designer you might think, but actually so very hard to cultivate in the real world. As everyone knows, risk-taking business entrepreneurs and us *difficult* creative types are not always the most natural of bedfellows.

One year, after we'd got to know him a bit better, Ron flew all the founders and principals of the businesses in which Yucaipa had invested to the sizeable area of Montana wilderness he owns for a mountain-biking/hiking/golfing/mingling company pow-wow. What an eye-opener! As well as meeting Puffy we were also introduced to the man who invented the McDonald's Happy Meal!

With our business relationship and friendship maturing we are still very grateful for that moment of soaring patriotism belted out by Christina to her hometown ice hockey crowd and for the connection that the song's performance forged with billionaire Burkle. Sometimes our plans haven't always sparkled and blinged in quite the brilliant cut, blemish-free manner that we imagined, however. Aside from the growth we have achieved due to Ron's investment, incidents such as a global financial meltdown can be tricky for a small jewellery business, whilst a war on the border of Russia and Ukraine will tend to throw a spanner in the works—especially when you have worked hard at nurturing a loyal retail and customer base in said same area. During such challenging times, having a partner who believes in you and your business, who happens to wear pants with deep pockets—from one of his own apparel brands, probably—can be the difference between survival and being caught with one's own trousers down. Did I mention that the in-flight dining service on-board Air Burkle 1 is second to none? God Bless America.

Jordan Bratman, Christina Aguilera and myself at a dinner prior to Christina hosting a Bombay Sapphire party for SW in Las Vegas

Watercolour and ink artwork of Murder She Wrote Eve Ring

CHAPTER 22

RODEO DRIVE

By 2008 SW had several stores around the world. We had moved from our bijoux shoebox on Duke Street, London into our *flagship* store on Mount Street. There were also stores in Assia's hometown of St. Petersburg, in Moscow, Kiev, Seoul, Vienna, and Geneva, but nothing in the very place we had built the business; the US. We needed to show the Yanks what we were made of.

At first, I explored New York—uptown, downtown, midtown, all around town—before deciding that New York is like at least four towns with luxury shopping enclaves everywhere. I couldn't make up my mind and people's advice just made it worse: "You belong downtown"; "You're a downtown brand"; "All the real luxury shopping is uptown —downtown is just fashion and hand-to-mouth types." As for the Meatpacking district, that was a whole other can of worms.

In the meantime, in a bid to get established in the US market, our sister brand Garrard had opened and closed a shop on Rodeo Drive, Los Angeles—a change in strategy left a store that had become surplus to requirements. Ron Burkle invited me to visit the vacant property before he let it go but I was hesitant. Los Angeles is a fickle place, just like the entertainment industry it exists to serve. I wanted to play a major role in the great American movie, not just a brief, walk-on part. I guess the least I could do was take a look.

The store's prominent position on the corner of Rodeo Drive—the main location for a key scene in the *Beverly Hills Cop* movie—and Wilshire Boulevard was irrefutably seductive. Exactly opposite was The Beverly Wilshire Hotel—location for much of *Pretty Woman*, a favourite fairy story of every woman of a certain age. If location, location, location are the three most important things for a property, then this multiple movie location was prime stuff.

Inside, the store and all its fixtures and fittings were circular. So much so, I actually felt giddy. There was an exit door that lead to a rear staircase and a second floor consisting of three offices, a small kitchen and a further back office, all standard stuff... except for the views. One office looked straight out over the Beverly Wilshire Hotel, the other down the length of Wilshire Boulevard and the third down Rodeo Drive; three of the most iconic views in LA.

I had an idea: "What if we knocked all the walls down, ripped the ceiling out and turned the fire exit into a sweeping staircase," I said out loud. "We could connect the ground level store with the space upstairs?" I was alone at

Watercolour and ink artwork of
Seven Deadly Sins Pride Ring

Stephen Webster flagship store,
Rodeo Drive, 2010

the time so no one objected. We hadn't moved in yet, but I already knew that this upstairs space wouldn't be about showing jewellery but an area where I could curate my personal collections and inspirational items, host intimate parties and entertain clients—once we had some. This imaginary place, of course, was still in my mind, but I was already visualising a radical concept that would send shock waves through the conventional, immaculately manicured retail community of Beverly Hills.

The next step was to meet Bill Wiley, Rodeo Drive's property representative and convince him to buy into my vision. I got lucky. With all the latest, luxury action gravitating to the centre of the Drive, its neglected extremities—the parts of Rodeo for which Bill was responsible—needed a new focus. So, much to my surprise Bill agreed that the change of use, from office to gallery, was a good idea. It slipped my mind to mention that I already had a name for the upper space: the "No Regrets Lounge."

We appointed a hip Los Angeles architect who had built some interesting restaurants around town and a few months later, just like I had imagined it, we had a jewellers and an upstairs space, connected by a sweeping Hollywood staircase. A welcome side effect of the refurb was that the store had now lost most of its carousel-like layout. We disguised the original showcases by covering them in black, faux crocodile and installed a specially commissioned, ceiling-high bronze tree, uplit with LED lights in the centre of the store's ground floor. The floor was poured concrete inlaid with iconic SW motifs generated in our design studio. Tracey Emin made us a huge neon artwork with a slogan, written inside a heart: "I promised to love you." Tracey said she always felt this particular neon belonged in a jewellers—a place where people get engaged or celebrate milestone occasions.

The upstairs space—once three rather boring offices—was now transformed into a huge loft with windows on all sides giving panoramic vistas of the neighbourhood. The ceiling was left raw and open, exposing the pipes and vents and structural metalwork that usually got covered up. There was also a bar, of course—no ordinary bar either—a "No Regrets Lounge" that was both cosy and brutalist, furnished with an oxidised expandable iron dining table—big enough to accommodate 24—and enough wall space to hang a sizeable show. It was, and is, amazing.

I found Matt, our store manager, just down the boulevard at Neiman Marcus, when I was hosting a show for our *Seven Deadly Sins* collection. Matt was drafted in to work on this particular off-site project as a sales person by

top The artist, the cook and the jeweller: Harland Miller, Mark Hix and myself, No Regrets Lounge, Beverly Hills, 2015

bottom With photographer Richard Young and Ron Burkle at the launch of Richard's exhibition of his Elizabeth Taylor photographs at the Beverly Hills boutique

top With Rankin and DJ Pete Tong at the launch of the Rankin for SW campaign at the Beverly Hills boutique in 2014

bottom Holding artwork gifts made by SW, with D*Face and Shepard Fairey, to mark the *In Conversation* between the two artists, held at the launch of the D*Face exhibition *Face To Face*

Neiman Marcus and despite not officially working in the precious jewellery department, seemed to be shifting more stuff than the other, *official* jewellery staff put together. Well aware that it's bad form to poach from your own, I held off tapping up Matt for a while, but the more qualified and totally unsuitable candidates I interviewed for the role of manager, the more I was drawn back to this young, dynamic guy. The job description was specific; I needed someone who would take ownership of our unique space, someone who loved art and food and popular culture, as well as having experience in jewellery sales. Someone who would give it all while being 6,000 miles from me and 3,000 miles from his closest boss in New York. Matt ticked all the boxes. I offered him the job and called the Neiman Marcus people. They were a little miffed but also knew this was the perfect opportunity for Matt and handed him over without much of a struggle.

We finally opened for business on 10th December 2010. The store was finished and full of jewels but we were determined to put on an exhibition on the upper floor so that people understood that this was not just another jewellers with an upstairs VIP space. With no local credentials and with such short notice there was no way we were going to get an artist of any calibre to show at the No Regrets Lounge in, of all places, Beverly Hills. For a while, our options were limited to some Monet prints from the gallery a few doors up, but that just wouldn't do—we needed to ruffle a few feathers. Fortunately, some years before, Assia and I had introduced Christina Aguilera and her husband Jordan to the street artist Banksy via the artist's London gallery, Lazarides. They'd become keen, early collectors of Banksy's work. So, Steve Lazarides, eternally grateful for the stellar introduction, loaned us a great selection of contemporary street art to hang at the opening.

Still, we needed more impact. After deciding that our massive window was too big for jewellery, I decided to give this city full of stylists the opportunity to style a window on Rodeo. After the opening we began a *stylist of the month*

Interior of the SW Beverly Hills boutique featuring Tracey Emin's *I Promise To Love You* neon

collaboration, handing over complete editorial control of the dedicated window to a different stylist each month. Boy, over the years, have they ever taken advantage of that artistic freedom, whether a bloody massacre-themed display or an installation titled *Crack Baby* by the artist Judith Supine, featuring, you guessed it, a painting of a crack-smoking baby. Sometimes, Matt and I have a bet that "this will be the one" that will provoke the Beverly Hills Cops into closing us down.

We opened with a bang not a whimper. After a big launch party we were written about in publications as diverse as the *Los Angeles Times* and the *Chicago Tribune*. The front cover of the *Financial Times*' luxury magazine, *How to Spend It*, dubbed us one of the most progressive jewellery stores in the world.

Upstairs, with the last two shows featuring the work of Britain's Harland Miller and street artist D*Face, both sell-outs, the No Regrets Lounge has earned its reputation as a successful and credible art gallery. Other highlights have included several visits from Mark Hix, the famous British chef who introduced an initially cynical, no-carbs Californian crowd to the yummy possibilities and points of difference of seasonal British cuisine. Alison Balsom, the UK's young classical musician of the year 2012, blew us a few tunes and then blew us away again when she played trumpet for her supper. Tracey Emin, the Dame of the British art scene, hosted a debate with a few of her favourite men—artist Mat Collishaw, Mark Hix and myself—later described by *The Hollywood Reporter* as one of the funniest and most natural "in conversation" events the writer had ever experienced. Photographer Richard Young has showcased some of the many candid images he has snapped in a decades-spanning career that began when he took a snap of Elizabeth Taylor at her birthday party back in 1974; which was a nice twist for me, as a decade after Richard had gate crashed her party, Liz was also the first celebrity for whom I ever made a piece of jewellery.

I like to think that Stephen Webster has helped make Rodeo rock again.

Interior of the SW No Regrets lounge in preparation for a performance by the then young classical musician of the year, Alison Balsom and her trumpet

CHAPTER 23

A MEMBER OF THE BRITISH EMPIRE

I began this book 38 years ago. The snail's pace with which I've filed copy is down to the fact that I am a jeweller not a writer and, despite a certain dexterity at the workbench, I can't type properly. My stabbing, single finger keyboard technique on the iPad provided hours of amusement to my colleagues in the office. I'm delighted that I have managed to recall so much of my life and career in some detail, as though the memories were all pieces of my jewellery, which, of course, they often are. Other moments I have lost forever. One thing is for sure, I've been blessed to experience a full, exciting and sometimes adventurous life… a life shaped unquestionably by jewellery.

A jeweller's bench is a compact and intense environment where everything required by the craftsman to apply his trade is at close hand. This has been the case for centuries. So, a few years back when I calculated that my trade had clocked up no fewer than five million air miles—make that 500,003,250-ish, I'm writing this chapter in a 747, bound for Boston—the extraordinary distance got me thinking. What was it about this particular jeweller that had turned him into a terminal nomad?

A recent exhibition at the Museum of London titled *The Cheapside Hoard* supplied some possible clues. The story behind the exhibition is set on the street where I served the second half of my apprenticeship, under the dandy jeweller John Donald, between 1979–81. The Cheapside Hoard refers to a treasure trove of jewellery dating back to the sixteenth century that lay undiscovered on London's Cheapside until exposed by demolition work in 1912. Hidden under the floorboards of what is thought to have been an old jeweller's shop or trading office, were hundreds of pieces of fine gold and gem-set jewellery. Such was the hoard's value and the extraordinary story of its discovery that everyone in the London jewellery industry knew about it.

The first exhibit of the show set the scene with a recreated jeweller's bench and workshop from Elizabethan times. My daughter Nika pointed out that these benches—the candlelight aside—were virtually unchanged from the workbenches we have now, and the ones at which I have worked at since the age of 16. The reason for this apparent lack of progress is that fine jewellery making is a craft that requires mainly hand skills. Just as in the case of musicians' instruments, our tools are extensions of the hand, each one perfected for a specific purpose. Few would argue that a sixteenth century Stradivarius violin could be improved with technology and the same theory, perhaps, in a more modest way, can be applied to the functionality of the centuries-old jeweller's tool case; although, we have lost a few bits of kit

Watercolour and ink artwork of Lady Stardust Pearl Ring

along the way, some of which were still in circulation when I was at art school. The Archimedean drill, for example, a favourite with the Ancient Greek smiths and Lord Olivier's sadistic implement of torture in the movie *Marathon Man*, was rendered redundant with the introduction of the overhead dental drill.

The main exhibition focussed on the hundreds of exquisite pieces that formed the "hoard" and the story behind them. The elements that interested me most were the variety of specialist techniques employed in the making of the pieces—enamelling, gemstone and gold carving, engraving and many forms of gold fashioning. Considering that these pieces were made 500 years ago the variety of stones used was astonishing, the origins of the gems spanning the far-flung and nether regions of the entire globe. Most would have been fashioned by indigenous people at the source and brought back to Britain along with all kinds of other bounty—potatoes, tobacco and rugs—by the maverick explorers, merchants and pillaging thieves of the day. Men, gone for years on end, returned with exotic treasures and creatures to bestow upon Queen Elizabeth in return for positions of power and status, if they were lucky. Perhaps even regal gratitude expressed in kind.

But without romancing the stones too much, I decided that my own life as a jeweller was fairly well represented by the exhibition too. As with every jeweller, my story had begun at the workbench, a semi-circular cut-out station and wooden peg, known as the business end. A hardwearing pigskin is draped as a soft tray under the working area where it catches every dropped diamond fragment and precious particle of gold dust, to be later smelted, assayed and sold for a cash bonus when a decent pile has accumulated. This kind of scam, by the way, no longer operates. Along with so many perks, tricks and fiddles, it came to an end many years ago, when those pesky HM tax inspectors started to scrutinise the industry more closely, suspecting that things may not be as kosher as they appeared down at Hatton Garden. Nowadays, with things 100 per cent above board, gold filings under the workbench are refined back to bullion.

In a similar vein to those aforementioned Elizabethan

My brother showing me an hilariously expensive tourmaline, Idar-Oberstein, Germany

looters, the other side of my life in jewellery has involved travel; lots and lots of travel. I have flown millions of miles in my pursuit of anything that could possibly be connected to the making, designing, inspiration, presentation and distribution of the jewellery we create. If that first million plus miles with American Airlines seemed outlandish, it's worth knowing that I've racked up another four million or so with British Airways—but in contrast to AA, they never wrote to me.

The craft of jewellery seduced me from the very first time I set foot in a workshop and has taken me to the four corners of the earth. I get to mix with fascinating, exotic and talented characters. There have been many successful business people, a few poets, many artists, musicians and singers, hunters and gatherers, a couple of faith healers and snake charmers—true, truuuussstt me—philanthropists and, of course, the people who work so hard behind the scenes of my glamorous industry. I've been down mines and dined with miners; I've met diamond cutters in India and Israel and stonecutters and carvers in Thailand and Germany. We have employed or worked alongside hundreds of highly skilled bench jewellers worldwide. Every single experience, in one way or another, started from my bench peg.

Despite its name, "Stephen Webster" is not a one man band or brand; this is an ensemble piece. My team are truly amazing and dedicated people. My brother David, himself a great craftsman—possibly better than me—is now a qualified gem hunter. Without my wife Assia I could never have built the business we have today. In head designer Claire Denham-Smith we have one of the best jewellery designers in London and a creative team that keeps the DNA of SW exciting and relevant. Kate Jarvis, who rose through the ranks from salesperson to our managing director, is a petite blonde who keeps us all in order while Tina does a sterling job of running SW USA, our second home. A further 50 or so talented and dynamic people make up the ever-expanding Stephen Webster organisation.

As we all know, time flies when you're having fun… and I have had plenty of fun. A fact recently recognised by the French Champagne board who took it on themselves

With D*Face, in front of his portrait of HM the Queen at the *Face to Face* exhibition, SW Beverly Hills boutique

Outside Buckingham Palace
with Assia, Nika and Amy, after
receiving my MBE in 2013

to publicly honour me for my contributions to the *Joie de Vivre* lifestyle. I accepted this award with dignity and the straightest face I could muster. Having all this *fun*, I barely noticed my migration from *enfant terrible* to senior citizen of the jewellery establishment.

Shouldering the gravitas that only elders can, I was not surprised to receive an invitation to dinner from Coutts of the Strand, my bank—not, as I anticipated as a gratuity for years of bank charges, but an invitation extended to various members of the British fashion and allied industries. Sitting directly opposite me at dinner was Caroline Rush, the newly appointed CEO of the British Fashion Council (BFC.) Over dinner I asked Caroline why it was that with fashion and fine jewellery now inextricably linked, the BFC had no initiative for upcoming jewellery talent? Without missing a beat, Caroline suggested that I form one. I deflected the offer with the excuse that I could barely manage my week as it was and changed the focus back to the free dinner. But we all know there is no such thing as a free lunch. Caroline persisted accordingly and I relented. Within a few months we announced Rock Vault, the first platform for emerging jewellery talent in the UK with me as curator/mentor.

Designers wishing to be included in Rock Vault are considered on the merit of their work and the BFC appoints a selection panel. Between us, we interview all applicant designers, each of whom have to bring examples of their most current work.

We announced the ten successful applicants and launched Rock Vault at London Fashion Week A/W 2012. Would it work? After all, instead of being in competition with each other, the designers now needed to get used to the idea of being mutually supportive. The powers of the commune prevailed and before the first LFW show was over, all the designers were sold on the power of ten. Now, all young and emerging jewellery talent want to be a part of Rock Vault.

In 2013, high on hope and hearing there was an entire ballroom going spare at the Couture show at the Wynn hotel, Las Vegas, I threw caution to the wind and secured it. The space came at a price for us, but I knew that if I was really going to use my years of experience to expedite the fortunes of young jewellers, I had to announce Rock Vault to the very city where, 15 years earlier, SW's rock star jewellery had been the talk of the town. The gamble in Vegas paid off and when I made the announcement back in London, the designers were thrilled. I'd be responsible for taking ten young people to their first US show in Sin City. What could possibly go wrong? Very little actually. We launched Rock Vault with a huge party on the first evening of the show

and with collective arms outstretched, the global jewellery industry warmly embraced the concept and our group of hitherto unfamiliar designers. The combination of top-shelf talent and the spirit of a mentoring programme resonated in a way that I could never have imagined. Americans, devoid of cynicism, welcomed us Brits as their own.

2015 marks Rock Vault's third trip to the show. Now, due to the nature of the initiative, designers have to graduate and make way for newcomers. With no external sponsorship I can only manage ten members at a time, with usually only two spaces becoming available each year. This keeps standards high and competition fierce.

2013 was a big year for another reason. One day, amongst the clothing catalogues and takeaway food flyers, my mail included a notification from the Prime Minister. On behalf of HRH the Queen, David Cameron was delighted to inform

HRH Prince Charles pinning on my MBE medal at Buckingham Palace in 2013 me that—on the condition that I accept it—I would be awarded an MBE at Buckingham Palace later that year. The award, the letter explained, was for training and skills to the jewellery industry. An MBE! Bloody hell! I couldn't believe it. How did the Queen know about my training and skills? I later found out that Assia and my friend Richard Jarvis had been busy in the wings supplying relevant details to the powers that be.

Driving into Buckingham Palace to receive my award, accompanied by Assia, Amy and Nika, all dressed to the nines, was most definitely the proudest day of my life. Many of the other honour recipients that year were Olympians who had won medals in the 2012 London Games. Having coffee in one of the palace's anterooms with so many athletic heroes, all waiting to join the procession into the palatial room where the honours are bestowed was a blast. From a gilded plinth HRH Prince Charles was knighting some and pinning medals on others. When it came to my turn to approach, bow and receive my medal, Charles remembered having met me on several occasions before—I had designed and manufactured the trophies for the Audi polo league, of which the Prince's Highgrove polo team had won plenty—and also recalled my role as director of Garrard, holder of his own royal warrant for jewellery and silverware. After posing for pictures outside the palace, we were joined by my dad, brother and the rest of our family at the Queen's favourite grocery store, Fortnum & Mason. The lunch was courtesy of the man at the top of the food chain, my good friend Ewan Venters.

From the estuary town of Gravesend and Medway college of Design to Buckingham Palace, my jewellery journey has been, frankly, bloody amazing. A heck of a ride! All 38 years of it. I've put diamond cocktail rings on the fingers of rockers, movie stars, artists and princesses. I've worked my fingers to the bone and raised a couple of digits to a few people along the way, but now my tired and increasingly inept single finger needs to stop punching this keyboard. Like I said when this book begun, I am a jeweller not a writer. I need to get back to my workbench.

Stephen Webster MBE

The *No Regrets* neon at the top of the stairs at the No Regrets Lounge, SW Beverly Hills store

No Regrets
Lounge

COLLECTIONS

CLOTH OF GOLD

The first full collection we made. All the pieces feature elaborate hand engraving, inspired by a pocket watch my father gave me for my twenty-first birthday. The gem set pieces and hand engraving give a rich tapestry-like effect to the gold surfaces, hence the name *Cloth of Gold*, borrowed from a meeting between King Henry VIII and Francis I of France in the French countryside near Calais in 1520. The two and a half week long extravaganza was so opulent it almost bankrupted the treasuries of both countries.

18k hand engraved yellow gold cuff
with pavé white diamonds

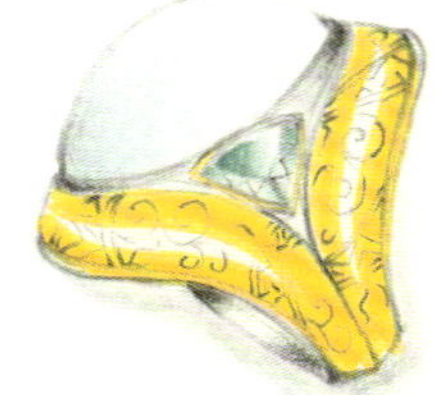

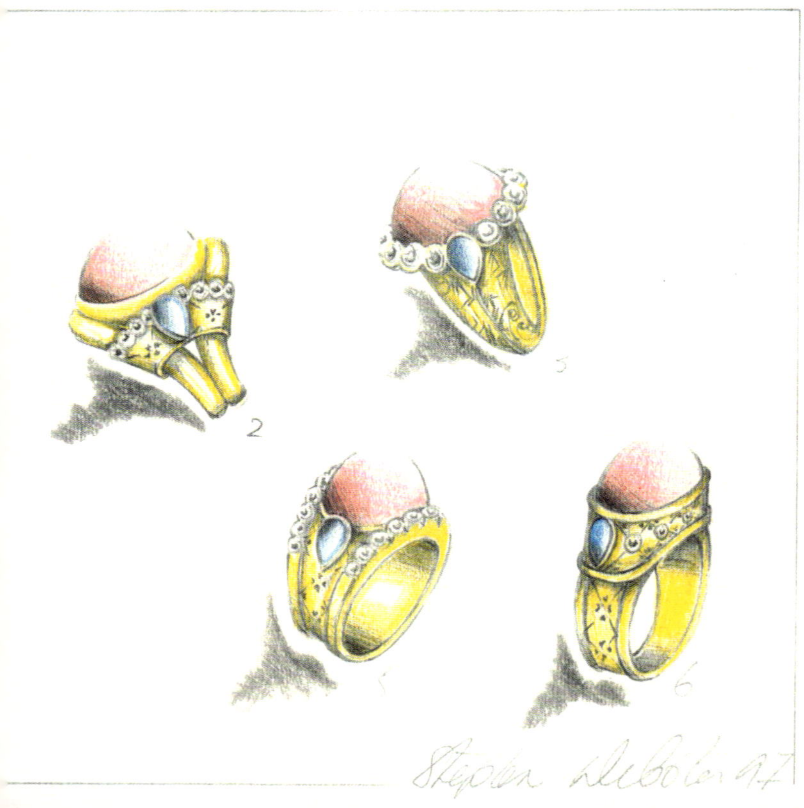
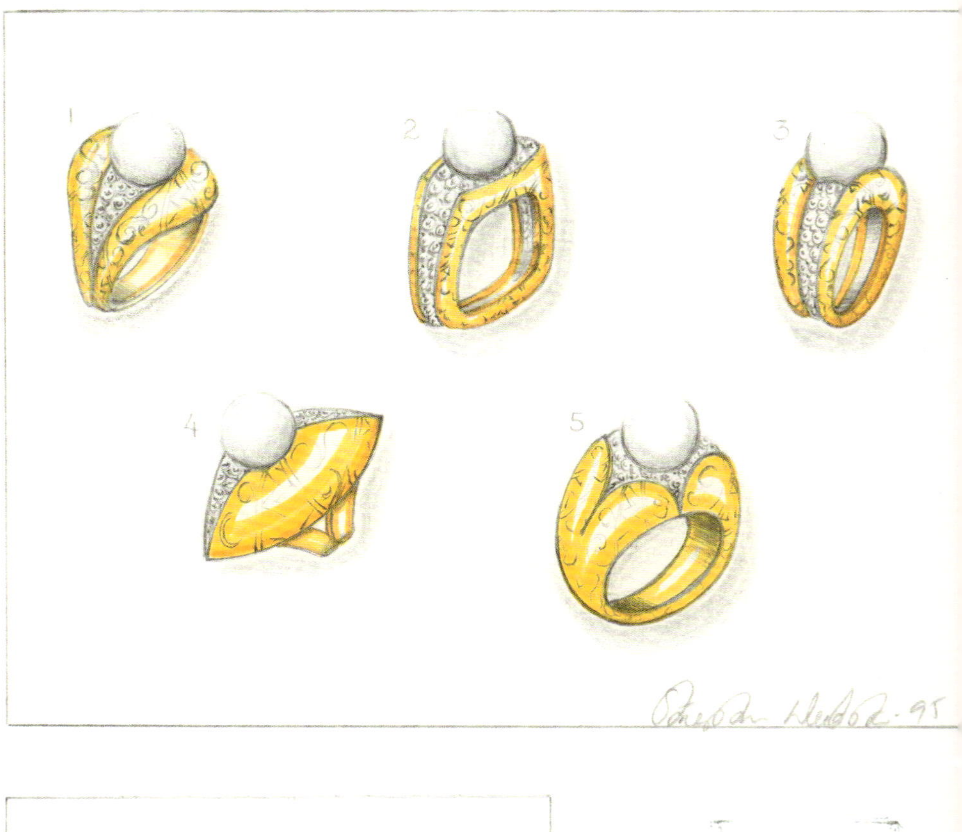

opposite Selected *Cloth of Gold* sketches

top 18k hand engraved yellow gold brooch

bottom 18k hand engraved yellow gold earrings

18k hand engraved yellow gold cuff with pavé white diamonds

opposite top 18k yellow gold drop earrings with pavé white diamonds, amethyst and south sea pearls

opposite bottom 18k yellow gold drop earrings with pavé white diamonds, aquamarine and bronze chrysoberyl

18k hand engraved yellow gold cuff with pavé white diamonds and buff top amethysts

opposite top 18k yellow gold ring with pavé white diamonds and rubellite tourmaline

opposite bottom 18k engraved yellow gold necklace with pavé white diamonds and rubellite tourmaline

18k hand engraved white
and yellow gold with pavé
white diamonds and
rubellite tourmaline

opposite
18k engraved white gold
collar with pavé white
diamonds and tanzanite

FEMME FATALE

Drawing inspiration from the alluring femme fatales of 1940s Hollywood, the luxury and edge of this collection sets it apart from the girl next door inspirations more normally found in the world of fine diamond jewellery. This exquisite, diamond only, limited edition collection features the unique WebCut™ diamond—courtesy of Dali Diamonds—a deco inspired cut, developed for the truly wicked femme fatale.

FEMME FATALE DETACHABLE EARRINGS
Platinum with pavé white diamonds
and WebCut™ diamonds

Sketch of FEMME FATALE PENDANT

opposite FEMME FATALE PENDANT Platinum with pavé white diamonds and WebCut™ diamonds

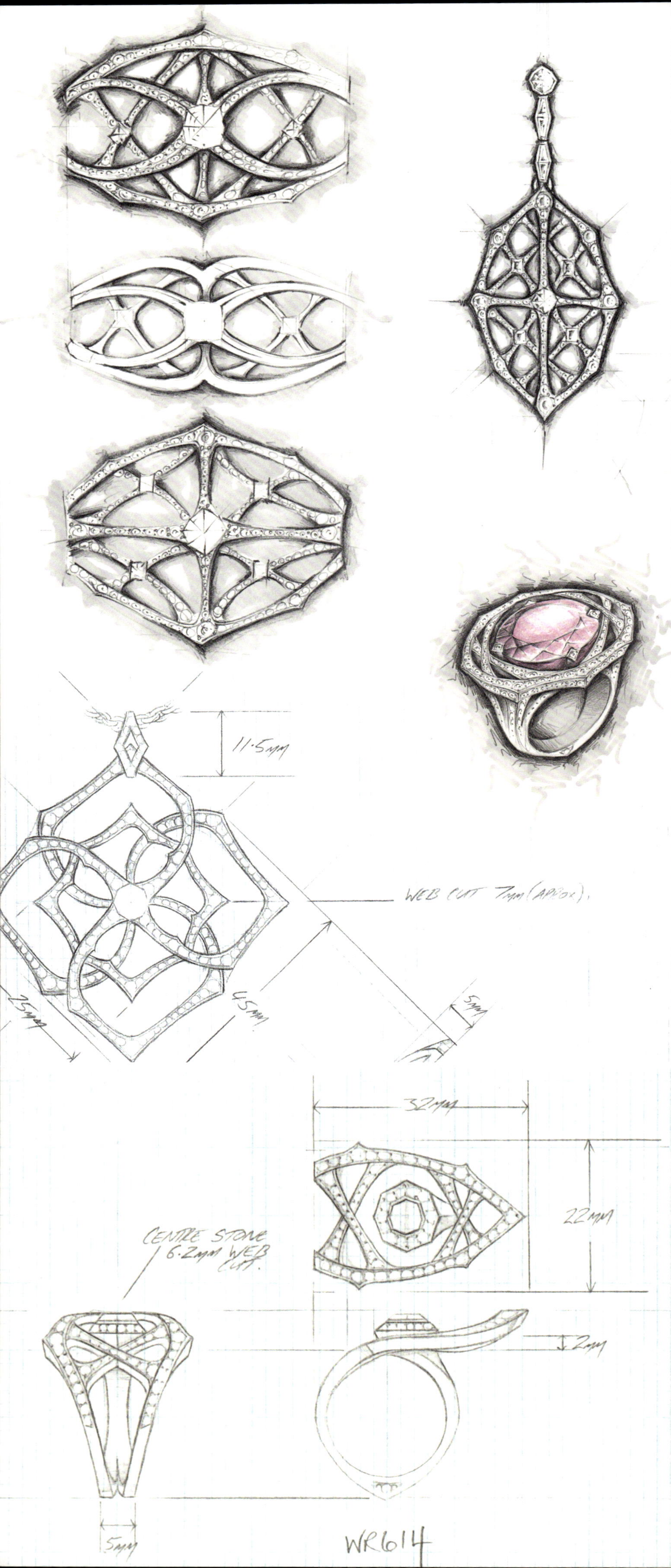
11·5MM
WEB CUT 7MM (APPROX).
25MM
45MM
5MM
32MM
22MM
CENTRE STONE 6·2MM WEB CUT.
2MM
5MM
WR614

FEMME FATALE DROP PENDANT Platinum with pavé white diamonds and WebCut™ diamonds

left top FEMME FATALE HALF TEMPLE RING Platinum with pavé white diamonds and a single WebCut™ diamond

left bottom FEMME FATALE COCKTAIL RING Platinum with pavé white diamonds and a single WebCut™ diamond

opposite Selected *Femme Fatale* sketches

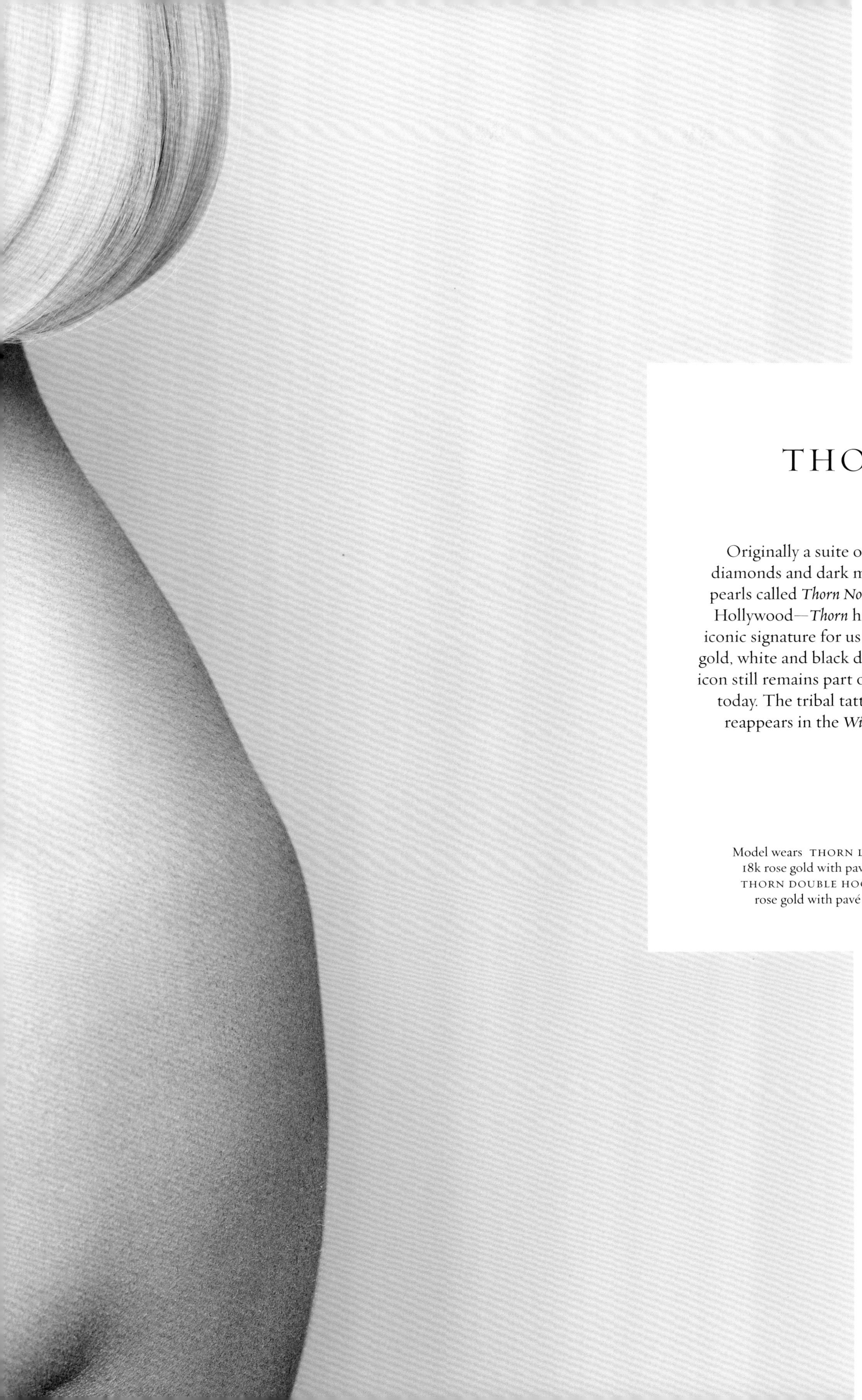

THORN

Originally a suite of 18k white gold, diamonds and dark mysterious Tahitian pearls called *Thorn Noir*—another nod to Hollywood—*Thorn* has become such an iconic signature for us that the minimalist gold, white and black diamond embellished icon still remains part of our core collection today. The tribal tattoo inspired motif reappears in the *Wild Rose* collection.

Model wears THORN LONG FINGER RING 18k rose gold with pavé white diamonds; THORN DOUBLE HOOP EARRINGS 18k rose gold with pavé white diamonds

top THORN TATTOO CUFF 18k white gold with pavé white and black diamonds

bottom THORN TATTOO EARRINGS AND PENDANT 18k white gold with pavé white diamonds

opposite Model wears DOM PERIGNON ROSÉ COCKTAIL RING 18k white gold with pavé white diamonds and pink tourmaline; DOM PERIGNON ROSÉ NECKLACE 18k white gold with white diamonds, pink sapphires and a Tahitian pearl

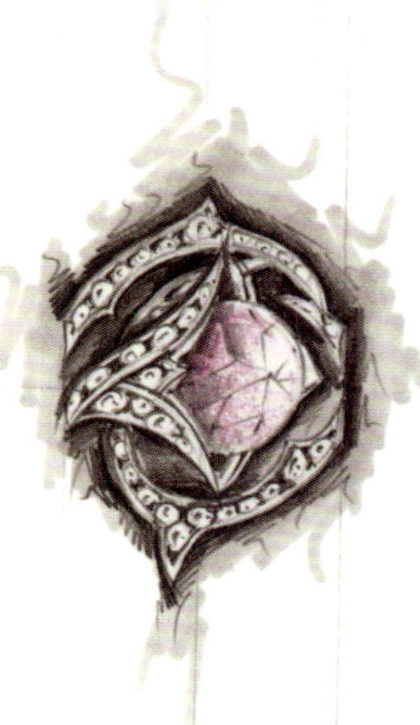

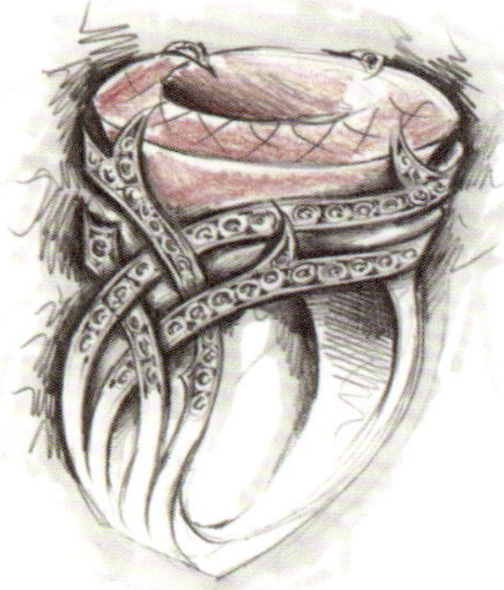

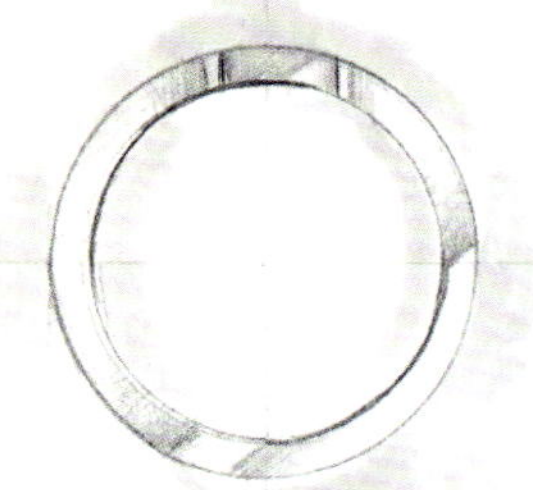

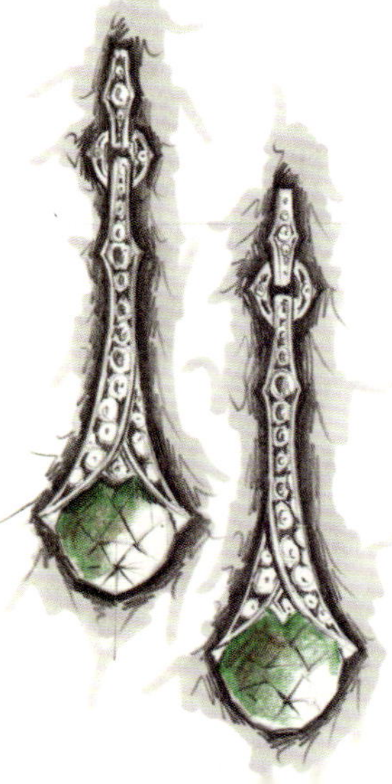

Selected *Thorn* sketches

opposite Model wears WILD ROSE CUFF 18k white gold with pavé white, black and brown diamonds and South Sea pearls; WILD ROSE EARRINGS 18k white gold with pavé white, black and brown diamonds and South Sea pearls

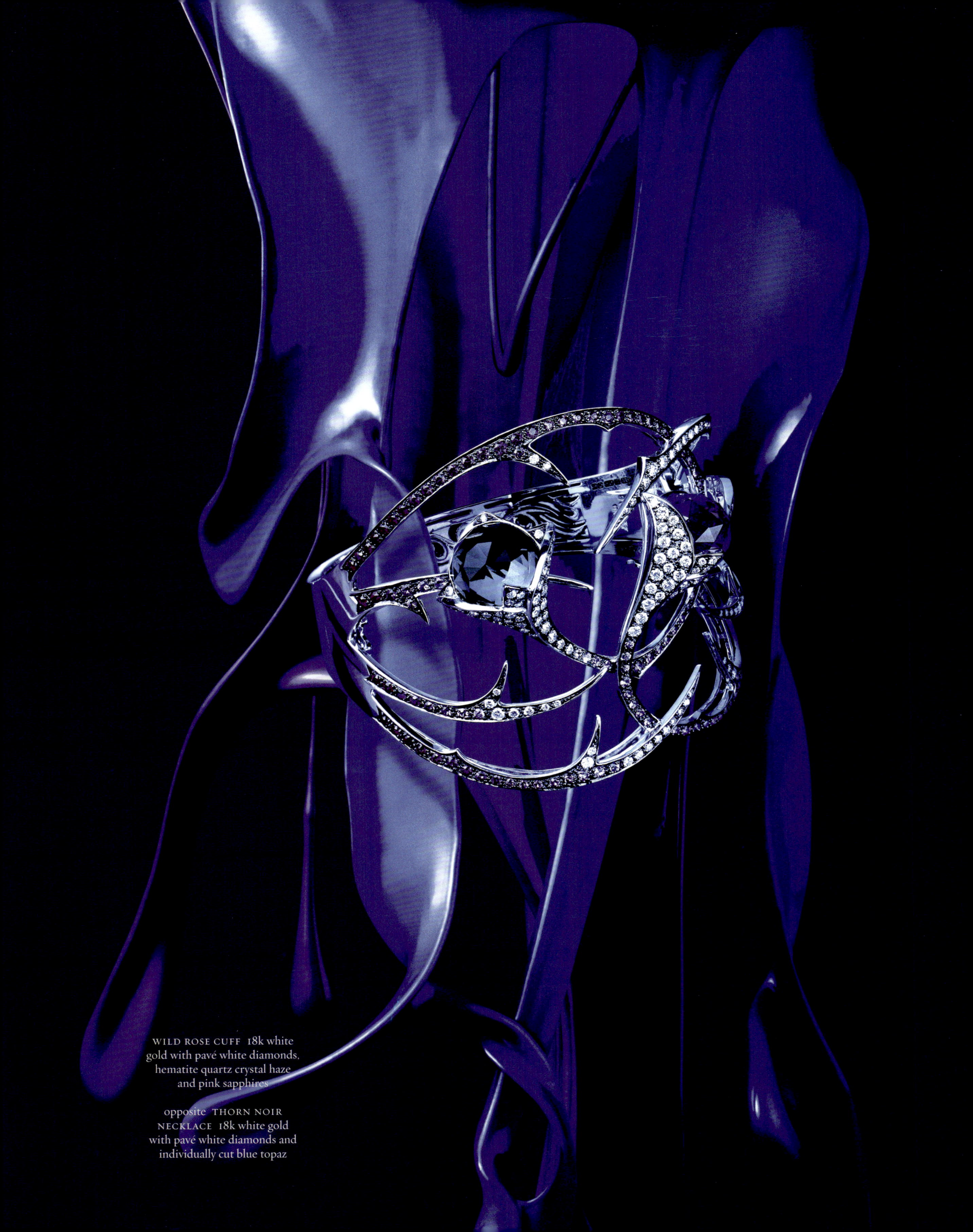

WILD ROSE CUFF 18k white gold with pavé white diamonds, hematite quartz crystal haze and pink sapphires

opposite THORN NOIR NECKLACE 18k white gold with pavé white diamonds and individually cut blue topaz

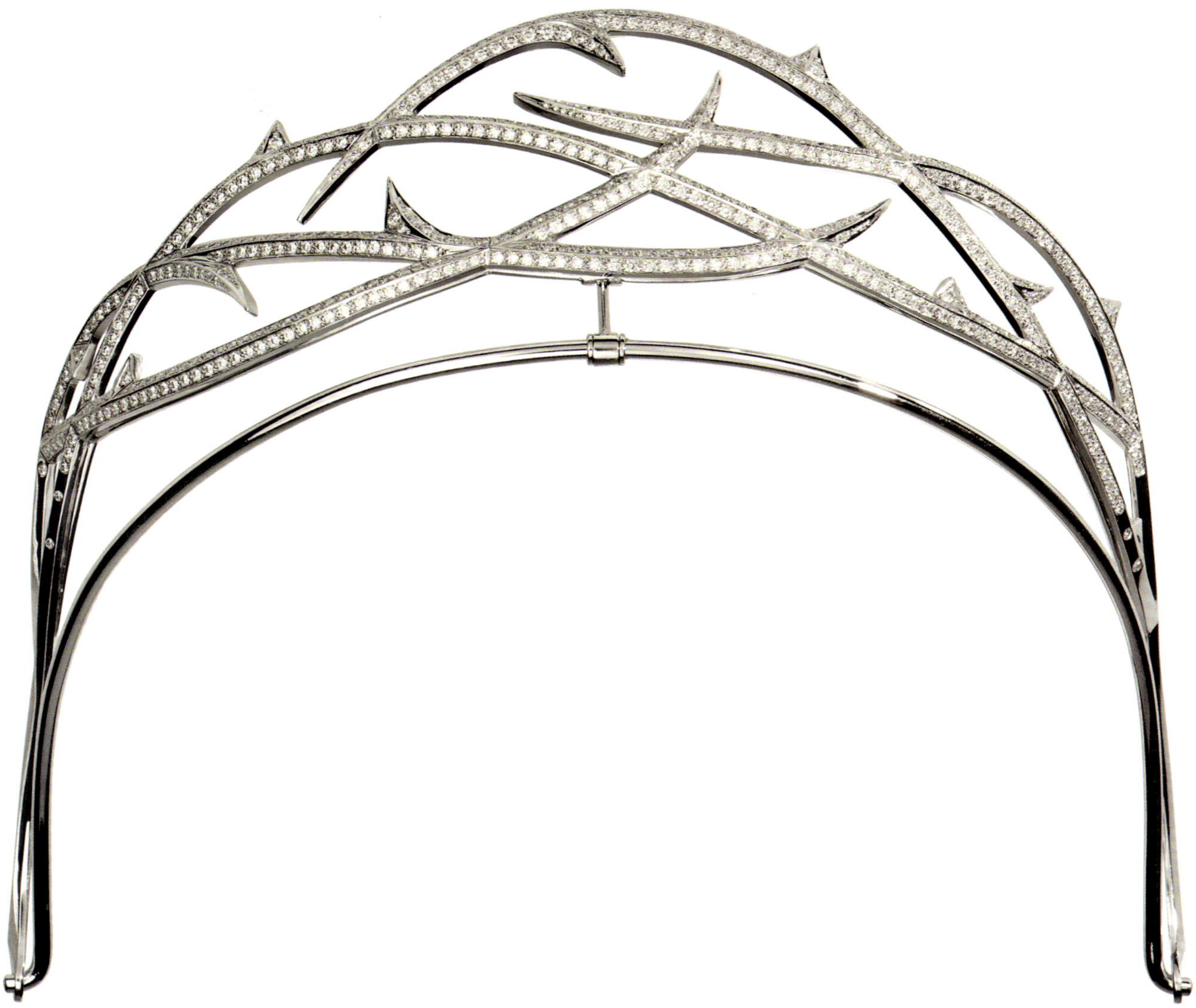

ONE OF A KIND THORN TIARA
18k white gold with pavé white diamonds

opposite Rosamund Pike wears THORN TIARA 18k white gold with pavé white diamonds

STEPHEN WEBSTER
SWISS MADE

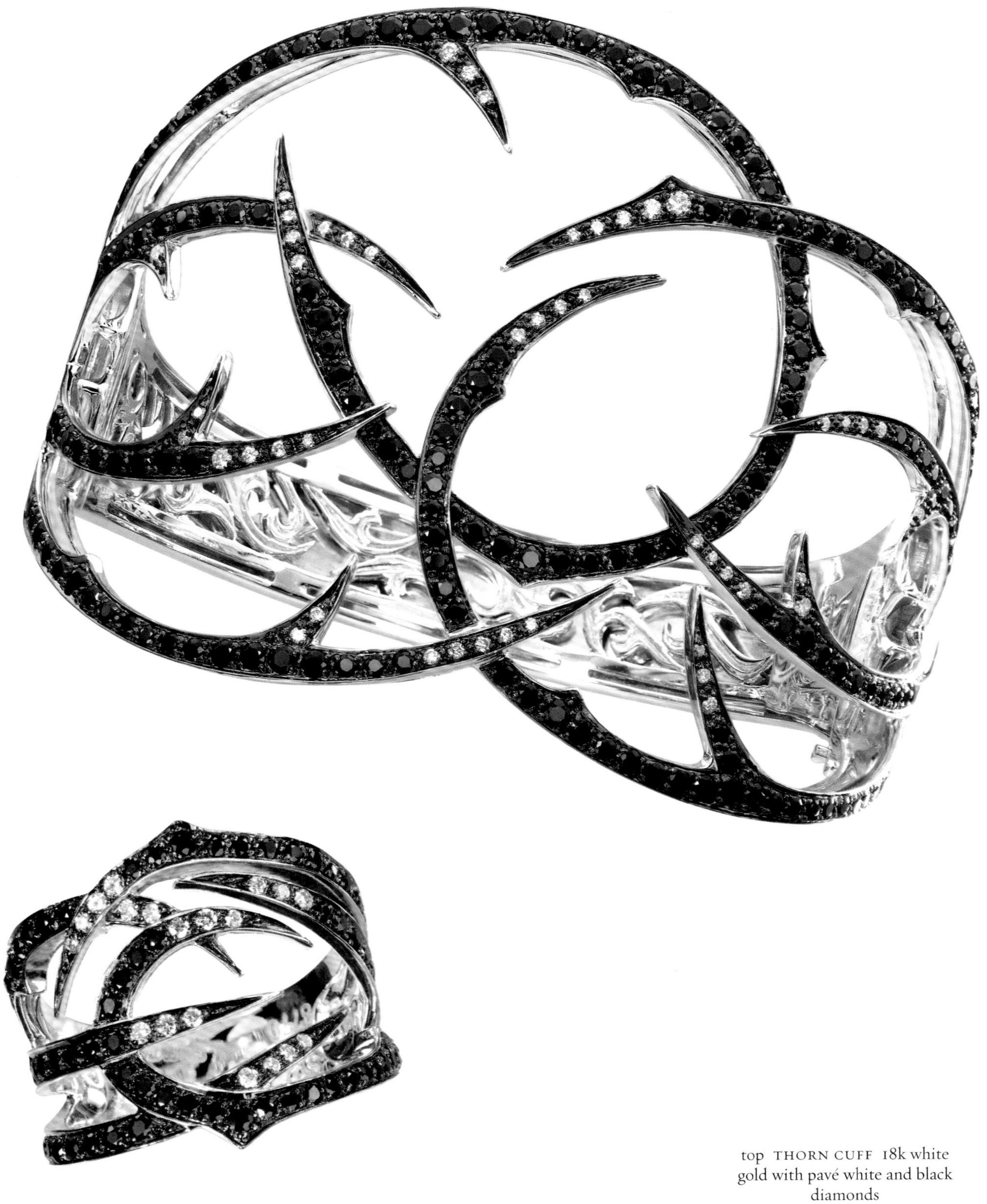

top THORN CUFF 18k white gold with pavé white and black diamonds

bottom THORN RING 18k white gold with pavé white and black diamonds

opposite THE LIBERTINE WATCH 18k white gold with pavé white diamonds, black mother of pearl and ray skin strap

RUSSIAN ROULETTE

The first time I set foot on Russian soil with my future wife Assia, a couple met us, he was carrying a Kalashnikov and she a beautiful bunch of flowers. It was at that moment that I began to understand the term *Russian Roulette*. Russia has embraced my creations, and me, and it is one of the most dynamic and exciting markets in the world. Every time I go my experiences are cultural, crazy and glamourous, with an element of danger. A *Russian Roulette* collection by SW just had to happen.

below RUSSIAN ROULETTE BRACELET
18k white gold with pavé white diamonds, chrysoprase and hematite

opposite RUSSIAN ROULETTE RING
18k white gold with pavé black diamonds, chrysoprase quartz crystal haze and hematite

Sketch of RUSSIAN ROULETTE COLLAR

RUSSIAN
25869

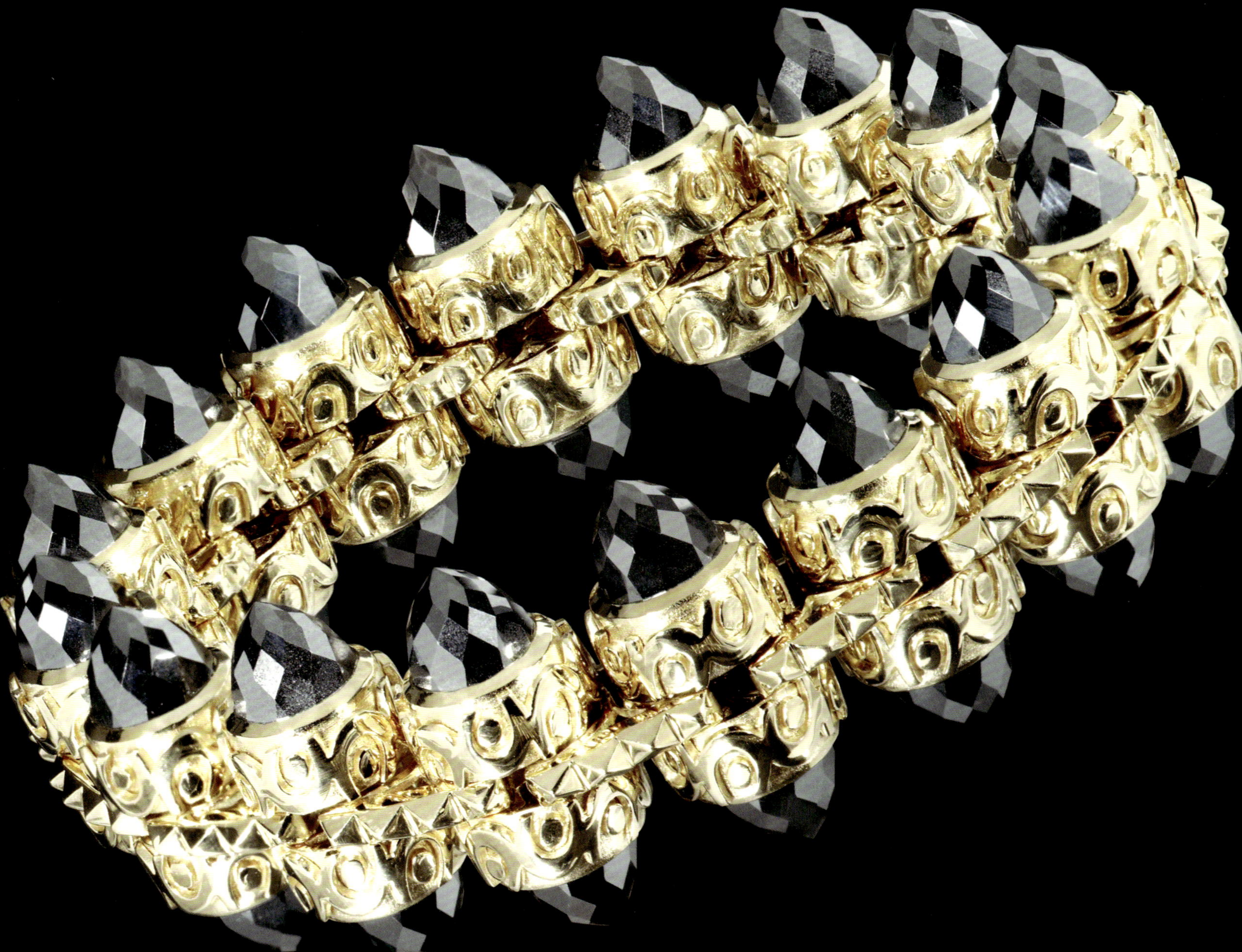

RUSSIAN ROULETTE BRACELET
18k yellow gold with hematite

opposite Selected *Russian Roulette* sketches

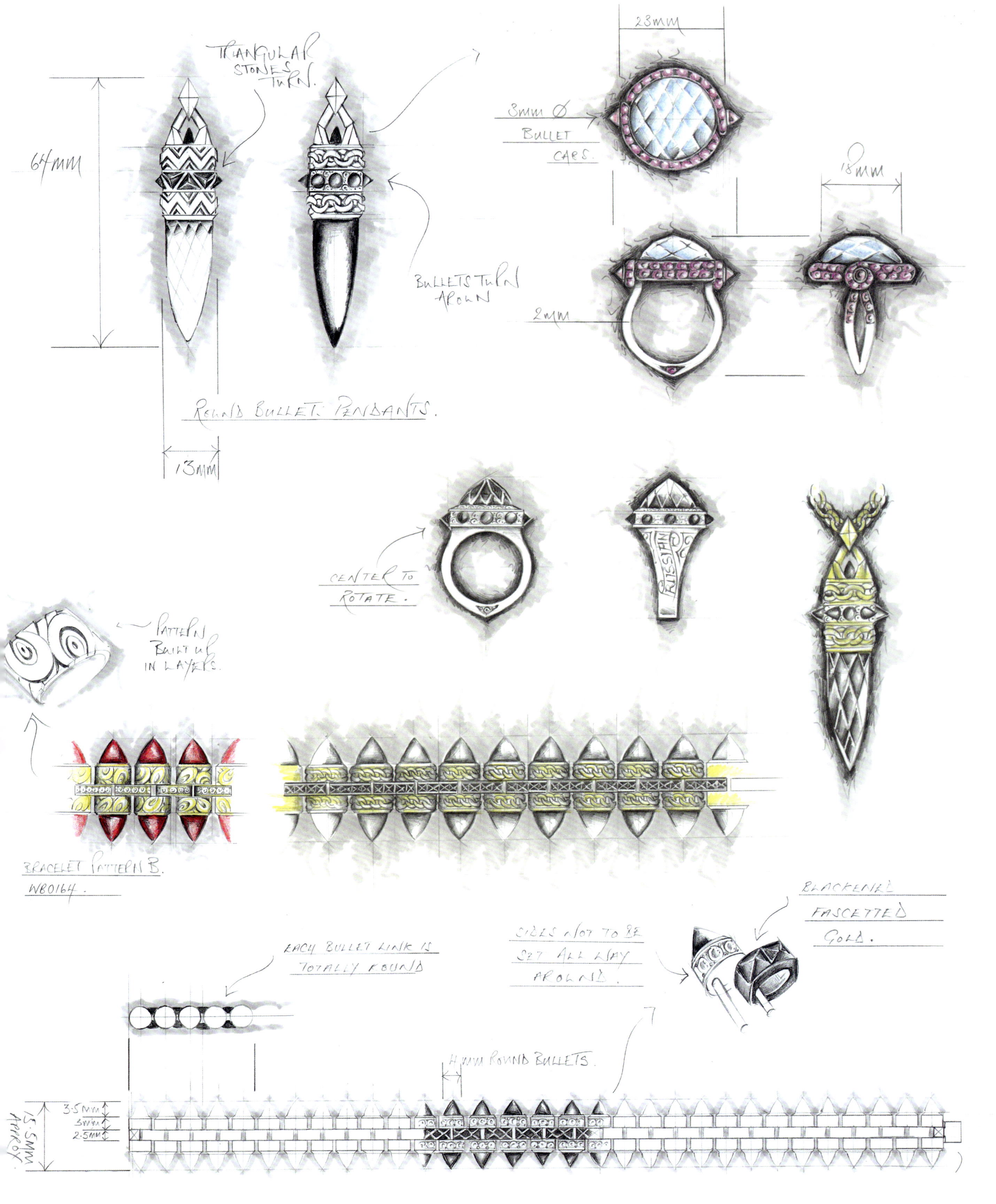
TRIANGULAR STONES TURN.
64MM
13MM
ROUND BULLET PENDANTS.
BULLETS TURN AROUND
23MM
3MM Ø
BULLET
CAPS.
18MM
2MM
CENTER TO ROTATE.
PATTERN BUILT UP IN LAYERS.
BRACELET PATTERN B.
WB0164.
EACH BULLET LINK IS TOTALLY ROUND
SIDES NOT TO BE SET ALL WAY AROUND.
BLACKENED FASCETTED GOLD.
4MM ROUND BULLETS.
3.5MM
3MM
2.5MM
15.5MM APPROX.

opposite top RUSSIAN ROULETTE BULLET HAZE RING 18k white gold with pavé black diamonds, coral and quartz crystal haze

opposite bottom RUSSIAN ROULETTE BULLET HAZE RING 18k white gold with pavé blue sapphires and turquoise quartz crystal haze

CRYSTAL HAZE

Probably our most recognisable signature, *Crystal Haze* is a concept, combining hand and laser-cutting techniques with materials as old as time. The magical effect is created by bonding a high dome of crystal clear, multifaceted rock crystal over a thin layer of natural precious stone. The cut rock crystal allows light to enter at hundreds of different angles producing a holographic *haze* of colour that moves as the stone is turned. The stones are usually surrounded by brilliant cut diamonds... the overall effect is striking! The *Crystal Haze* stones come in a variety of vibrant colours using opaque materials such as lapis, blue green and white agate, ruby, rhodochrosite, cornelian, chrysoprase, chalcedony, turquoise, silver, rainbow obsidian and black and white mother of pearl. *Crystal Haze* has run through many collections for almost 20 years.

Christina Aguilera wears CRYSTAL HAZE BOULDER COLLAR 18k white gold with pavé white diamonds and hematite quartz crystal haze; CRYSTAL HAZE DAGGER EARRINGS 18k white gold with pavé white diamonds and hematite quartz crystal haze; CRYSTAL HAZE THREESOME RING 18k white gold with pavé white diamonds and hematite quartz crystal haze

above CRYSTAL HAZE CLASSIC BRACELET 18k white gold with pavé white diamonds and hematite quartz crystal haze

Sketch of CRYSTAL HAZE CLASSIC BRACELET

opposite CRYSTAL HAZE FAN RING 18k white gold with pavé white diamonds and turquoise quartz crystal haze

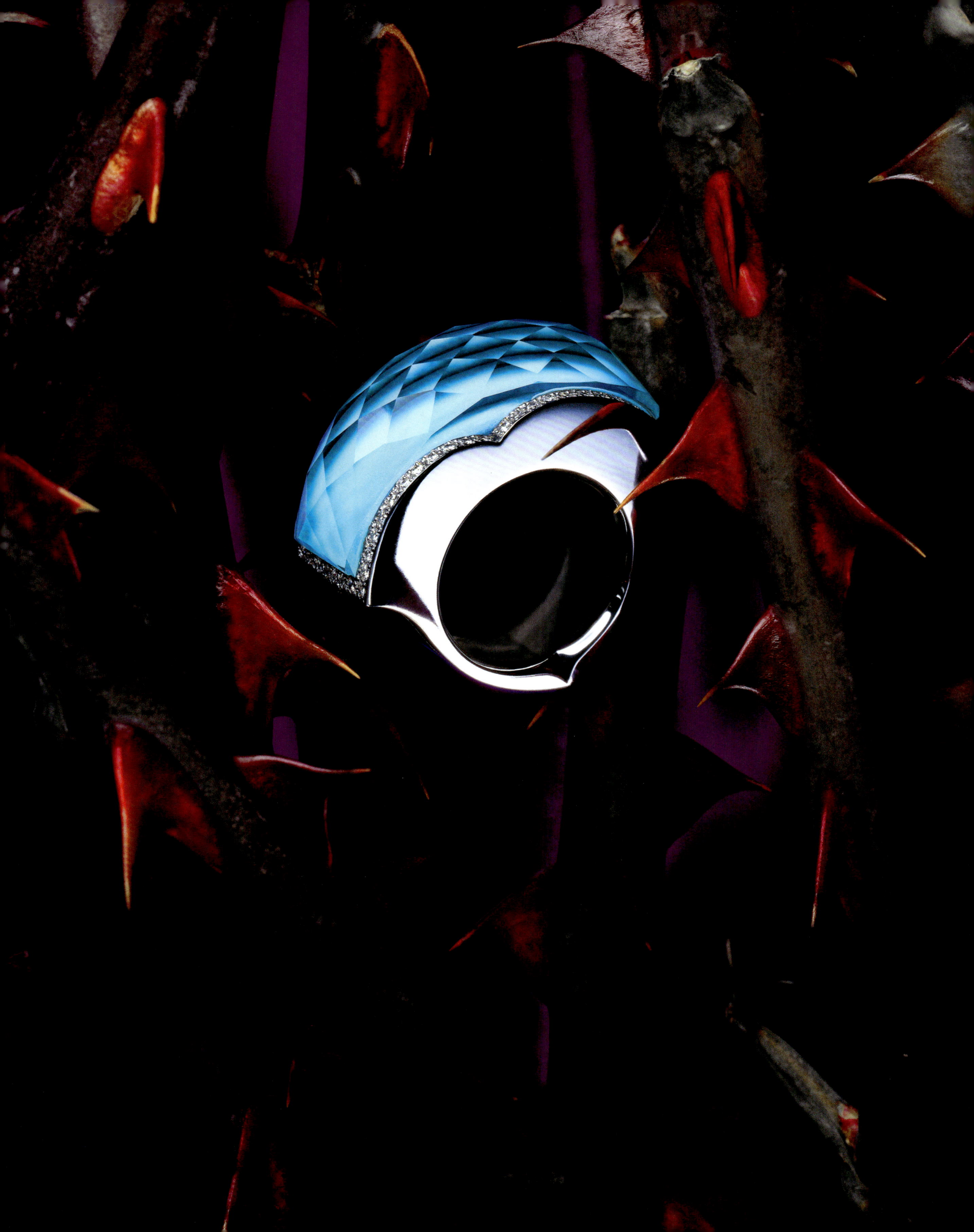

top Sketch of CRYSTAL HAZE CLASSIC RING

bottom Sketch of LOVE HAZE PENDANT

opposite LOVE HAZE PENDANT
18k white gold with pavé white diamonds and hematite quartz crystal haze

CRYSTAL HAZE JEWELVINE RING 18k white gold with pavé black diamonds and red coral quartz crystal haze

opposite Dita von Teese wears CRYSTAL HAZE DECO RING 18k white gold with pavé black and white diamonds and red coral quartz crystal haze

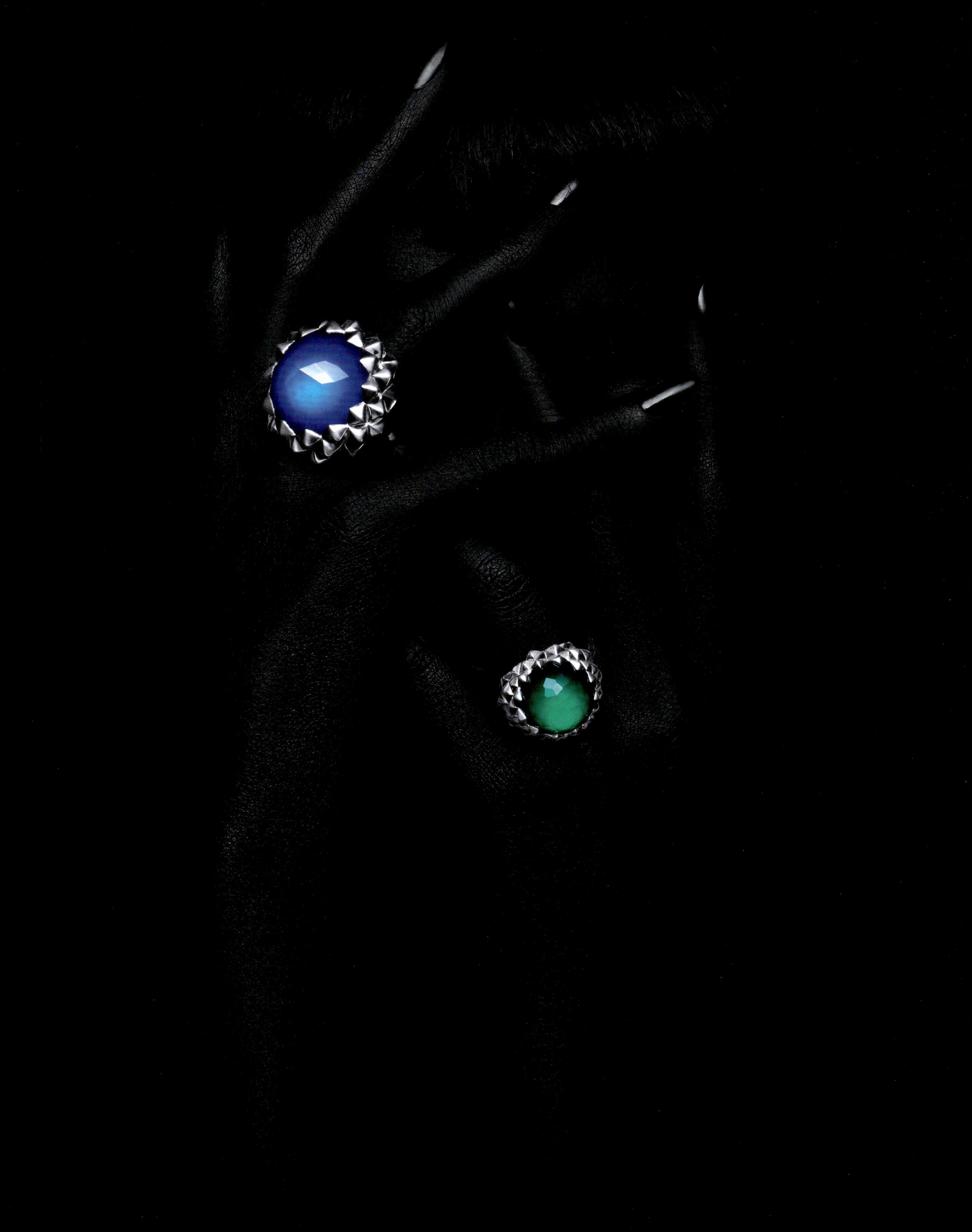

Model wears DECO HAZE LONG DROP EARRINGS 18k white gold with pavé black diamonds, black opal quartz crystal haze and blue sapphires; DECO HAZE LONG FINGER RING 18k white gold with pavé black diamonds, black opal quartz crystal haze and blue sapphires

opposite Model wears SUPERSTUD CRYSTAL HAZE RING Sterling silver with blue agate quartz crystal haze; SUPERSTUD CRYSTAL HAZE RING Sterling silver with chrysoprase quartz crystal haze

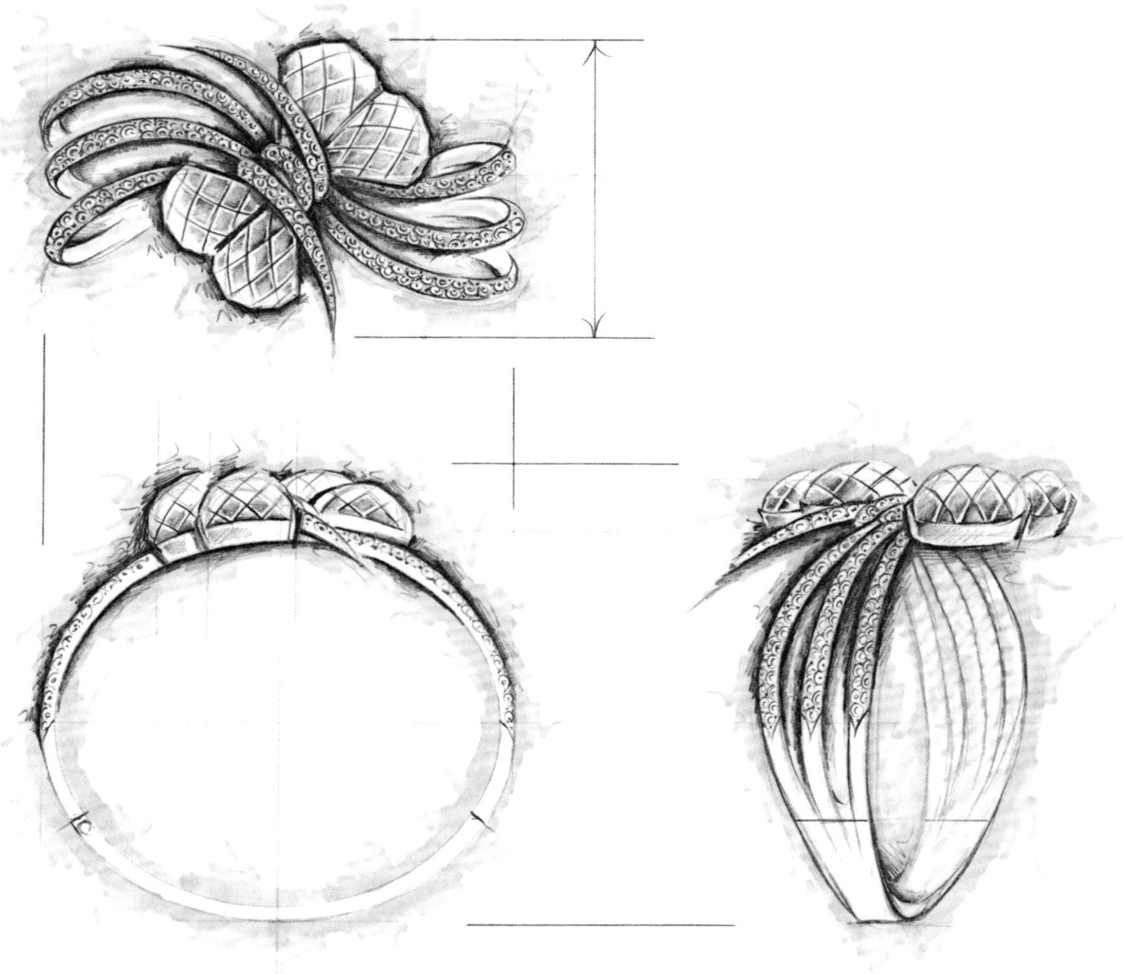

Sketch of FORGET ME KNOT BOW CRYSTAL HAZE CUFF

opposite Model wears FORGET ME KNOT BOW CRYSTAL HAZE CUFF 18k white gold with pavé black diamonds, black opal quartz crystal haze and blue sapphires

JEWELS VERNE

A collection drawing inspiration from one of my favourite books as a child—*20,000 Leagues Under the Sea*—the nineteenth century, sub-nautical fantasy novel by French author, Jules Verne. The aquatically themed, fantastical collection is comprised of pieces as whimsical and detailed as the Victorian machines and creatures described in the book. *Jewels Verne* far exceeded our expectations, due to it being our then, most creative collection to date, out of which crawled two of our best ever selling rings: the Crab followed by the Lobster. Due to its success, and on a crustacean high, the following year we launched *In Deep*, featuring more inspirations from the seafood buffet.

JEWELS VERNE FIGHTING FISH BROOCH
Illustration by Rory Dobner

top JEWELS VERNE CRAB PINCER PENDANT 18k rose gold with pavé white diamonds and moonstone and pink opal quartz crystal haze

middle JEWELS VERNE CRAB RING 18k rose gold with pavé white diamonds and pink opal quartz crystal haze

bottom JEWELS VERNE CRAB PINCER RING 18k rose gold with pavé white diamonds and moonstone and pink opal quartz crystal haze

opposite Christina Aguilera wears JEWELS VERNE CRAB RING 18k white gold with pavé black diamonds, black opal quartz crystal haze and blue sapphires; FLY BY NIGHT CHANDELIER EARRINGS 18k white gold with pavé white and black diamonds

opposite top JEWELS VERNE AQUARIUM PENDANT 18k white gold with pavé black and white diamonds, blue sapphires, black opal quartz crystal haze and hematite cabochons

opposite bottom JEWELS VERNE AQUARIUM DOUBLE FINGER RING 18k white gold with pavé black and white diamonds, blue sapphires, black opal quartz crystal haze and hematite cabochons

opposite Selected *Jewels Verne* sketches

JEWELS VERNE LOBSTER RING 18k white gold with pavé black diamonds, amethyst and white mother of pearl quartz crystal haze

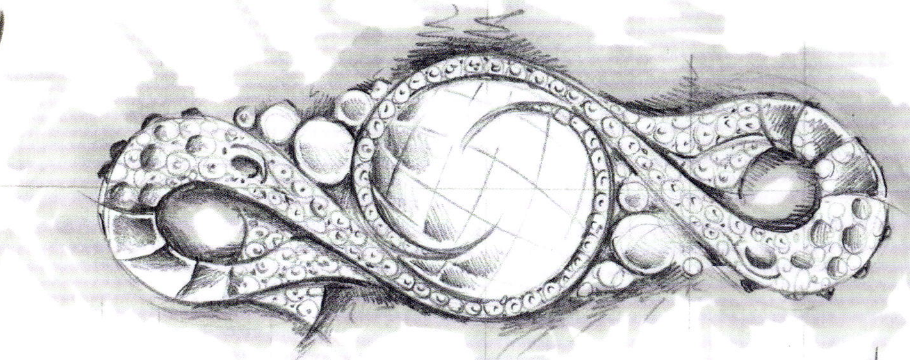

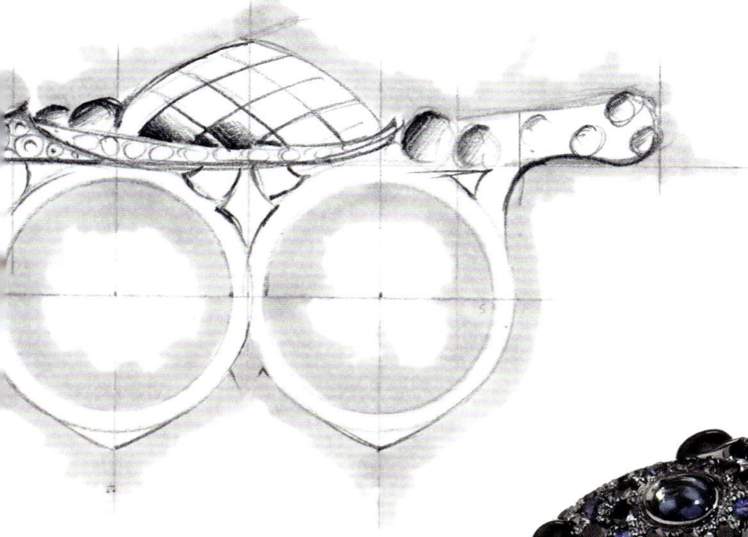

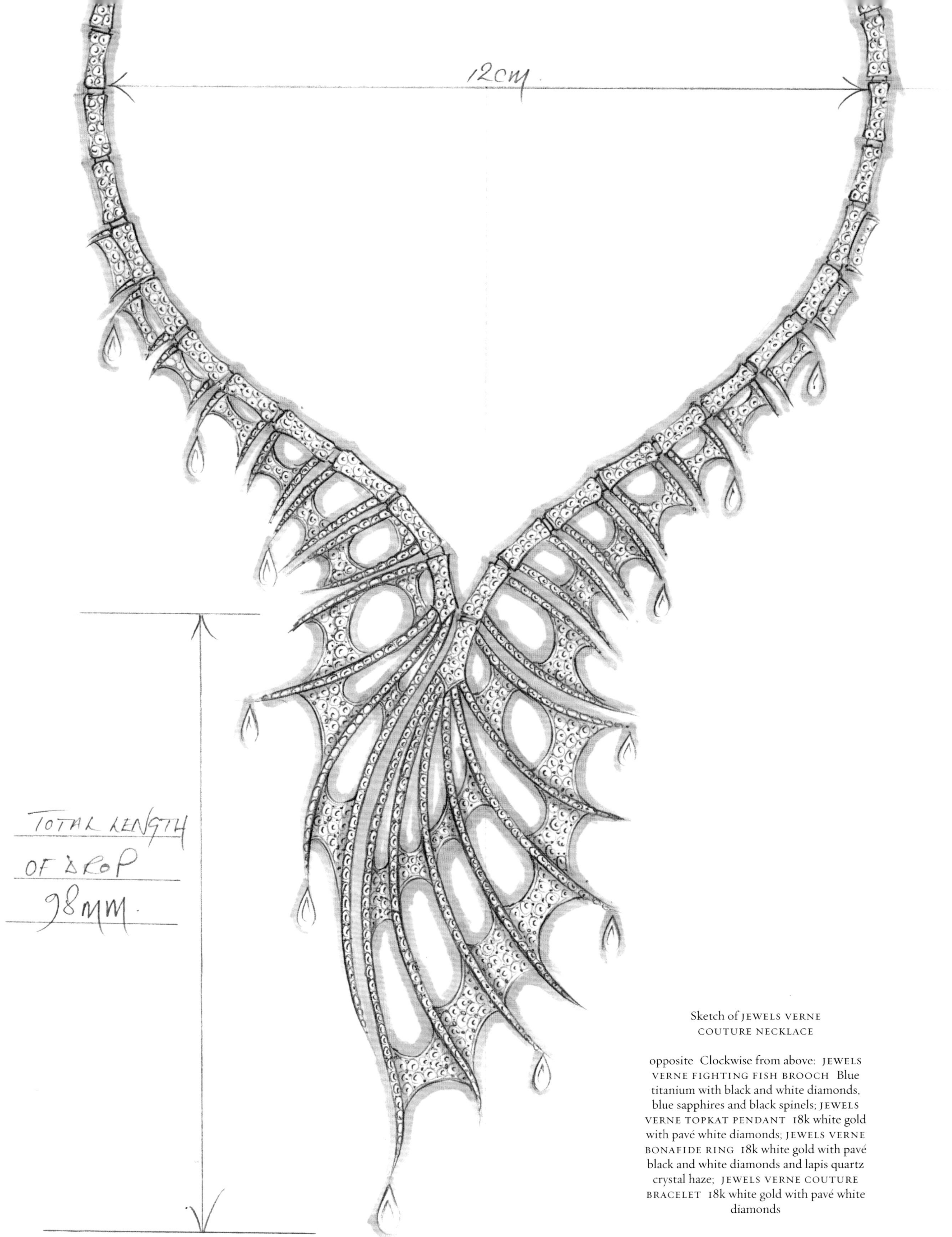

Sketch of JEWELS VERNE COUTURE NECKLACE

opposite Clockwise from above: JEWELS VERNE FIGHTING FISH BROOCH Blue titanium with black and white diamonds, blue sapphires and black spinels; JEWELS VERNE TOPKAT PENDANT 18k white gold with pavé white diamonds; JEWELS VERNE BONAFIDE RING 18k white gold with pavé black and white diamonds and lapis quartz crystal haze; JEWELS VERNE COUTURE BRACELET 18k white gold with pavé white diamonds

JEWELS VERNE FIGHTING FISH BROOCH Blue titanium with black and white diamonds, blue sapphires and black spinels

top Sketches of JEWELS VERNE FIGHTING FISH EARRING and BROOCH

bottom JEWELS VERNE FIGHTING FISH EARRINGS Blue titanium with black spinels, blue sapphires and white diamonds

clockwise: JEWELS VERNE STINGRAY RING 18k white gold with pavé black diamonds and emeralds; JEWELS VERNE PUFFER FISH PENDANT; 18k white gold with pavé white diamonds and amethysts; JEWELS VERNE SPIDER CRAB CUFF 18k white gold with pavé black diamonds, black opal quartz crystal haze, black onyx cabochons and blue sapphires; JEWELS VERNE TOPKAT PENDANT 18k white gold with pavé white diamonds; JEWELS VERNE STINGRAY BROOCH 18k white gold with orange and yellow sapphires, white and brown diamonds and ruby eyes; JEWELS VERNE LANGOUSTINE BROOCH 18k white gold with black opal quartz crystal haze, black and white diamonds, blue sapphires and black onyx cabochons; JEWELS VERNE BONAFIDE CRYSTAL HAZE RING 18k white gold with green agate quartz crystal haze and black and white diamonds; JEWELS VERNE BONAFIDE CRYSTAL HAZE BRACELET 18k white gold with hematite quartz crystal haze and white diamonds

top JEWELS VERNE SPIDER CRAB CUFF 18k white gold with white diamonds and black spinels

bottom Sketch of JEWELS VERNE SPIDER CRAB CUFF

opposite JEWELS VERNE SHARK JAW BRACELET 18k white gold with pavé white diamonds

SEVEN DEADLY SINS

Seven cocktail rings, each a sin and each with a backstory; a collection that emerged, perhaps a little too easily from the design studio, provoking us to ask, "just how bad we really are?" Each sin features beautiful bold gemstones such as Mexican fire opal, Pakistani peridot, African tanzanite, garnet and diamond, Brazilian amethyst and aquamarine. A combination of craftsmanship, rich material and dark humour: perhaps a true reflection of SW?

Seven Deadly Sins moodboard

envy
greed

SEVEN DEADLY SINS LUST RING
18k white gold with pavé white
diamonds and tanzanite

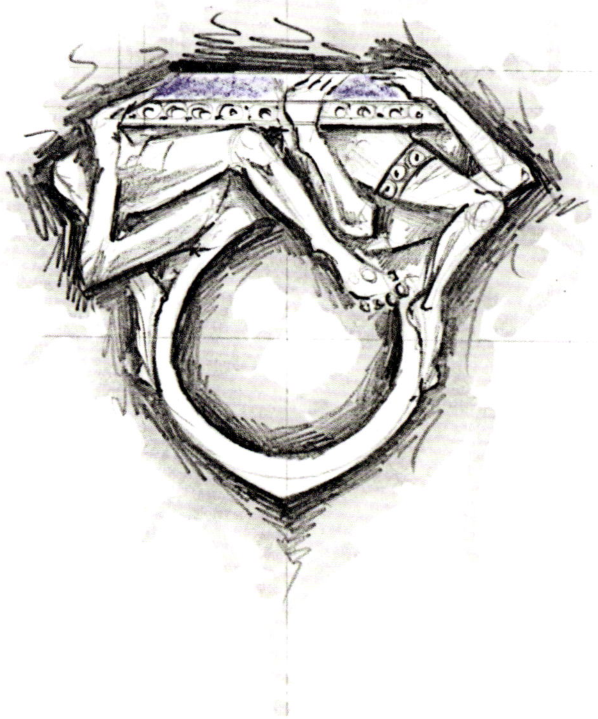

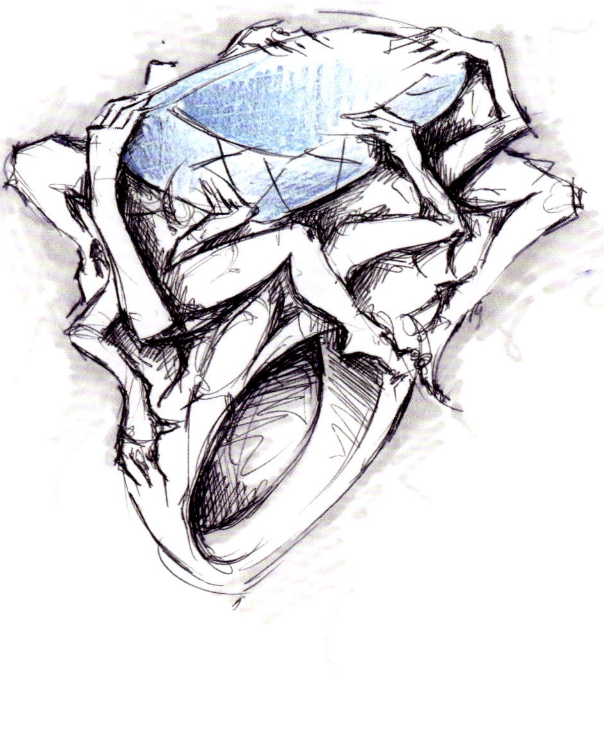

Sketches of SEVEN DEADLY SINS
LUST RING

SEVEN DEADLY SINS ENVY RING
18k white gold with pavé white and black diamonds, peridot and tsavorites

opposite SEVEN DEADLY SINS PRIDE RING Blue titanium with amethyst, pink and blue sapphires and white diamonds

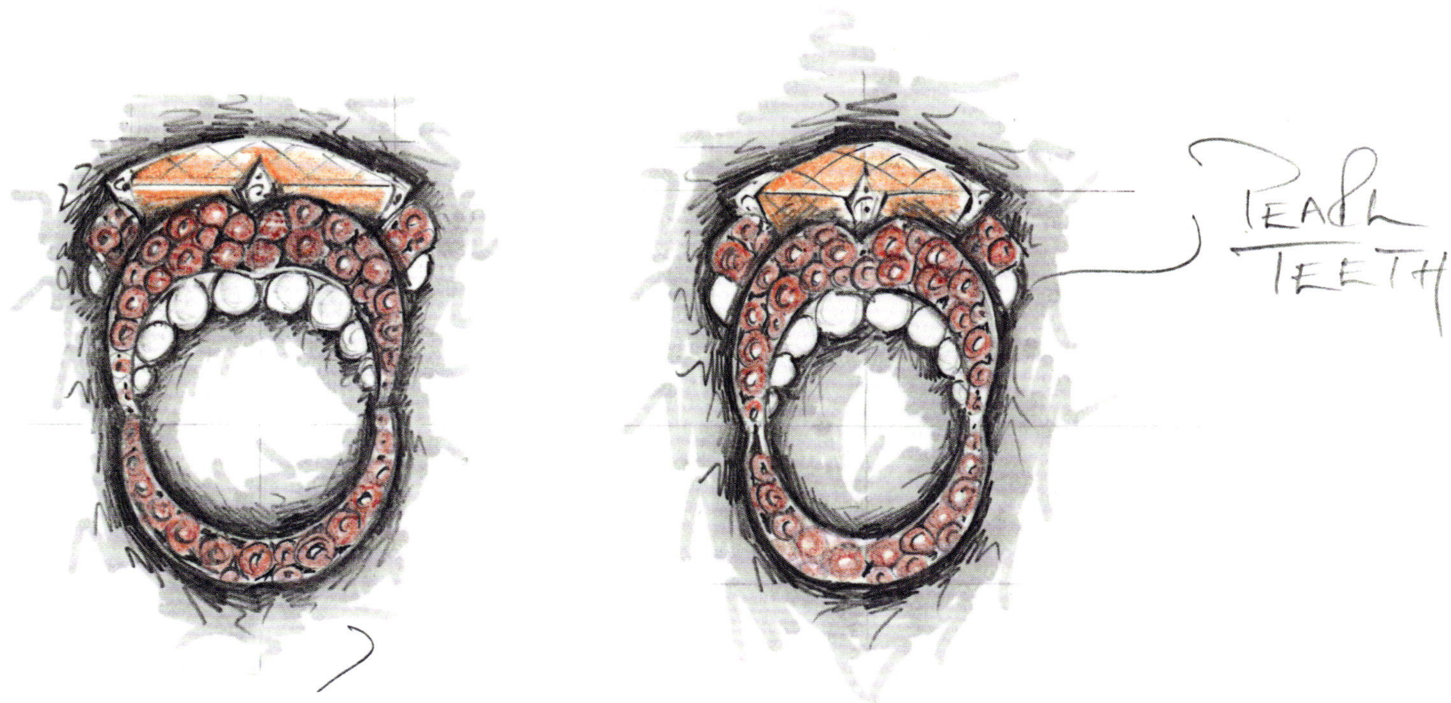

Sketch of SEVEN DEADLY SINS GLUTTONY RING

opposite SEVEN DEADLY SINS GLUTTONY RING 18k white gold with fire opal, rubies, white agate and white diamonds

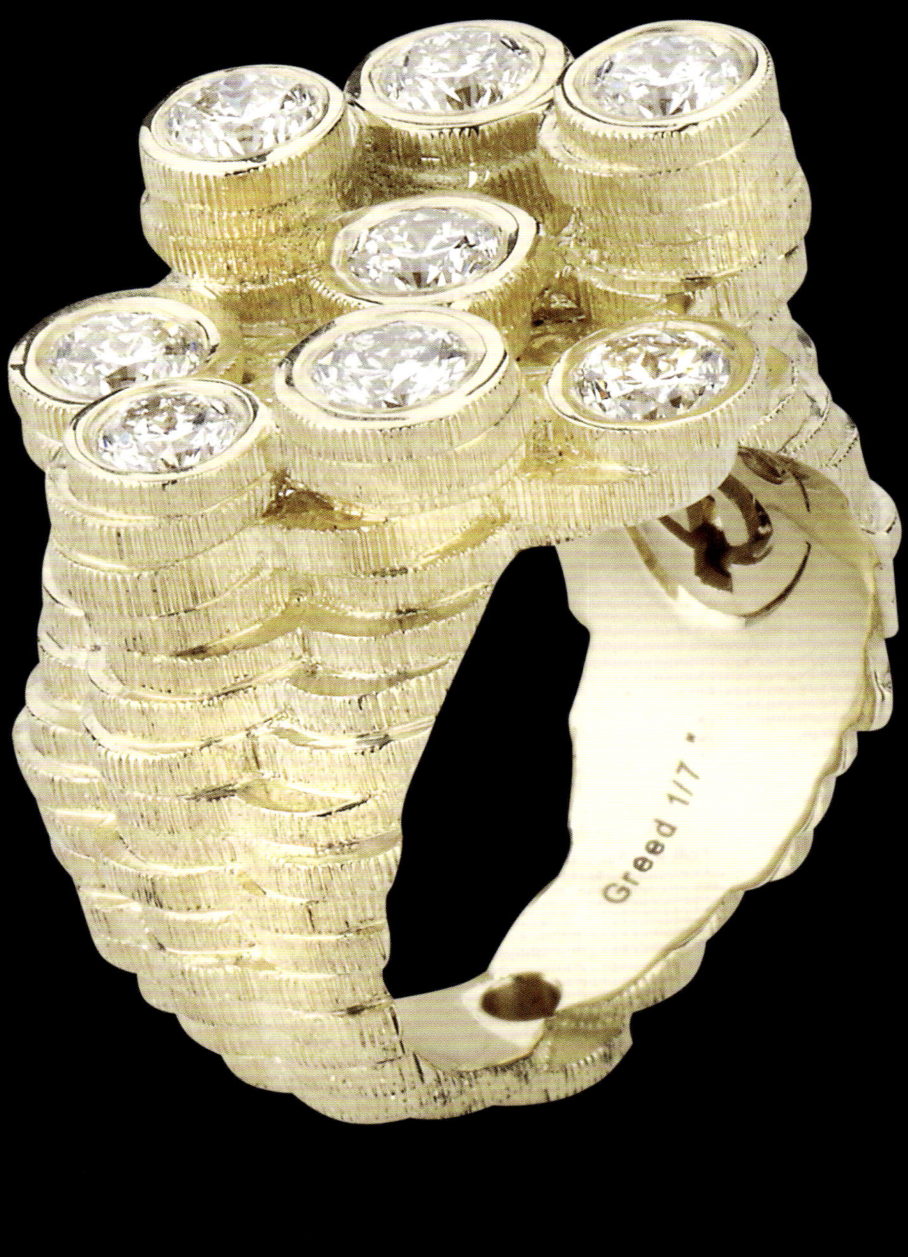

SEVEN DEADLY SINS GREED RING 18k yellow gold and white diamonds

SEVEN DEADLY SINS SLOTH RING 18k yellow gold with aquamarine, red enamel and white diamonds

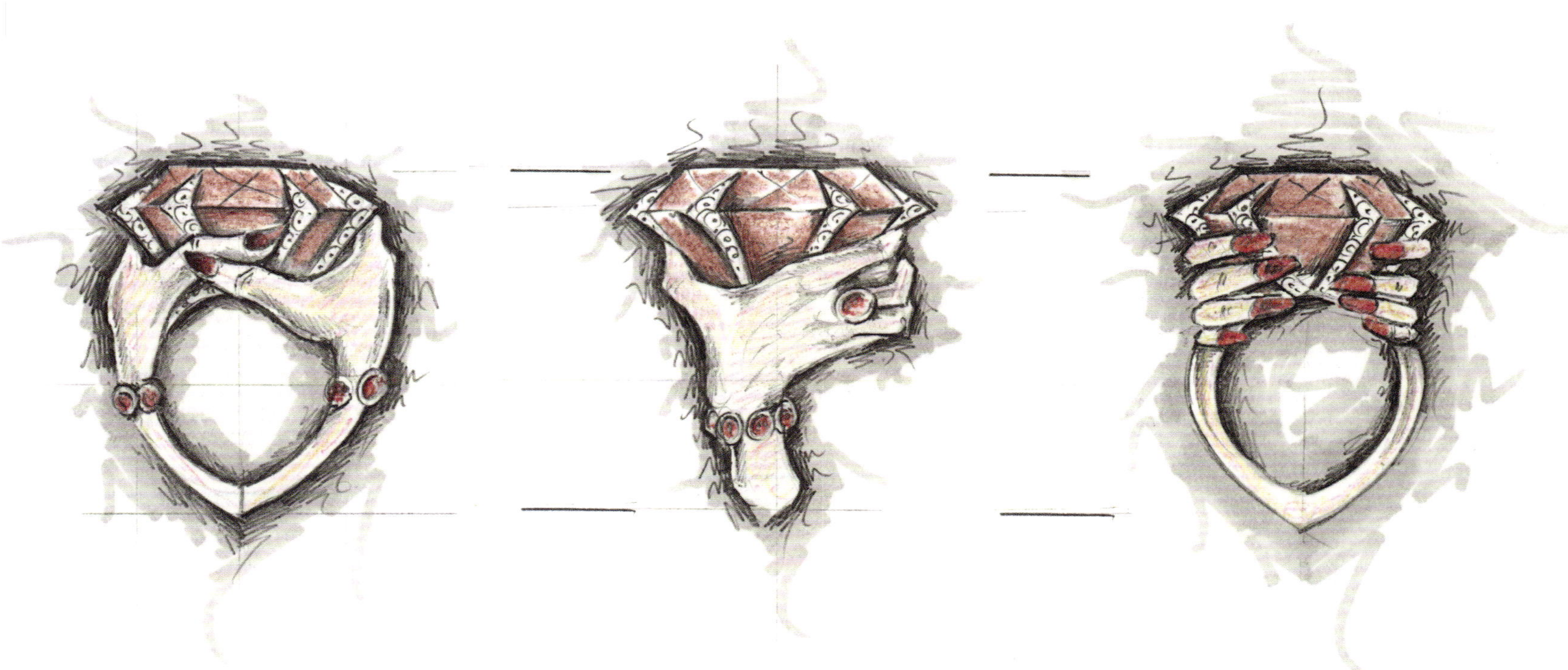

Sketches of SEVEN DEADLY SINS WRATH RING

opposite SEVEN DEADLY SINS WRATH RING 18k rose gold with red garnet, rubies, white and black diamonds

MURDER SHE WROTE

A collection of *whodunit* questions and murderously desirable diamonds, rubies, emeralds and sapphires. In the very English tradition of murder and a cup of tea, *Murder She Wrote* encompasses many tales of deceit, revenge and jealousy set in the idyllic surrounding of a thatched cottage. This collection knows there's a trail of blood and jewellery on the croquet lawn, the kitchen floor, and more often than not, the bedroom.

Model wears MURDER SHE WROTE POISON APPLE RING 18k rose gold with tsavorites and white diamonds; MURDER SHE WROTE POISON APPLE RING 18k rose gold with rubies and white diamonds

top Sketch of MURDER SHE WROTE POISON APPLE RING

bottom MURDER SHE WROTE POISON APPLE RING 18k rose gold with black and white diamonds

MURDER SHE WROTE EVE RING
18k rose gold with pavé black
diamonds and rubies

top MURDER SHE WROTE SMOKING GUN NECKLACE 18k yellow gold with pavé white diamonds

bottom MURDER SHE WROTE GIRL WITH A GOLDEN GUN RING 18k yellow gold with pavé white diamonds and citrine

opposite MURDER SHE WROTE VAPE PIPE Sterling silver, titanium, white and black diamonds and green enamel

MURDER SHE WROTE BANG CUFF 18k white gold with hematite quartz crystal haze, white diamonds and ray skin

opposite Erin O'Connor wears MURDER SHE WROTE BANG CUFF

left MURDER SHE WROTE DAGGER PENDANT 18k white and rose gold with pavé black and white diamonds and ruby drop

right Sketch of MURDER SHE WROTE DAGGER PENDANT

opposite MURDER SHE WROTE BLEEDING HEART TWO FINGER RING 18k rose gold with pavé black and white diamonds, red garnet quartz crystal haze and ruby drop

MURDER SHE WROTE BANG RING
18k white gold with black opal
quartz crystal haze, blue sapphires,
white and black diamonds

opposite Maxine Peak wears
MURDER SHE WROTE CRYSTAL
HAZE RING 18k white gold with
pavé white diamonds and turquoise
quartz crystal haze; MURDER SHE
WROTE BANG RING 18k white
gold with pavé white diamonds and
white mother of pearl crystal haze;
THORN CUFF 18k white gold
with pavé white diamonds

FLY BY NIGHT

Is it a bat? Is it a bird? Is it a moth? Is it a butterfly? No it's a *Fly By Night*. A nocturnal, winged, fantastical creature; illusive, magical and beautiful if ever caught and studied. Inhabiting only the most enchanted of forests, *Fly By Night*s are said to be made out of diamonds, sapphires, rubies, gold and the rarest of gems: the *Crystal Haze*. Only the lucky few know if this is fact or fiction.

Model wears FLY BY NIGHT CRYSTAL HAZE RING 18k white gold with pavé black diamonds and black opal quartz crystal haze; FLY BY NIGHT CRYSTAL HAZE RING 18k white gold with pavé black diamonds and ruby quartz crystal haze; FLY BY NIGHT CRYSTAL HAZE LONG EARRINGS 18k white gold with pavé black diamonds, black opal quartz crystal haze and blue sapphires

FLY BY NIGHT CRYSTAL HAZE RING 18k rose gold with pavé white diamonds and pink opal quartz crystal haze

opposite Model wears FLY BY NIGHT CRYSTAL HAZE PENDANT, RING AND EARRINGS All 18k rose gold with pavé white diamonds and pink opal quartz crystal haze

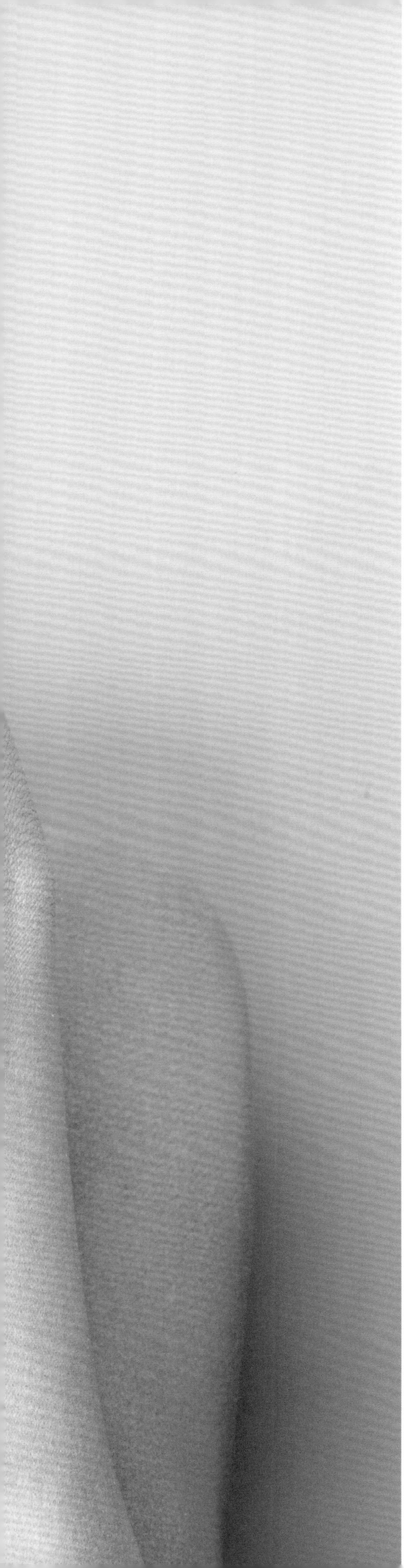

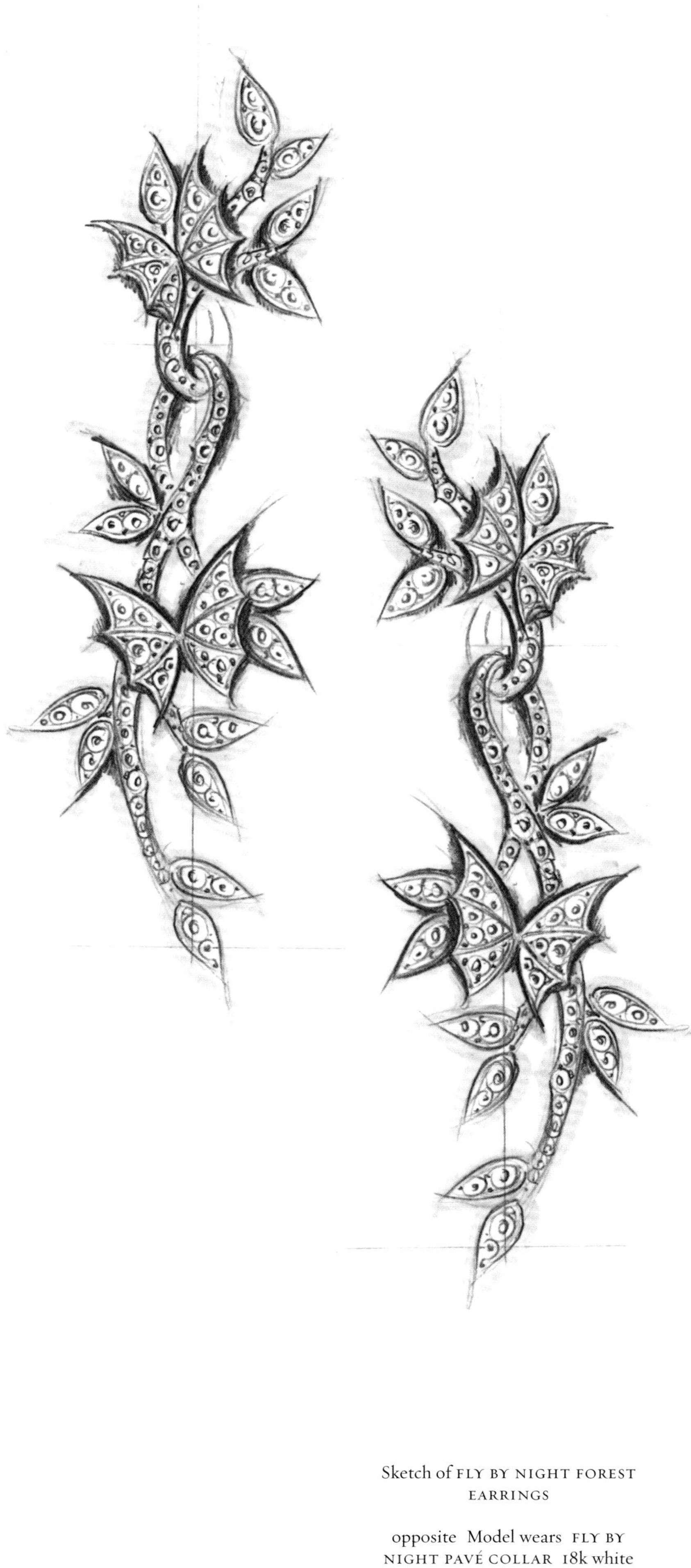

Sketch of FLY BY NIGHT FOREST EARRINGS

opposite Model wears FLY BY NIGHT PAVÉ COLLAR 18k white gold with pavé white diamonds and tanzanite; FLY BY NIGHT PAVÉ RING 18k white gold with pavé white diamonds

top and opposite FLY BY NIGHT FOREST EARRINGS 18k rose gold with pavé white and black diamonds and rubies

bottom and opposite FLY BY NIGHT FOREST LONG FINGER RING 18k rose gold with pavé white and black diamonds and rubies

top Sketch of FLY BY NIGHT PAVÉ OVAL EARRINGS

bottom Sketch of FLY BY NIGHT PAVÉ CHANDELIER EARRINGS

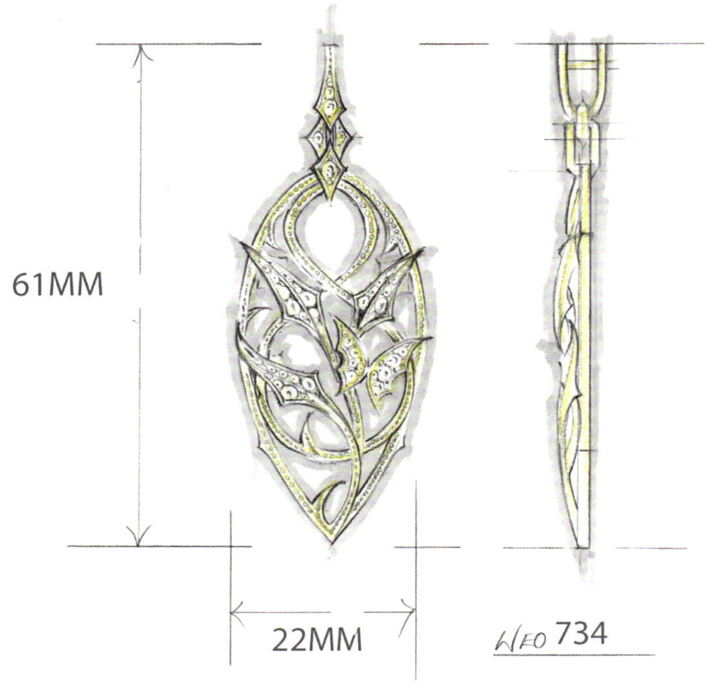

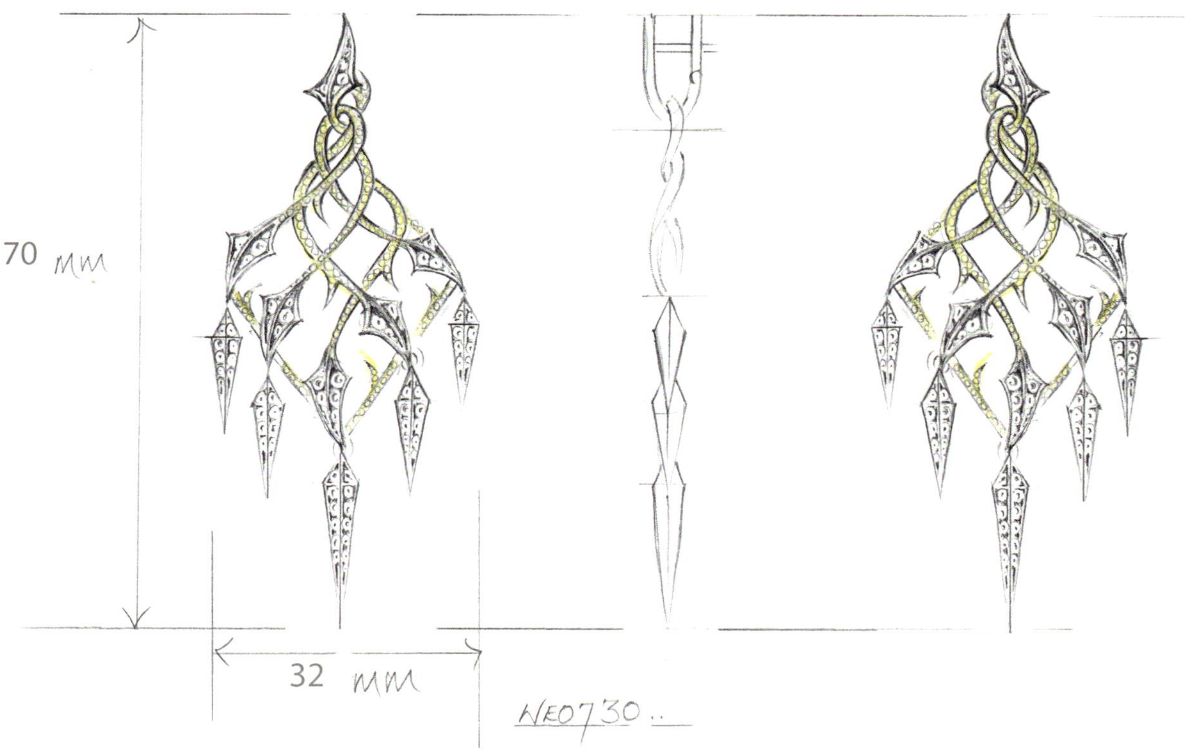

opposite top FLY BY NIGHT PAVÉ BROOCH 18k yellow gold with pavé white diamonds

opposite middle FLY BY NIGHT PAVÉ RING 18k yellow gold with pavé white diamonds

opposite bottom FLY BY NIGHT PAVÉ OVAL EARRINGS 18k yellow gold with pavé white diamonds

Sketch of one of a kind
FLY BY NIGHT COLLAR
Created for Swarovski

opposite Model wears one of a kind FLY BY NIGHT COLLAR at Swarovski Runway Rocks event, Shanghai, 2013. Sterling silver with Swarovski genuine gemstones and single Swarovski crystal
Created for Swarovski

Sketch of FLY BY NIGHT TIARA

opposite FLY BY NIGHT TIARA with Swarovski crystals. Created for Swarovski for the Vienna Opera Ball, Austria, 2014

MAGNIPHEASANT

We paid tribute to the British Isles with a fine jewellery collection inspired by the plumage of England's iconic game bird, the pheasant. *Magnipheasant* explores the elegant form created by a swathe of feathers, brought to life in a riot of colourful and exotic precious gemstones. Though classic in its inspiration, this collection showcases double and triple-finger cocktail rings, earrings with detachable drops and statement ear cuffs. Set with an extraordinary rainbow of marquise-cut coloured stones, including rubies, amethysts, emeralds, tourmalines, garnets, blue topaz, tanzanite, fire opal and pavé diamonds, this is our vibrant and imaginative take on fine jewellery-as-storytelling.

MAGNIPHEASANT COLLAR 18k white gold with pavé black diamonds, citrine, amethyst, rhodolite, red garnet, blue topaz, peridot and iolite

left MAGNIPHEASANT COCKTAIL RING 18k white gold with pavé black diamonds, red garnet, rhodolite and amethyst

middle Sketch of MAGNIPHEASANT COLLAR

right MAGNIPHEASANT LONG EARRINGS 18k white gold with pavé black diamonds, red garnet, rhodolite and amethyst

MAGNIPHEASANT BRACELET
18k white gold with pavé black
diamonds, citrine, amethyst,
rhodolite, red garnet, blue topaz,

MAGNIPHEASANT PAVÉ OPEN WING RING 18k rose gold with pavé white diamonds

opposite FLIGHT OF MAGNIPHEASANT PAVÉ PENDANTS AND EARRINGS 18k rose and white gold with pavé white and black diamonds

Model wears MAGNIPHEASANT PAVÉ EAR CLIP 18k white gold with pavé white diamonds

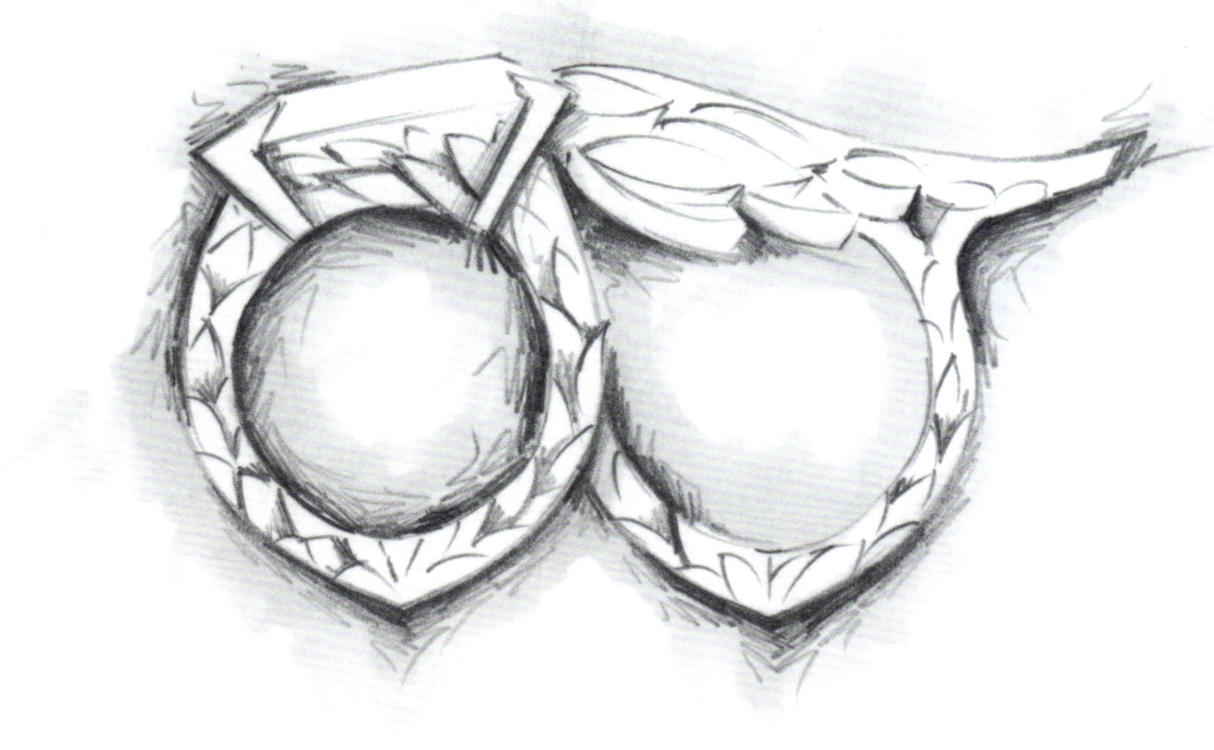

top MAGNIPHEASANT PLUMAGE TWO FINGER RING 18k white gold with pavé black diamonds, fire opal, rubies and yellow sapphires

bottom Sketch of MAGNIPHEASANT PLUMAGE TWO FINGER RING

opposite MAGNIPHEASANT PLUMAGE LONG EARRINGS 18k white gold with pavé black diamonds, fire opal, rubies and yellow sapphires

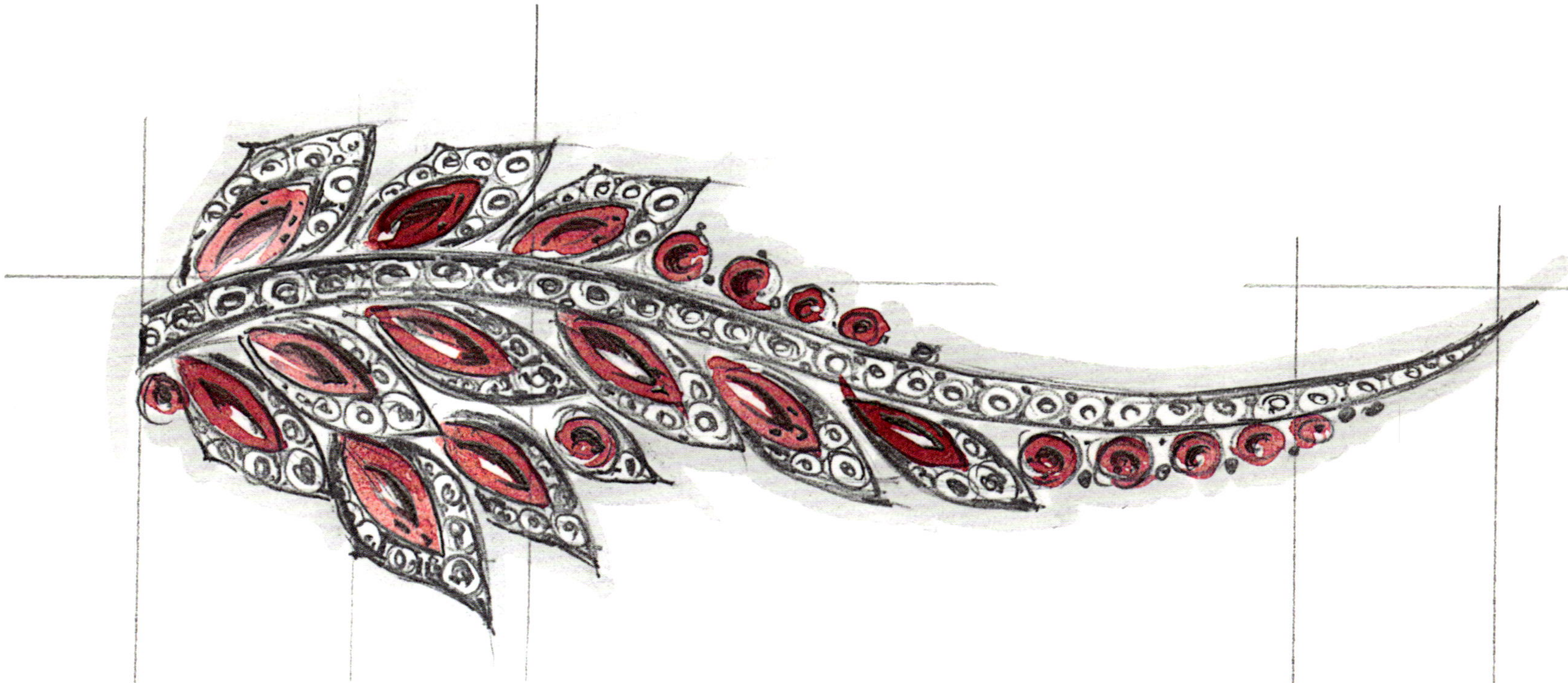

top Sketch of MAGNIPHEASANT PLUMAGE THREE FINGER RING

bottom MAGNIPHEASANT PLUMAGE THREE FINGER RING 18k white gold with pavé white diamonds and Gemfields™ rubies

opposite MAGNIPHEASANT PLUMAGE EAR CLIPS 18k white gold with pavé white diamonds, and Gemfields™ rubies

MAGNIPHEASANT PLUMAGE COLLAR 18k white gold with tanzanite, aquamarine and pavé white diamonds

LADY STARDUST

Inspired by my musical icon, David Bowie, the *Lady Stardust* collection expands on the famous lightning bolt motif featured on the *Aladdin Sane* album cover. We captured the Thin White Duke's pioneering style by translating this symbol of glam rock music into beautifully articulated bracelets, elegant drop earrings, striking cocktail rings and pendants set with colourful *Crystal Haze* stones and pearls. Drawing further on traditional British imagery, this collection also reflects the classic *herringbone* motif. This chevron-like design is accentuated by the use of white and black diamond pavé as well as brightly coloured sapphires which have been set to create a *dip dye* effect, graduating through the full colour spectrum, including Bowie's trademark orange and red.

LADY STARDUST CRYSTAL HAZE RING 18k white gold with pavé yellow and orange sapphires and red coral quartz crystal haze

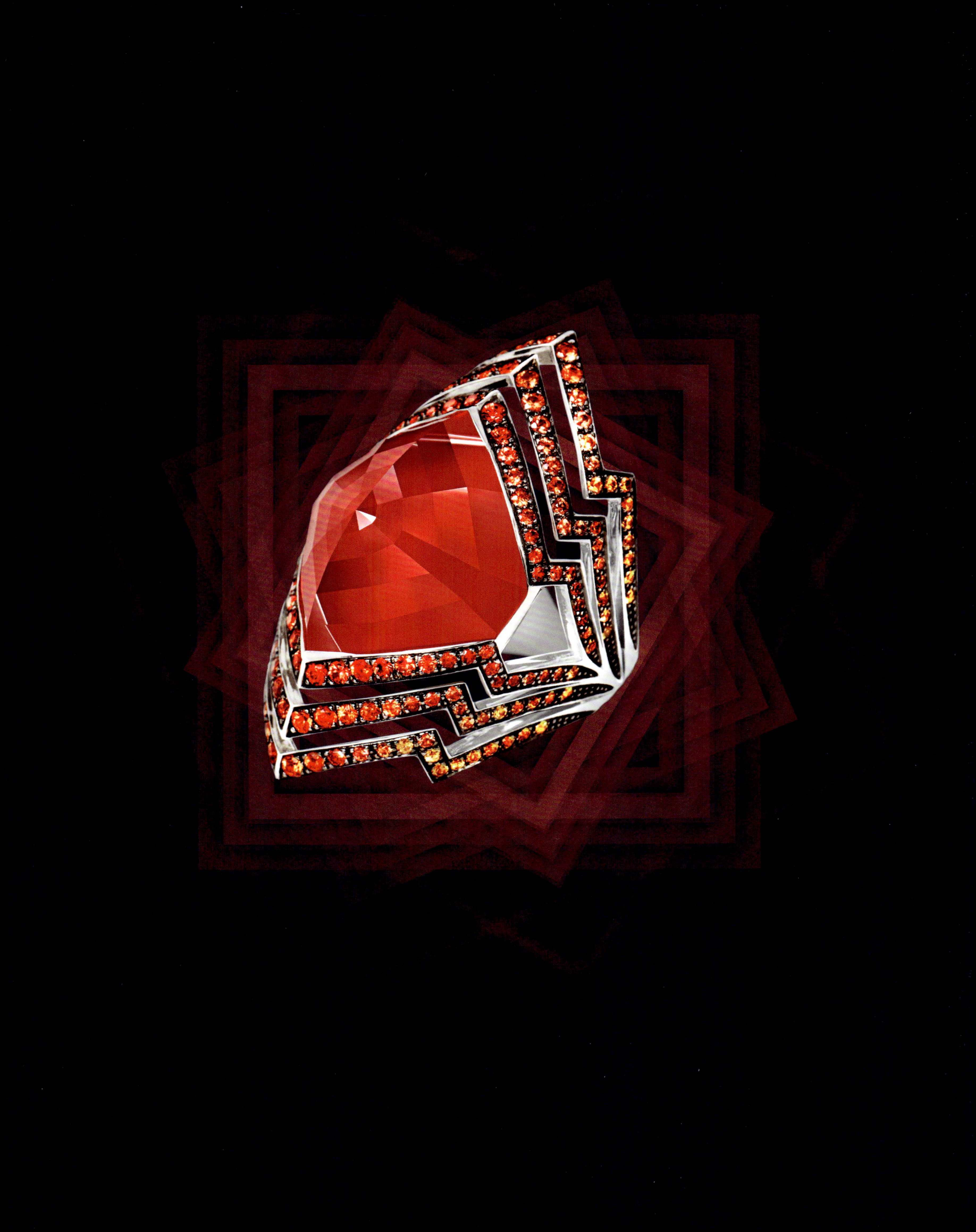

opposite top LADY STARDUST CRYSTAL HAZE RING 18k white gold with pavé yellow and orange sapphires and red coral quartz crystal haze

opposite bottom LADY STARDUST LONG EARRINGS 18k white gold with pavé yellow and orange sapphires

below LADY STARDUST EARRINGS 18k white gold with triangle-cut and pavé black diamonds

top LADY STARDUST CRYSTAL HAZE PENDANT 18k white gold with pavé white and black diamonds and green agate quartz crystal haze

bottom LADY STARDUST CRYSTAL HAZE LONG EARRINGS 18k white gold with pavé white and black diamonds and green agate quartz crystal haze

opposite LADY STARDUST CRYSTAL HAZE RING 18k white gold with pavé white and black diamonds and green agate quartz crystal haze

previous LIFE ON MARS, LADY STARDUST CRYSTAL HAZE RING 18k white gold with pavé white and black diamonds, black opal quartz crystal haze and blue sapphires

above LADY STARDUST CRYSTAL HAZE RING 18k white gold with pavé white and black diamonds, amethyst, white mother of pearl crystal haze and purple sapphires

opposite LADY STARDUST DECO EARRINGS 18k white gold with pavé white diamonds, amethysts and purple sapphires

above and opposite
LADY STARDUST REVERSIBLE
PEARL TASSEL BRACELET
18k white gold with pavé white
and black diamonds, emeralds,
Tahitian and South Sea pearls

Model wears LADY STARDUST EARRINGS 18k white gold with pavé white diamonds, amethysts and purple sapphires; LADY STARDUST NECKLACE 18k white gold with pavé white diamonds, amethysts and purple sapphires; LADY STARDUST RING 18k white gold with pavé white diamonds, amethysts and purple sapphires; LADY STARDUST PEARL RING 18k white gold with pavé white and black diamonds, Tahitian pearl and amethysts

top and bottom
LADY STARDUST NECKLACE
18k white gold with pavé
white diamonds, amethysts
and purple sapphires

middle LADY STARDUST
WIDE CUFF 18k white
gold with pavé white
diamonds, amethysts and
purple sapphires

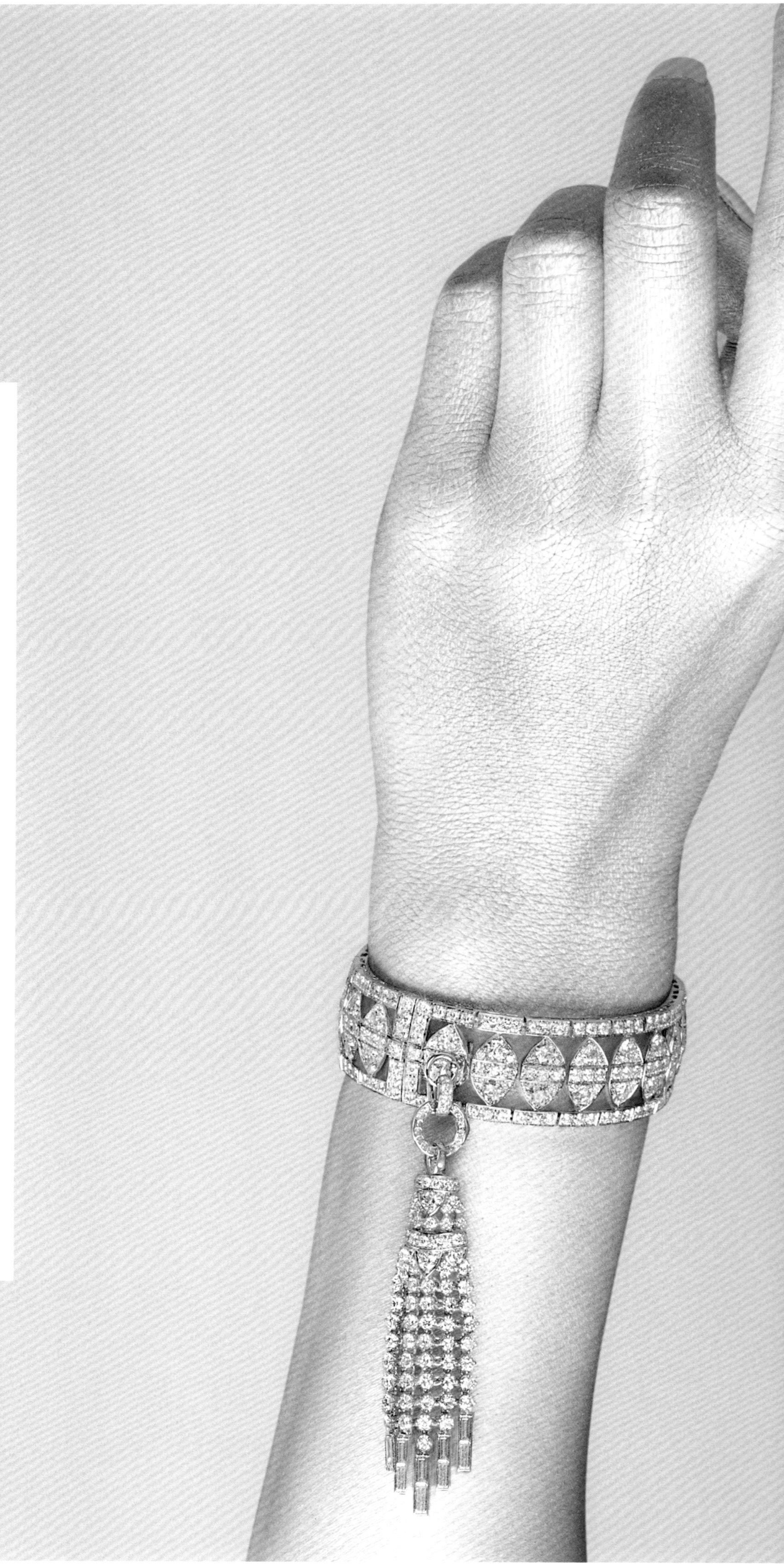

COUTURE VOYAGE

My life, shaped by jewellery, has taken me to the far flung corners of the earth. A jeweller can function from a very small space, I did for my early years. Very soon after my training, jewellery started to take me places. Years later I have lost count of all those places. *Couture Voyage* is a collection of special pieces inspired by some of my favourite destinations. The USA has always been important to me and features heavily but so do some more unlikely places such as Azerbaijan's Caspian Sea, Africa, China and, of course, Russia. A sort of jewellery expedition.

Model wears COUTURE VOYAGE NEW YORK BRACELET 18k white gold with pavé, baguette cut and Forevermark™ white diamonds; COUTURE VOYAGE NEW YORK EARRINGS 18k white gold with pavé, baguette cut and Forevermark™ white diamonds

top COUTURE VOYAGE NEW YORK EARRINGS 18k white gold with pavé, baguette cut and Forevermark™ white diamonds

bottom COUTURE VOYAGE NEW YORK EARRINGS 18k white gold, baguette cut and pavé emeralds

opposite COUTURE VOYAGE NEW YORK BRACELET 18k white gold with pavé, baguette cut and Forevermark™ white diamonds

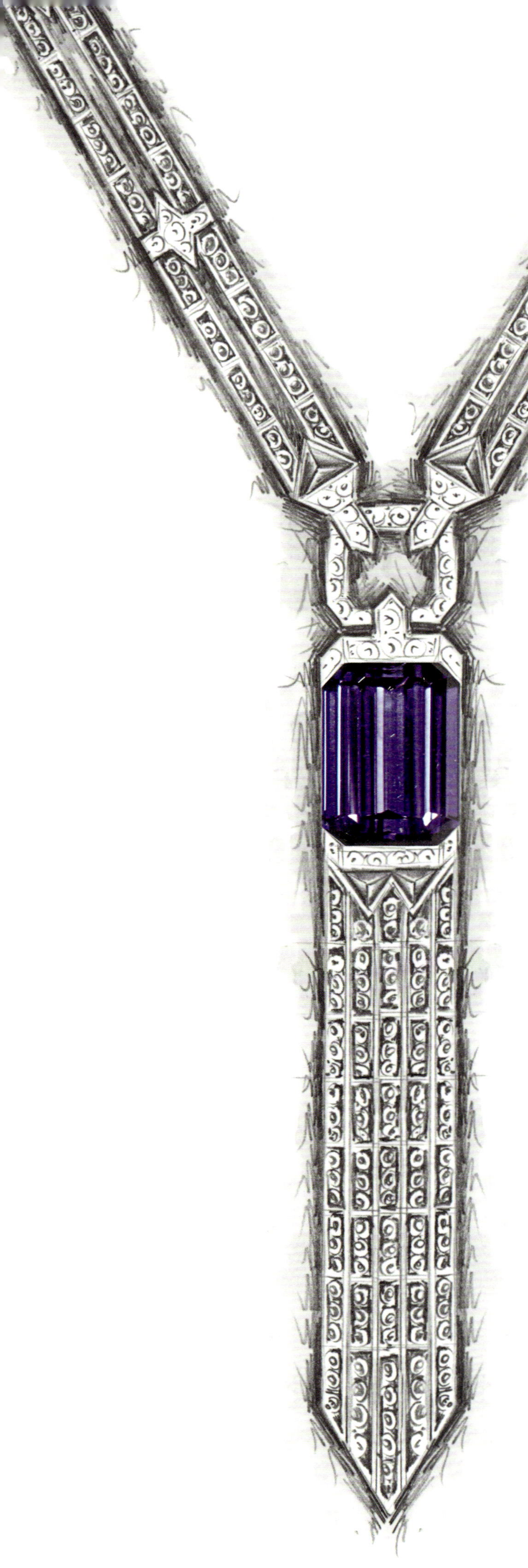

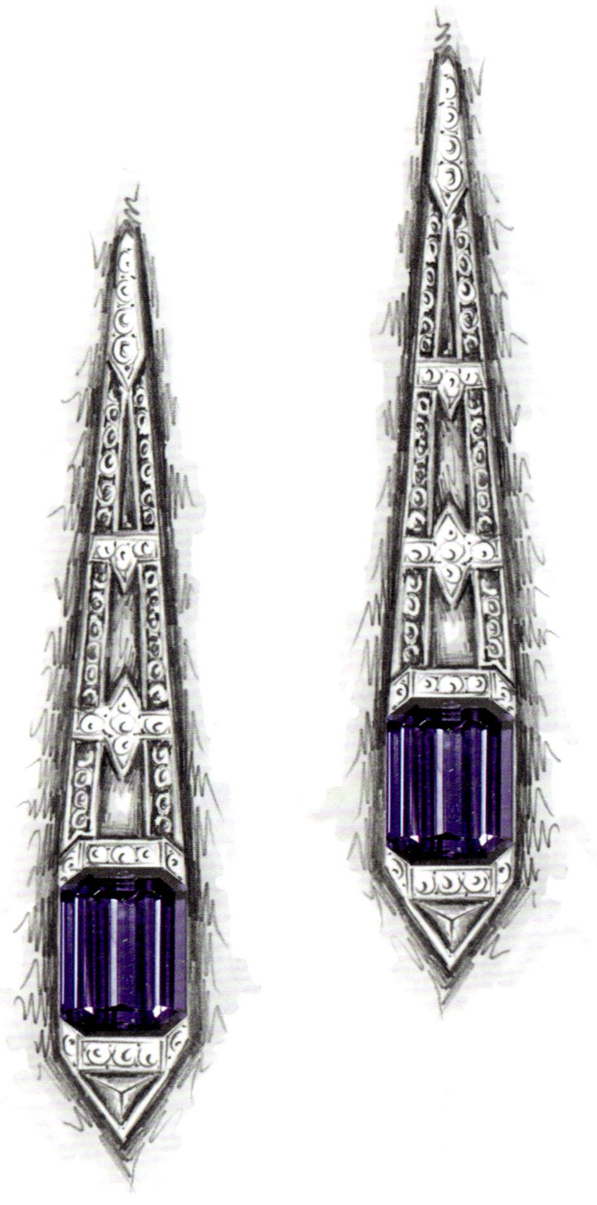

left Sketch of COUTURE VOYAGE NEW YORK DECO PENDANT

right Sketch of COUTURE VOYAGE NEW YORK DECO EARRINGS

left COUTURE VOYAGE MIAMI EARRINGS 18k rose gold with pavé white diamonds

right COUTURE VOYAGE MIAMI PENDANT 18k rose gold with pavé white diamonds and morganite

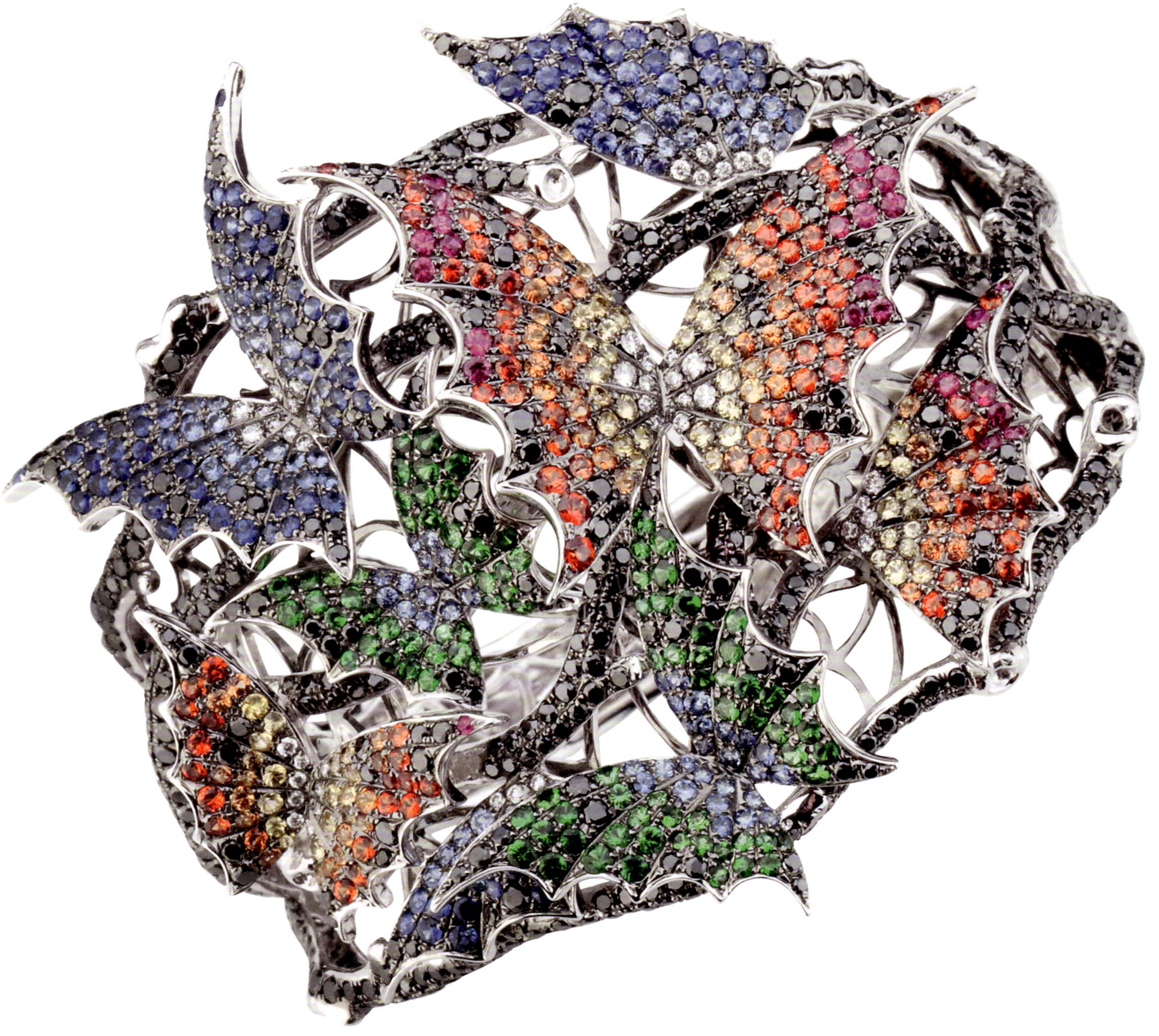

COUTURE VOYAGE AFRICA CUFF
18k white gold with pavé white and black diamonds, blue sapphires, tsavorites, orange sapphires and yellow sapphires

left COUTURE VOYAGE AFRICA EARRINGS 18k white gold with white and black diamonds, blue sapphires, tsavorites, orange sapphires and yellow sapphires

right COUTURE VOYAGE AFRICA RING 18k white gold with white and black diamonds, blue sapphires, tsavorites, orange sapphires and yellow sapphires

Africa suite sketches

opposite Daisy Lowe wears BELLE EPOQUE PENDANT 18k white gold with pavé black diamonds, emeralds and onyx cabochons BELLE EPOQUE ARMOUR-DILLO LONG FINGER RING 18k white gold with pavé black diamonds and emeralds; BELLE EPOQUE CHANDELIER EARRINGS 18k white gold with pavé black diamonds and emeralds

right BELLE EPOQUE PENDANT 18k white gold with pavé black diamonds, emeralds and onyx cabochons

below BELLE EPOQUE ARMOUR-DILLO LONG FINGER RING 18k white gold with pavé black diamonds and emeralds

COUTURE VOYAGE CHINA GIRL DRAGON BROOCH 18k white gold with pavé and single 5ct Forevermark™ white diamond

COUTURE VOYAGE CHINA GIRL DRAGON RING 18k rose gold with rubies, white diamonds and a white South Sea pearl

MEN'S

14 years ago, *Rayman* was our first full collection for men. Despite the fact that there were virtually no retail environments able to showcase a jewellery collection for men at the time, we persevered and eventually the market started to understand and embrace the concept. Over the years, inspired by history, intricacy, urban environments and popular culture, we have provided collections that have resonated with men; in turn, discovering that despite using much of the same material, what men want is intrinsically different to what women want.

Photograph by SW

selected RAYMAN RINGS
Sterling silver and 18k yellow gold

opposite RAYMAN BRACELET
Sterling silver

RAM'S HEAD BRACELET
Sterling silver with 18k yellow gold and pavé white diamonds

opposite TONY WARD WEARS RAM'S HEAD BRACELET
Sterling silver with 18k yellow gold and pavé white diamonds

BLEEDING HEART PENDANT
18k white gold with pavé white diamonds, onyx and rubies

opposite JONATHAN RHYS MEYERS WEARS LONDON CALLING SHIELD RING 18k yellow gold, pavé black sapphires and black mother of pearl

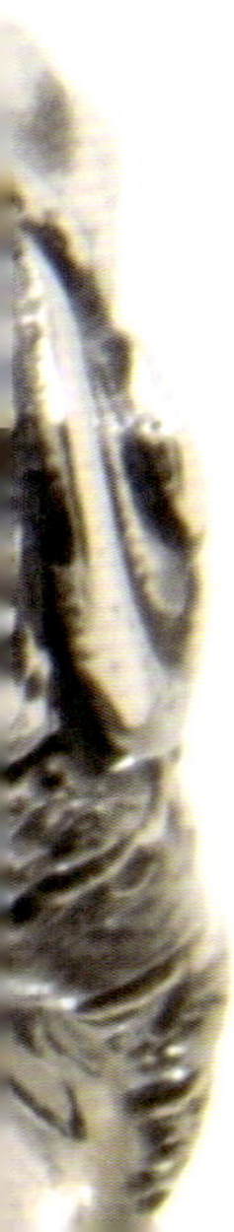

clockwise: KNOWLEDGE RING 18k yellow gold with ruby eyes; LONDON CALLING SIGNET RING Sterling silver, 18k yellow gold and bloodstone; LONDON CALLING GARGOYLE RING Sterling silver, 18k yellow gold, onyx and ruby eyes; RAM SKULL RING 18k white gold, pavé white and black diamonds; ONE OF A KIND CARVED SKULL RING 18k yellow gold and citrine with diamond eyes; LONDON CALLING SIGNET RING Sterling silver, 18k yellow gold whisky quartz; KABUKI MASK RING 18k yellow gold, pavé white diamonds and ruby eyes; LONDON CALLING SIGNET RING Sterling silver, 18k yellow gold ammalite; KNOWLEDGE RING 18k white gold, pavé white diamonds and ruby eyes

ENGLAND MADE ME SIGNET RING 18k rose gold with pavé white diamonds

left ENGLAND MADE ME REVOLUTIONARY BRACELET 18k rose gold with pavé black and white diamonds, single gypsy set white diamond and white mother of pearl inlay on a matt black ceramic link bracelet

right ENGLAND MADE ME CHURCHILL BRACELET 18k rose gold with pavé white diamonds and white mother of pearl inlay on a matt black ceramic link bracelet

All shown on matt ceramic link bracelets

top HALF CORONA CLASP
18k rose gold, oxblood enamel, pavé black diamonds

bottom CHURCHILL CLASP
Sterling silver, malachite inlay, pavé black sapphire

top ENGLAND MADE ME REVOLUTIONARY CLASP 18k rose gold with pavé black diamonds, black enamel, gypsy set emerald and black mother of pearl inlay

bottom ENGLAND MADE ME HALF CORONA CLASP 18k yellow gold with pavé white diamonds, gunmetal enamel and black mother of pearl inlay

opposite left NO REGRETS RAVEN'S SKULL BRACELET Sterling silver with bull's eye beads

opposite right LONDON CALLING RAVEN'S HEAD ROSARY Sterling silver with bull's eye beads

LONDON CALLING SWITCHBLADE PENDANT Sterling silver

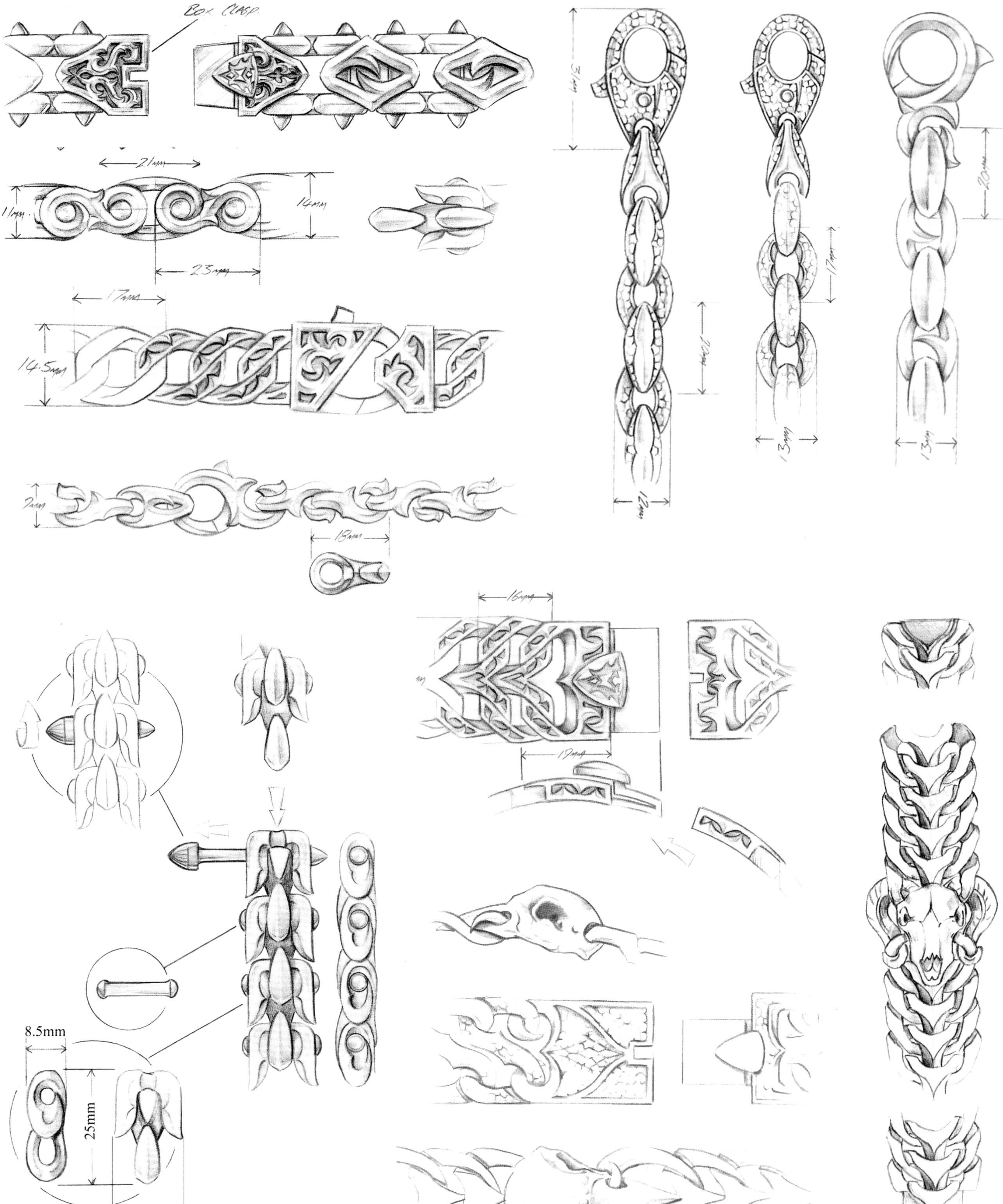

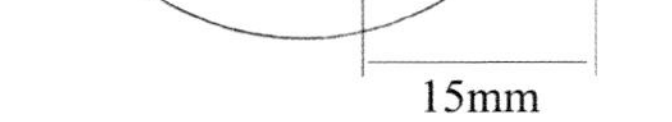

Selected men's bracelet sketches

opposite Selected men's sterling silver bracelets

clockwise GARGOYLE CUFFLINKS 18k white gold, pavé black sapphires and rubies; BULLDOG CUFFLINKS Sterling silver with red enamel; CANCER CUFFLINKS Sterling silver with black mother of pearl quartz crystal haze; SCORPION CUFFLINKS Sterling silver with pavé black sapphires and red garnet; CRYSTAL HAZE CUFFLINKS 18k white gold with lapis quartz crystal haze

opposite HAMMERHEAD CUFFLINKS Sterling silver with pavé blue sapphires

No Regrets
No Regrets

NO REGRETS BELT Gift from SW team on 50th birthday. Sterling silver with 18k rose gold and leather

opposite and overleaf
Stephen Webster custom design
No Regrets Harley Davidson tank

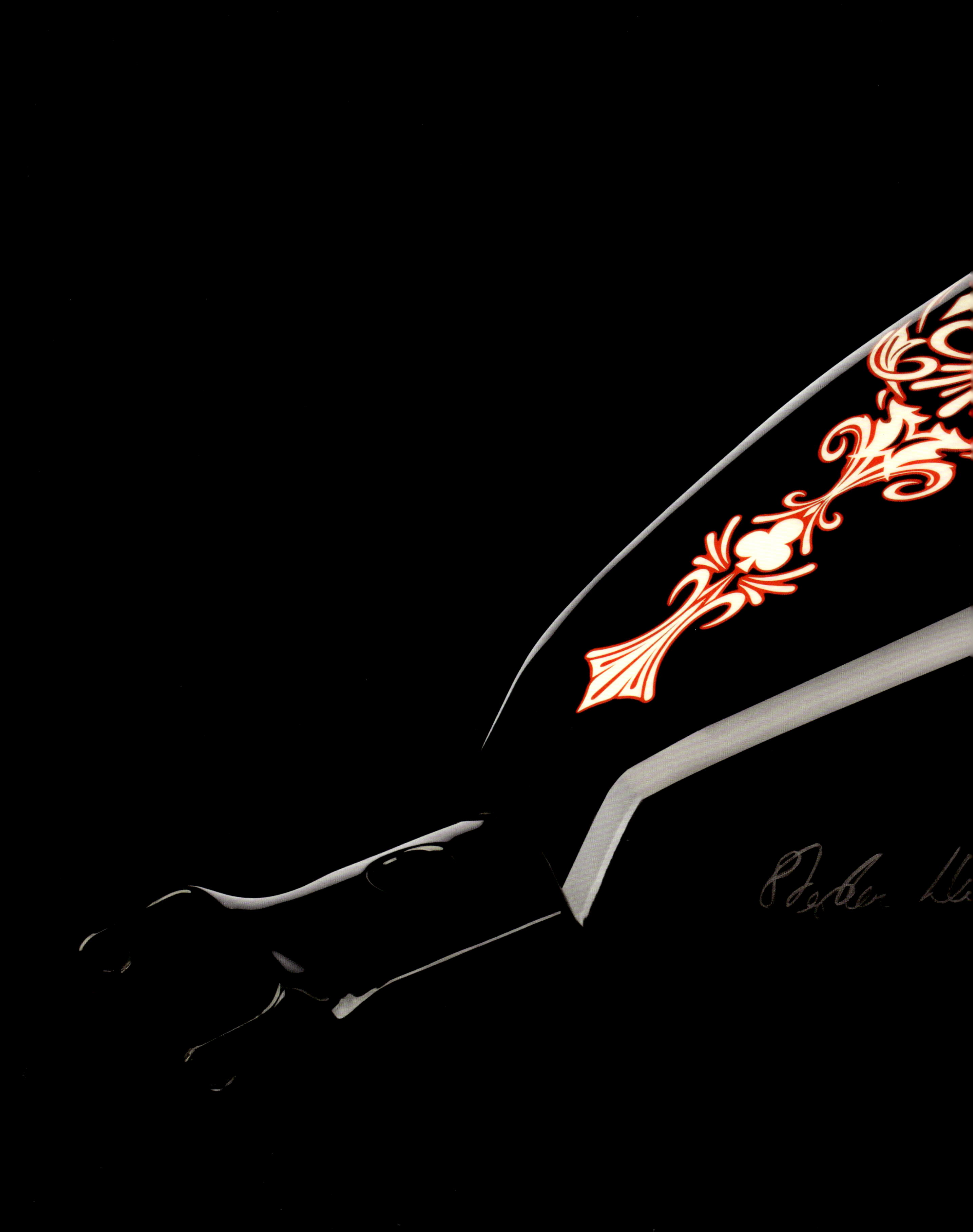

Harley
Davidson

ONE OF A KIND

Throughout my career I have always made *one of a kind* pieces. Usually defined by design often for an individual, or simply because I chose to make just one. In jewellery terms unique pieces tend to be of higher value than collection pieces, often containing rare and valuable gem stones. One could argue that every gem is different therefore every piece is a *one of a kind*. The reality being, clients would not be impressed by discovering that the individual piece they had acquired was unique simply because of this fact. One of a kind should mean just that; a piece that can never or will never be made again. These are a few examples of our bespoke or *one of a kind* pieces.

Peter Turner
Helen for Dom Perignon Vintage Rosé, 2010
Wearing John Galliano and Stephen Webster
Watercolour, graphite pencil, charcoal and ink

top One of a kind DOM PERIGNON VORTEX RING 18k white gold, white diamonds and featuring a rare 3ct pink-orange oval cut diamond

bottom One of a kind DOM PERIGNON STAR PENDANT 18k white gold, white diamonds and featuring a rare 11.19ct pink emerald cut diamond

opposite DOM PERIGNON ROSÉ COLLECTION in celebration of 1993 Vintage Rosé 18k white gold with pink tourmaline, morganite, pink sapphires and white diamonds

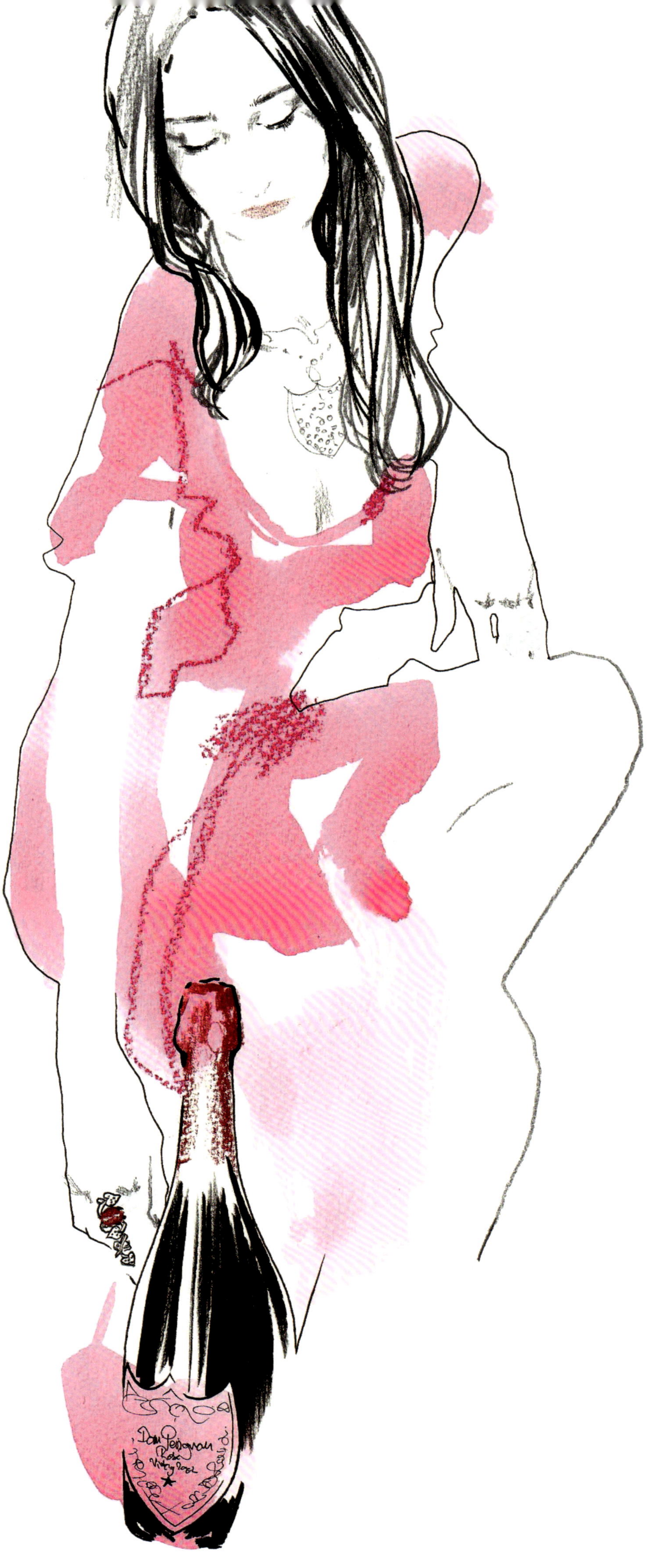

DOM PERIGNON DARK JEWEL EARRINGS 18k white gold with rubellite tourmaline and pavé black and white diamonds

opposite DOM PERIGNON DARK JEWEL LONG FINGER RING 18k white gold with rubellite tourmaline and pavé black and white diamonds

below and opposite Peter Turner
Helen for Dom Pérignon Vintage Rosé, 2010
Wearing John Galliano and Stephen Webster
Watercolour, graphite pencil, charcoal and ink

POMEGRANATE RING 18k white gold with 62.66ct Pakistani peridot, white diamond pavé and cabochon cut mixed peridot, tourmaline and black jade

GOLDMINE RING 18k yellow gold with 20.08ct spessartite mandarin garnet and mixed cabochon cut garnets

Render of JEWELS VERNE GIANT SQUID COLLAR for a 99ct Santa Maria aquamarine

opposite JEWELS VERNE AQUARIUM RING 18k white gold with pavé white diamonds and 77.8ct tanzanite

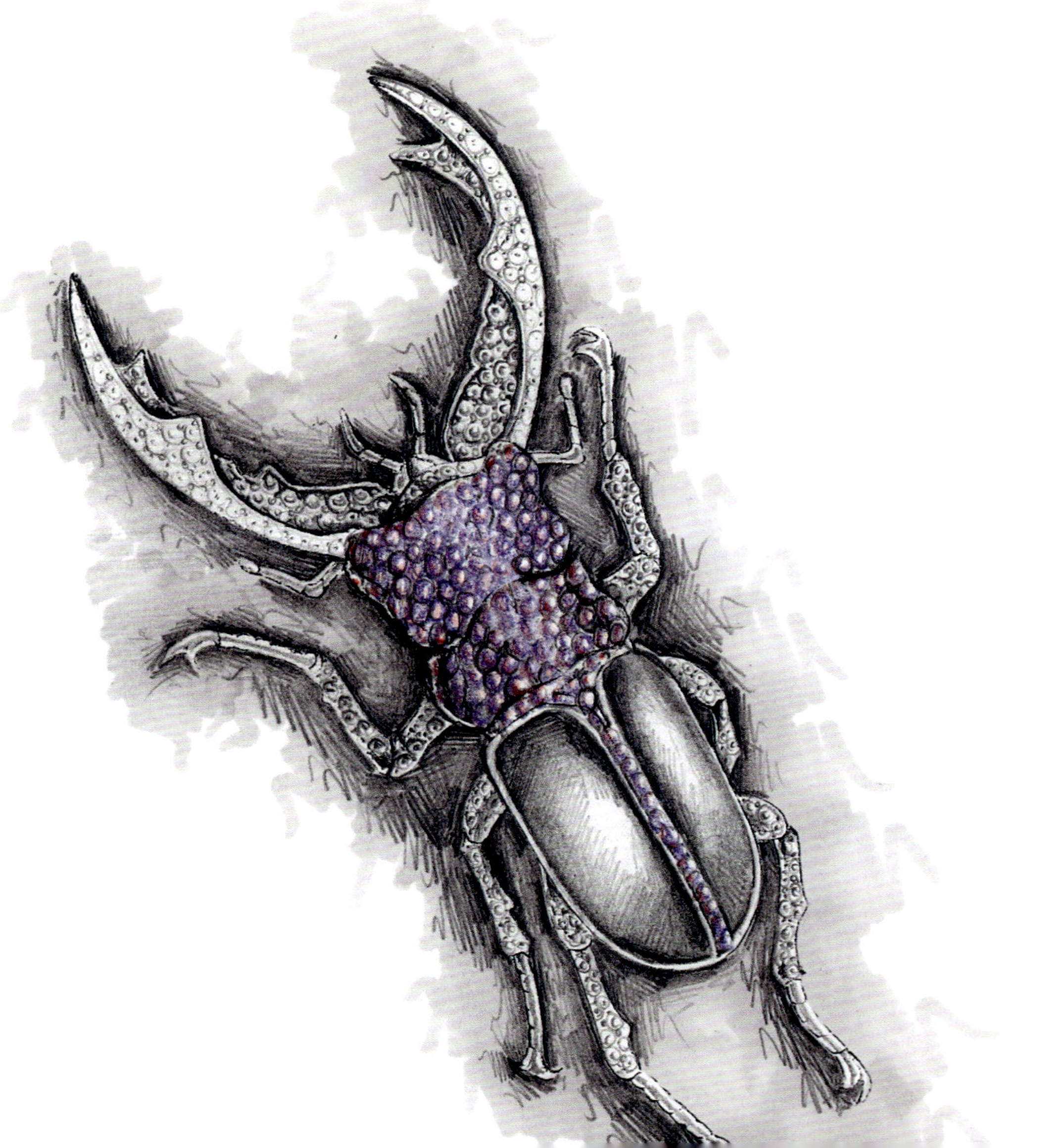

top STAG BEETLE BROOCH 18k white gold with pavé white and black diamonds, black mother of pearl and amethysts

bottom Sketch of STAG BEETLE BROOCH

top Sketch of SCORPION BROOCH

bottom SCORPION BROOCH
18k white gold with pavé white, black and brown diamonds and rubies

above CELESTIAL EARRINGS
18k white gold with pavé white diamonds and 16.8ct pear-shaped zultanite gemstones

opposite top and bottom Sketches of CELESTIAL SHIELD COLLAR and TWO-FINGER RING

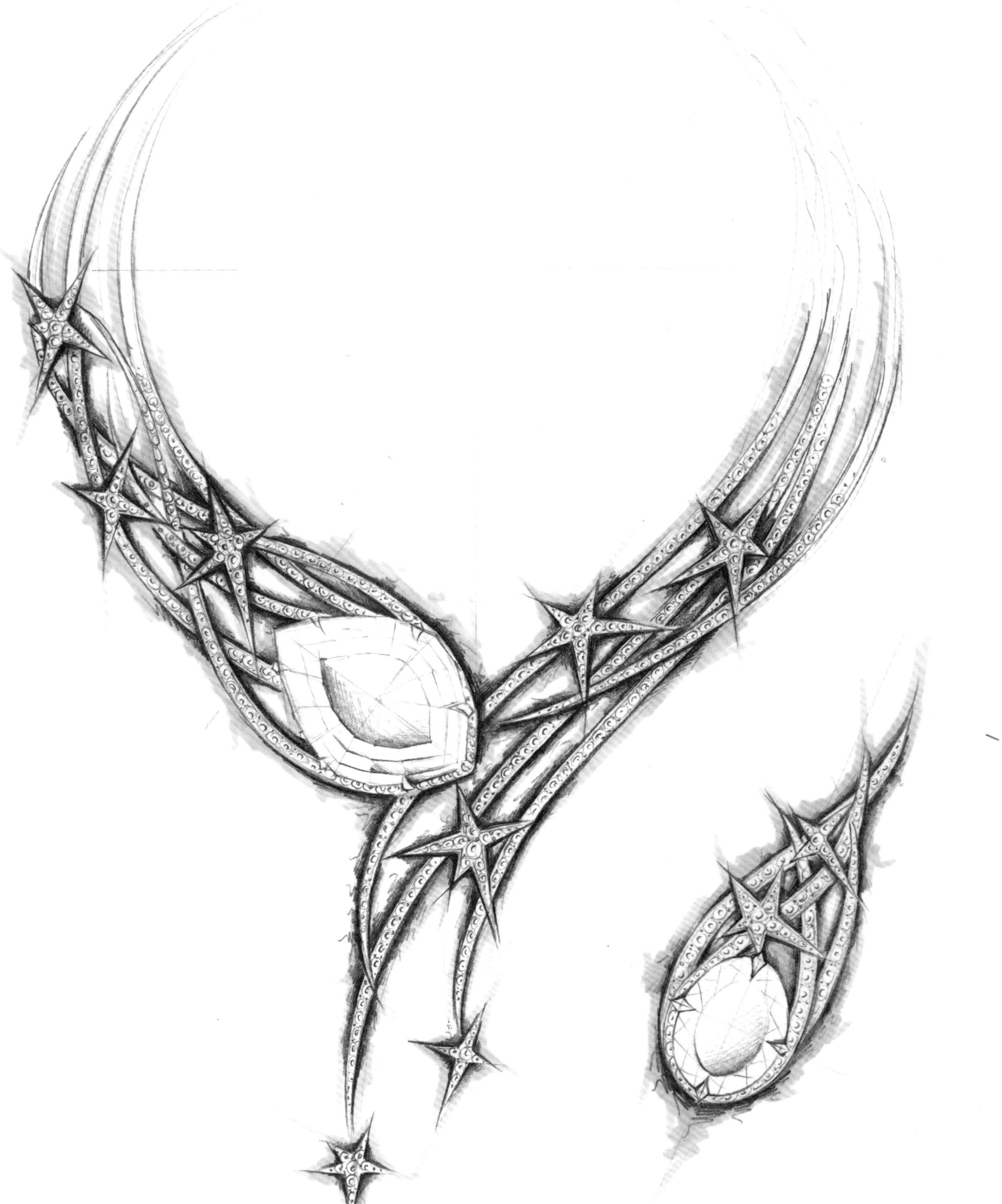

Bespoke TREE OF LIFE BRACELET
18k white gold with round,
pear and pavé white diamonds

opposite SIMPOR FLOWER
TWO FINGER RING 18k yellow
gold with white and yellow
diamonds

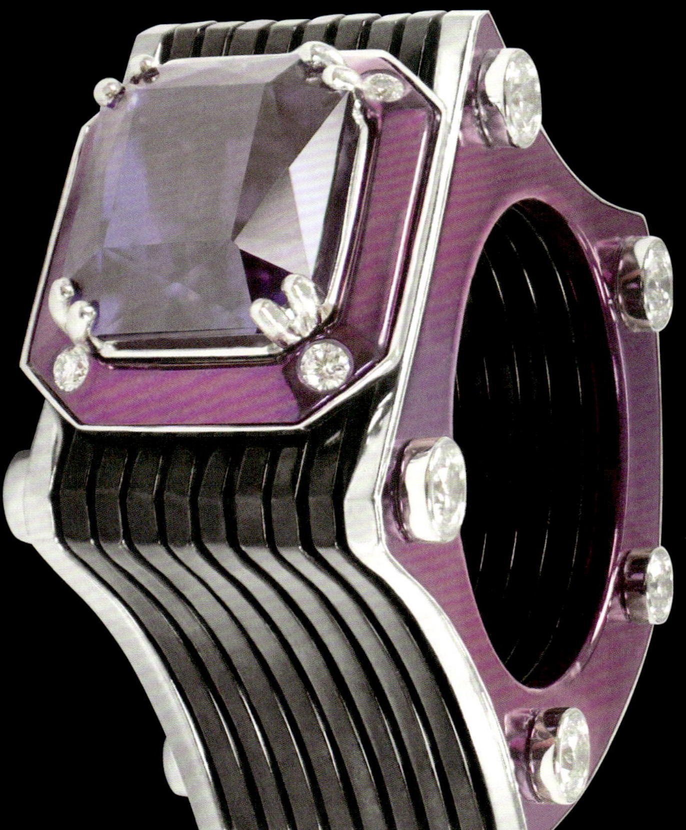

Men's ring 18k white gold with titanium, white diamonds and colour change sapphire

opposite Stephen Webster 30th anniversary custom design Harley Davidson Fatboy motorbike

CRYSTAL HAZE CUTLERY SET
Hand-forged sterling silver with hematite quartz crystal haze

opposite JEWELS VERNE CHAMPAGNE GLASSES Sterling silver with 18k yellow gold, South Sea and Tahitian pearls

THE CABINET OF CURIOSITIES

A couple of solid gold geezers, Stephen Webster and Jimmy Nesbitt, after a day on the Isle of Dogs

SOLID GOLD GEEZER

John Cooper Clarke

Solid gold geezer that
Got a girl in a million +vat
She wears her hair in a platinum plait
Keeps it underneath a Fabergé hat
Kisses him in the mouth and spat
Solid gold geezer that

Solid gold geezer that
From the solitaire pin through the mink cravat
To the snake eye studs on his kid shade spats
Solid gold geezer that

Solid gold geezer that
Lives in a solid gold flat
Sunshine slants through golden slats
And can't find anything matte

Solid gold geezer that
Lives in a solid gold flat
Sunshine slants through golden slats
And can't find anything matte

Solid gold geezer that
Freezer shy of any snack packs
What! You wanna get fat
Wipe your feet on the way out Jack
He's happy you can't argue with that
BRASS PLAQUE SAYS: FACT
Solid gold geezer that

Self made aristocrat
Life of Riley down pat
Ghetto fabulous binge tat
And a caviar guzzling cat
Home is where it's at
Just him her and that ball of fur
Solid gold geezer that
Solid gold geezer that
I seen the figures and I read the stats
Solid gold geezer that

I AM A JEWELLERY MAN

Stephen Webster

I am a jewellery man
I have a master plan
When all is told, if it's made of gold
I am the man who can

When asked by many, what do I sing?
I reply, no one, I'm the king of bling
Acoustic guitar, I would love to play
But heavy metal has become 'my way'

A life in fashion would have been nice
But not a patch on peddling ice
Chocolates and flowers, good to send
If only diamonds weren't a girl's best friend

For some 'brass knuckles' will do the job
But it's gold for me, I'm a jewellery snob
To leave an impression on someone's chin
Four sovereign rings, a guaranteed win

Platinum's more precious, we know it is
For me, 9 carat is the real showbiz
Those Europeans may consider it trash
But here, us Brits demand flash for cash

It's my business to add some lustre
To almost any unkempt cluster
Come upstairs to see my jewels
You'd be surprised who that one fools

There's a pearl necklace for the one
Who wants to come and join in the fun
Even though, I make gold rings
My skills can spread over many things

Whatever in life you choose to pursue
There are ups and downs, you know it's true
So for the times that don't quite go to plan
You can always turn to the jewellery man

Bling King grabber machine, bought to raise money for MacMillan nurses who cared for my mother when she was ill with cancer

BLING KING

WEBSTER'S JEWELLERY DICTIONARY

AMETHYST The ancient Greeks and Romans believed this rich purple gem could protect the wearer from alcoholism. When I lived in California I met a woman who slept with a large amethyst crystal under her pillow, she was taking no chances. Coloured stones are all about the colour, valued by the richness and hue of the material. With this in mind Amethyst is great value for money; a top grade Bolivian or Brazilian specimen will give you real bang for your buck. And remember if you do struggle with the temptation of the demon drink, try an amethyst mocktail ring.

MY COUSIN BERYL Aquamarine sounds and is beautiful, the same goes for Emerald. Beryl on the other hand has old aunt written all over it. It's not surprising then that both these gems, which are actually Beryls, use aliases. Beryl comes in blue or aqua and yellow and pink, which is known as Morganite, so named because JP Morgan bought a nice one from Tiffany back in the day. When Beryl has chromium in its makeup it becomes Emerald.

CARATS NOT CARROTS There are many carats in jewellery, though none suitable for a Lancashire hotpot. Carats are used to determine the weight of gem stones and pearls; one carat = 0.2 grams. A 5ct diamond weighs 1 gram. Then the other unrelated carat is used as a gauge of pure gold against other alloys. Pure gold is 24k or 999 parts pure out of a maximum 1000. 18k gold means a piece of jewellery has 750 parts pure gold. 9k is the lowest at only 375 parts. The rest may as well be a carrot. Simple really!

MEET THE GARNETS A family of gems occurring in many colours and locations, including the Almandine, more affectionately known as Carbuncle, a reddish/brown gem which has adorned jewellery dating back to the Saxon times. The Demantoid, a favourite of Tsars and wealthy Victorians, was known as the emerald of the Urals. Today, Garnets such as bright mandarin Spessartine or burgundy Rhodolite are often used in modern jewellery. Tanzanian green Tsavorite/garnet can fetch a cool million dollars.

WHAT IS THE REAL COLOUR OF GOLD? Gold in its raw state, no matter where the ore is mined or panned or gathered, is a rich yellow metal. 24k of pure gold is considered too soft for practical use in most jewellery so over the years different metals—alloys—have been introduced in order to make the pure metal more hard wearing and go further. These alloys can be any colour. Using metallurgy and mystery, men in white coats can make the yellow more pink, more white or more yellow.

JADE Whether Jadeite or nephrite, green, lavender, black or white—the purest white is known as mutton fat and is very rare—Jade is steeped in mystery and belief, and has a hold over the Chinese-speaking world like the most beautiful of concubines. Every person has at least a piece, which equates to a lot of pieces. Unlike other gemstones, jade has no crystal structure, tough and sticky as well as hard, normal lapidary skills of the gem cutter don't apply. Jade can only be fashioned by a jade master. Like everything from China, change is in the air, a new generation of masters, bored with the same beads, bangles and Buddhas are producing incredible modern masterpieces in this material that the West will never fully understand but can enjoy.

JEWELLERY AMULETS Fashions come and go but the protective qualities of precious materials mean that jewellery amulets are going nowhere and everywhere at the same time. Embedded in history and the handle of a Samurai warrior's sword or the plus size crucifix favoured by the Christian crusader or the evil eye sported by the spiritually secular. Amulets will always be the perfect gift for those who believe they believe.

OPALS As luck would have it, during the Middle Ages, opals were, in fact, massively lucky. It wasn't until 1829 when Sir Walter Scott included a chapter of bad luck in his novel *Anne of Geierstein* that the gem's luck changed. Opals by nature contain up to 22 per cent water. Therefore, if they are stored badly in environments that aren't humid enough there is a chance the water along with the luck could run out. This will cause crazing. Like most things that become crazed there is the question of value, with the exception of comic value, which doesn't apply to gems in general. SW recommends you keep your opals in a damp place like Britain and never on top of the oven.

PEARLS Pearls are back, only this time without the twinset. Extraordinary things pearls; along with coral they are a totally organic component considered precious enough for fine jewellery. Mary I, the original pearly queen, adored her pearls, in particular a conker-sized South Sea specimen known as La Peregrina. Eventually, along with almost everything else, this beauty found its way into Elizabeth Taylor's jewellery box. Over the past few years Chinese freshwater oysters have been producing pearls of steroid enhanced proportions in an array of colours, the price of these are far lower than the more established varieties meaning more girls can enjoy their very own set of pearls.

SEMI-PRECIOUS Like semi-detached or semi-qualified, semi-precious suggests something not quite top shelf. In normal circumstances I would be the first to agree. Officially, precious could only be applied to the big four; diamond, sapphire, ruby and emerald. However, having recently viewed a glorious 40ct Mozambique Red Spinel valued at just short of €4 million, or three intense fuchsia Morganites with a price tag of €150,000 or A grade Tanzanite's starting at €2,000/ct, it makes one wonder if referring to these or the many other exotic gems with eye watering price tags as anything other than plain precious would fall under the trade descriptions act.

TANZANITE I am compiling this entry from high camp on mount Kilimanjaro, currently at 4,600 m (summit tonight.) Last time I visited Tanzania I descended 1,500 m down the only Tanzanite mine on the planet, located below the foothills of Kilimanjaro. Tanzanite, a Zoisite mineral, was only discovered in 1967 by a part time tailor and gold prospector, Mererani de Souza. One of the rarest and most beautiful of gemstones it is blue/purple in colour with flashes of red, unquestionably exotic and 100 per cent African.

I AM TITANIUM Recent years have seen the introduction of a few non-precious materials to the notoriously rigid world of fine jewellery. One such newcomer, found in many of the collections of the Bond Street establishment, is Titanium. Formally the reserve of the avant garde jeweller, thanks to modern technology, this high-tech, super light exotic can be fashioned into almost as many forms as the far more compliant precious metals. What's the point you may ask? By using electrical currents Titanium has the unique quality of being able to be coloured to almost any shade, including grey but also pink, purple, red, blue and green, allowing it to be tonally matched to almost any coloured gem stone. It's like magic.

VERMEIL: GOLD PLATING OF AN INFERIOR CORE METAL When I was a jewellery apprentice in Hatton Garden, London's jewellery quarter—more like an eighth really it was so small—people used to talk in terms of microns of gold plate. 20 microns would last you at least 20 years and flash guilding of a micron was so thin that it could be stripped off with a potent dose of morning breath. There was also another term bounding around known as *rolled gold*. As far as I know, the trade's description act of 1850 saw the end of that. Vermeil is of course a clever ploy to add mystery and confusion to a good old fashioned guilding of the lily.

Liberty Ross wearing the
Stephen Webster for Swarovski
FASHION ROCKS PENDANT

clockwise: ASTRO BALL VIRGO PENDANT Sterling silver with white cubic zirconia pavé, yellow gold plating and topaz crystal; ASTRO BALL LIBRA PENDANT Sterling silver with black and green cubic zirconia pavé, yellow gold plating and blue violet crystal; ASTRO BALL SCORPIO PENDANT Sterling silver with black and red cubic zirconia pavé and sapphire crystal; ASTRO BALL SAGITTARIUS PENDANT Sterling silver with white cubic zirconia pavé, yellow gold plating and jet crystal; ASTRO BALL CAPRICORN PENDANT Sterling silver with black cubic zirconia pavé, yellow gold plating and topaz crystal; ASTRO BALL AQUARIUS PENDANT Sterling silver with blue cubic zirconia pavé, yellow gold plating and blue violet crystal; ASTRO BALL PISCES PENDANT Sterling silver with black cubic zirconia pavé, yellow gold plating and blue sapphire crystal; ASTRO BALL ARIES PENDANT Sterling silver with white cubic zirconia pavé, yellow gold plating and jet crystal; ASTRO BALL TAURUS PENDANT Sterling silver with brown cubic zirconia pavé, yellow gold plating and topaz crystal; ASTRO BALL GEMINI PENDANT Sterling silver with white cubic zirconia pavé, yellow gold plating and blue violet crystal; ASTRO BALL CANCER PENDANT Sterling silver with black cubic zirconia pavé, yellow gold plating and sapphire crystal; ASTRO BALL LEO PENDANT Sterling silver with black cubic zirconia pavé, yellow gold plating and jet crystal

HOROSCOPES

Stephen Webster

Leo
23 July–23 August
Gazing into my Astro Ball I see a familiar image: Leo the Lion. King of the Forest, and the most dominating of the sun signs. Due to their outgoing and imposing demeanour, Leo's can often be labelled as bigheaded, but sometimes this is just big hair. Proud and confident, Leo's seek respect and adoration.

Cancer
22 June–22 July
Gazing into my Astro Ball, I see a crab. Not just any crab but Cancer, the Webster Crab. Secretive and at times sensitive, a Cancer will give you a nip and tuck if tormented. Having powerful character, Cancer is the nurturer of the zodiac and will protect and cherish those they love. Responsive and loyal, crabs scour the ocean's edge adapting to an ever-changing environment.

Gemini
22 May–21 June
Gazing into my Astro Ball I see perhaps the most exciting sign. The two characters of Gemini love to chatter. Intelligent and considerate, there is nothing loose about the talk of a Gemini. Like a persuasive tattoo artist, they like to leave their mark on everyone they meet.

Taurus
21 April–21 May
Gazing into my Astro Ball I see a bull in a china shop. Taurus is powerful, stubborn, influential and smart. Stupidity is the red cloth that will send a Taurus charging. Completely loyal, once befriended, a Taurus is a friend for life. A Taurus has immense perseverance, even when others have given up, the Taurus rages on: a great partner in the pub quiz.

Aries
21 March–20 April
Gazing into my Astro Ball I see a powerful ram. Bestowed with boundless energy, enthusiasm and determination. Arians are independent go-getters. Their upbeat and magnetic personality entices others to follow their lead, and it's usually their way or the highway.

Pisces
20 February–20 March
Gazing into my Astro Ball, I see two fish but no chips. Nervous and easily agitated, Pisceans are agile and quicker than you are. Fishermen have to make an early start to stand a chance with these slippery *sole* mates. Sacrificial and generous, these lagoon-dwellers can also drift towards the negative.

Virgo
24 August–23 September
Gazing into my Astro Ball I see
an intelligent and analytical sign.
Virgo may be a feminine sign,
but don't confuse that with being
weak. On the contrary, Virgos are
strong and demanding. They have
a constant drive to improve and
perfect, their motives honest and
never malicious.

Libra
24 September–23 October
Gazing into my Astro Ball I see an
unusual sign. Libra, the only sign
not represented by a being. Librans
are well mannered and polished
quite rightly feeling superior over
those hell for leather animal signs.
They are able to put themselves
in other's shoes and see things
through another person's point of
view. Relaxed and mellow, Librans
are the types you need on life's
roller coaster ride.

Scorpio
24 October–22 November
Gazing into my Astro Ball, I see a
creature that loves to find a secret
place. A Scorpio never wanders
from a single-minded vision.
Intense and persuasive, a Scorpio
can be undisputed champion of the
world, always in control. Scorpios
are very deep—there is always
more than meets the eye.

Sagittarius
23 November–22 December
Gazing into my Astro Ball I see a
hunter and athlete. Sagittarius is a
curious explorer, a nomad. Forever
optimistic, Sagittarians make great
fans of underperforming football
teams. Their optimistic outlook
and positive disposition attracts
good fortune.

Capricorn
23 December–20 January
Gazing into my Astro Ball I see
someone I almost don't recognise.
Mature, serious and mentally
stable, Capricorns can be tricky.
On the surface this is the sign
for analytical accountants but dig
deep and there is an ambitious,
hardworking rock star.

Aquarius
21 January–19 February
Gazing into my Astro Ball, I see
someone who is gazing back at
my Astro Ball. Aquarius will get
into your head to find the truth.
Completely schizophrenic, these
shy extroverts often deviate from
the crowd and go their own way.
The water torture techniques
administered by Aquarius will get
to the bottom of it no matter how
adverse the situation.

overleaf left Tom and Assia Webster, *London Calling* launch

overleaf right Tracey Emin and I at the Dickensian Punk themed *London Calling* launch at Wilton's Music Hall, 2008

THE MILLION DOLLAR ARM

Stephen Webster

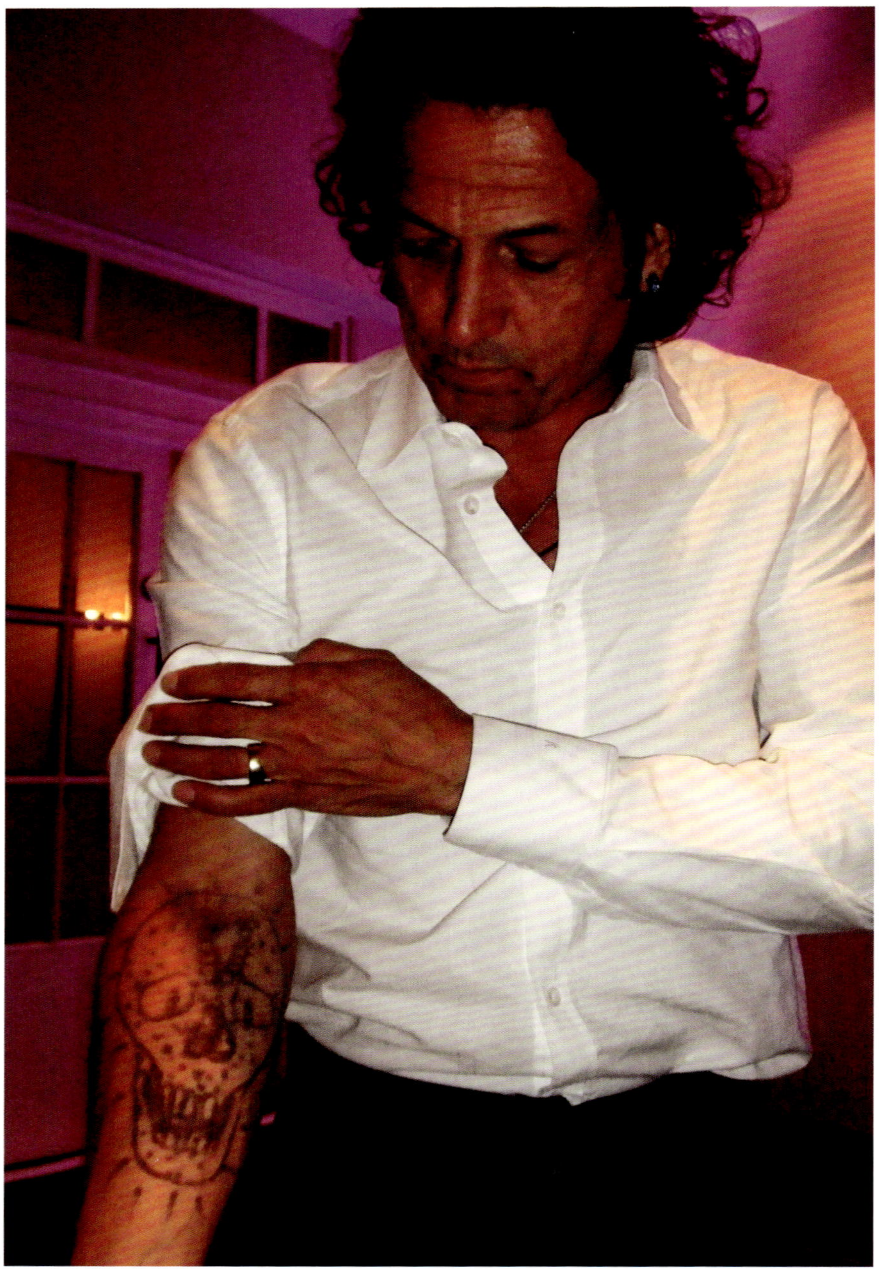

The year I moved to Canada, 1981, there was much talk of the contribution the Canadian Space Agency had made to NASA's space shuttle programme. The contribution was in the form of an arm. No ordinary arm, this arm cost $110 million—the most expensive limb ever back in 1981. Employed on the shuttle to capture, repair and deploy satellites, even position astronauts, it was known as Canadarm. This 15 metre long mechanical version of a human arm was so revolutionary and successful, it inspired massive interest and progress in space age electronics from the Canadian Agency, eventually leading to the 17 metre, and even more flexible, Canadarm II.

My arm story is nowhere near as impressive as either Canadarm or Canadarm II. The value involved was also over a hundred times less, but nonetheless it was a million dollar arm, and unlike the Canadian versions, which function for up to 30 years, this one lasted a week.

The story starts where most things come to an end—or at least the night does—at the Groucho club in London's Soho. I had been fulfilling my role as an ambassador for Jaguar, which mostly meant just driving about in the new car they gave me every nine months. Every now and again the ambassadors would get invited to a variety of events, some sporting, some cultural and others that ended in a watering hole in Soho.

A few of us were gathered upstairs in an ambassadorial group, talking things Jaguar, when who should interrupt us—in a way that only he can—but the creative director of British arts himself, Damien Hirst. Realising he hadn't joined a gathering of the Soho anarchists society, he changed the subject. "Roll up your sleeve," he said to me, "I've got a present for you." Knowing that we both had more than our fair share of skulls in our closets, he produced a Sharpie from somewhere—probably an assistant—and drew a skull on my forearm. Taking into account the sartorially required low lighting of the venue and the small hour of the morning, it wasn't a bad likeness at all.

When I got home I was careful to wash only my hands and no further up my arm. In the morning I called the Mrs, who was elsewhere at the time; "I've been given a Damien Hirst" I told her. Assuming I was mistaken, she went on to talk about something more pressing. I repeated, "I've been given a Damien Hirst and what's more, by the man himself!" Finally the penny dropped, "What? Are you kidding?" "I'm not kidding, I ran into him last night in the Groucho and he gave me an original skull picture," "it must be a print," "it's not a print, I watched him do it." "What was he doing, some kind of show in the Groucho last night?" "Not really, well, only his usual." With the conversation getting more convoluted, I broke the bad news that unless we could persuade him to finish the job and put me—or at least some of me—in formaldehyde, this gift was temporary. Nonetheless, for that moment I had a million dollar arm and a great story.

At work—sporting short sleeves despite the chill in the air—I showed my design team, who were, quite rightly, as impressed as I obviously was. Dan, my menswear designer at the time, had been a tattoo artist before joining SW. We toyed with the idea of tattooing over it, so that my arm would not only retain its value but would most likely increase on the secondary market. Finally, we all agreed that this, whilst being a solution, would also mean that I would be permanently committed to the rather large, very obvious and somewhat crude skull covering my entire forearm. It was decided that I should protect it as much as possible without committing to anything that I might regret in the morning, so to speak.

After the first day, despite having lost that Sharpie saturated ink definition—it didn't quite have the intensity of the new work of the night before—it was, however, still very evident. I would shower with my arm out the door; absolutely no towel use in the surrounding area! I wore short sleeves, no sleeves—although my family and staff were not fans of that look—or loose sleeves, almost as bad. In other words, for the following few days, nothing came into contact with my artwork. By midweek, despite my best efforts, it was plain to see that it was disappearing. Come Thursday, I was actually having to describe it, as well as show it. It was a disaster to have expected that by taking precautions, indelible ink may have some kind of permanence to it. After all, when your kids get it on the carpet or sofa, it's there forever.

Desperate times call for desperate measures; I wrapped my arm and art in cling film for the night. Unfortunately this made my forearm—not normally an area prone to perspiration—sweat like a boiled ham, making things even worse. By Friday, like the old drunk in the pub of the watering holes of Soho, I could be found with my sleeve rolled up, outlining to anyone who would listen, roughly where there had once been an original Damien Hirst.

It could be seen as performance art—definitely graffiti art—a case for art versus ownership or the perfect combination of art and biology. Whatever you call it, I call it art theft. At the start of a week, for once in my life, I had a million dollar arm; by the weekend I was back to being just another blank canvas, one the other hand, I still had an arm.

THE CARDIGAN *A short story written at 35,000 ft*

Stephen Webster

Through virtually the entire boarding process there was just a tiny old lady and myself in our row. Having come to terms with my economy status, and the flow of passengers having slowed to a halt, I placed all my reading materials, Blackberry and glasses on the empty chair between us; sort of marking the territory, indicating that the seat may not be empty. I desperately needed to sleep on the flight having been up until 5am the morning before at a fundraiser in Palm Beach Gardens, at the palatial home of my friends and clients the Healey's. This was followed by the usual way too early wakeup call from the driver taking me to Miami airport for the last leg of this final trip before Christmas.

Suddenly the plane listed to one side. People gasped. Levelling off as quickly as it had tipped, there she was. Eyes focussed into a mid space somewhere up the aisle; she waded forward, struggling to squeeze between the aisle seats. The 3 ft gap in reality was nowhere near wide enough. You could feel the collected bated breath of 200 passengers. Everyone praying "don't let it be me, please don't let it be me." 350 pounds of morbid obesity heading our way. I crossed myself but it was to no avail. Those deep-set little piggy eyes had spotted me. This was her perfect spot... a larger than normal gap between a small weak man and a skeletal Floridian woman, she could own the centre ground.

By prising the back of the seats forward she created her path, her way in. The only thing she didn't do was beat her chest. Once in front of the centre seat she turned, and like a massive cartoon hen, she hovered above her nesting place. I watched open mouthed as, first of all, her rear end was sat on both armrests at once and even a little beyond. Slowly the weight of the upper body was enough to sink the lower part down onto the cushion leaving a substantial roll over each armrest. Acting like a cookie cutter, the part of her filling the seat cavity must have formed a perfect square, all the dough being forced into each corner. I wanted to tut very loudly but what was the point? The damage was done, she was in.

After takeoff, in an attempt to use the loo, I went to get up but was jerked back into my seat. My cardigan was open and at some point during the lowering process one part of it had got sucked into the vacuum that had been created. This was going to be a problem. First of all to make her stand up was obviously going to involve heavy lifting equipment. Probably something like a winch, pulley and sling contraption favoured by roadside assistance. The second thing was that she was snoring. God give me strength. I pulled and pulled but the cashmere was stretching and becoming misshapen. There was only one thing to do—slip it off. First one arm and shoulder, then the turn in a confined space, then over the second shoulder, then out.

Managing this, I got up, climbed over the row in front—the only way out—and went to the loo. Repeating the climbing manoeuvre I returned to my seat. Now I realised it was chilly. At first I tried to cope with it but it was a futile effort. I needed to put my cardigan back on!

Let's just say Harry Houdini would have been proud of the contortion I pulled off pulling that cardigan back on. It made me sweat but despite this it was now staying on, still with one wing trapped, my movements were now restricted for the entire rest of the journey. Oh well, only five more hours to go. I just hope the beast doesn't get hungry when she wakes and wants to order food. She may have her own nosebag. Like an insuppressible turret's tick, I won't be able to stop myself from passing comment if she so much as opens her mouth when the food trolley goes by. Something to the tune of: "Haven't you put me through enough already" or simply "Oh for fuck sake woman."

I think I need to go to the loo again before we land. Lord, please help me hold it in.

On a fully restored 1957
“Black Russian” Ural motorcycle
and sidecar combination,
St Margaret’s Bay, Kent

To Assia, Amy and Nika. The three most precious gifts.

Thank you to Tom and Jean, never could parents have given more love and encouragement. To David, who has put up with me in a way that only a brother can and still gives everything he has to our business. To Assia, who took me and the jewellery industry by storm and without whom I would still be in the basement.

To Claire, who is the best jewellery designer I could ever hope to have met and work alongside—a special thanks for her visual contribution to this book, including the 12 artistic impressions of our jewellery and the limited edition print. To Tracey Emin, for contributing the foreword and her *David Essex or Ken Dodd?* portrait and Rory Dobner, for his amazing drawings of our crab and fighting fish pieces. To John Cooper Clarke, for dedicating *Solid Gold Geezer* and Mick Jones, for the use of *London Calling*. Thank you also to Neiman Marcus, Swarovski and Dom Perignon for use of their imagery; and Rankin, Amelia Troubridge, Richard Young, Stefanie Keenan and Andrei Bronnikov for their photography. Thank you also to Simon Mills for the editing of my words.

To Kate, Tina and every member of the Stephen Webster team, who never cease to amaze me—don't worry, God also knows you're good. To Brian Hill, who taught me what craftsmanship is all about; Mike Ridding, for introducing me to gemstones; Richard Jarvis, for sticking his neck out when no one else would. To Tim and Corrina, Gordon and Angela, for being early angels; Brian and Craig, for showing a bench jeweller how business works; Christina and Jordan, who did what they said they would and to Ron Burkle, for putting his money where his mouth is and remaining a great partner.

To Joe Hage, who continues to give me good advice and with Rob Payne, Phoebe Adler and the HENI team has turned a lot of therapeutic musing into this beautifully bound volume.

And finally, to all our clients and friends, who allow us the luxury to do what we believe we do best.

Portrait by Rankin

Picture Credits

Tim Beddow: pp.344–345. © Tim Beddow
Alexander Beer: p.284. © Alexander Beer, courtesy Tony Ward
Dave Bennett: p.102. © Dave Bennett
Andrei Bronnikov: pp.153, 154, 164, 165, 175, 179, 181. © Andrei Bronnikov
Tzu Chen Chen: p.98. © Tzu Chen Chen
Mat Collishaw: p.276. © Mat Collishaw, courtesy Daisy Lowe
Claire Denham-Smith at Stephen Webster: pp.6, 14, 41, 72, 77, 86, 95, 123, 124, 132
Ian Derry: p.287. IAN DERRY/CHILLI MEDIA, courtesy Jonathan Rhys Meyers
Thomas Dobbie: p.307. Courtesy Thomas Dobbie and Moët Hennesey
Rory Dobner: pp.8–9, 188–189. © Rory Dobner
Douglas Duebler 3: p.162. © Douglas Duebler 3
Tracey Emin: p.10. © Tracey Emin. All rights reserved, DACS 2015
Entertainment Weekly: p.80. © Entertainment Weekly, 2015. All rights reserved
Getty Images: p.129 Bottom. Photo by Ari Perilstein/Getty Images for Stephen Webster
Eli Green: p.135. © Eli Green
Claire Harrison: p.185. Photo by Claire Harrison www.claireharrisonphotography.com
Iakovos Kalaitzakis: pp.214–215. © Iakovos Kalaitzakis, fashion editor: Rebekah Roy, courtesy Laura at Select
Stefanie Keenan: pp.106, 120, 121, 126–127, 128 top, 128 bottom, 129 top, 130, 131, 139. © Stefanie Keenan
Lane Crawford: p.237. Courtesy of Lane Crawford
Luciana Val & Franco Musso: p.167. © Luciana Val & Franco Musso, courtesy Rosamund Pike
Craig McDean: p.190. © Craig McDean/Art+Commerce, courtesy Christina Aguilera
Vincent Peters: p.177. © Vincent Peters, courtesy Tristan Godefroy and Christina Aguilera
Photoshot: p.16 left. ABACA/Photoshot. All rights reserved.
Rankin: p. 16 right, 158–159, 161, 184, 186–187, 221, 225, 226–227, 228, 230–231, 266, 268–269, 306, 337, 338, 339. © Rankin, courtesy Aisha at Models1, Flo Drom at Select, Erin O'Connor at Models1, Maxine Peake, Aisha at Models1, Veronika Vilim at Wilhelmina and Lindsay Lohan
David Slijper: p.331. © David Slijper, courtesy Liberty Ross
Swarovski: p.239. © Swarovski
Alistair Taylor-Young: pp.232–233. © Alistair Taylor-Young, courtesy Neiman Marcus and Gertrud Hansen at Unique Models
The Sunday Times/News Syndication: pp.88–89, 134. *The Sunday Times*/News Syndication, photo: Andrew Testa
Travis Rathbone Studio: p.240. © Travis Rathbone Studio, courtesy Schön! magazine
Amelia Troubridge: pp.118, 182, 326–327, 340, 341. © Amelia Troubridge, courtesy Dita von Teese and Christina Aguilera
Chris Turner: p.194. © Chris Turner at Process, Kara Sims Design, courtesy Schön! magazine
Peter Turner: pp.304–305, 308, 309. © Peter Turner, *Helen for Dom Perignon Vintage Rose*, wearing John Galliano and Stephen Webster, watercolour, graphite pencil, charcoal and ink, 2010
Stephen Webster: pp.3, 4–5, 17, 18, 20 top, 20 bottom, 21, 22, 23, 24, 26 top, 26 bottom, 29, 30, 31, 32, 36, 37, 38, 39, 40, 42, 44, 45, 46, 47, 48, 49, 50, 51, 52, 54 top, 54 bottom, 55, 58 top, 58 bottom, 59, 60, 62, 63, 64, 66 top, 66 bottom, 67, 68, 70, 71, 74, 75 top, 75 bottom, 78, 82, 84, 85, 90, 92, 94, 96, 97, 104, 107, 108, 110, 111, 114 top, 114 bottom, 115, 117, 136, 137, 142–143, 144, 145, 146, 147, 148, 149, 150, 151, 155, 156 left, 156 right, 157, 160, 163, 166, 168, 169, 170, 171, 172, 173, 178, 180, 183, 186, 191, 192, 193, 195, 196, 197, 198–199, 200–201, 202–203, 204, 205, 206, 207, 208, 209, 210, 211, 212, 213, 216, 217, 218, 219, 220, 222, 223, 224, 229, 231, 232, 234, 235, 236, 238, 242, 243, 244, 245, 248, 249, 250, 251, 252–253, 255, 256, 257, 258, 259, 260–261, 262, 263, 264, 265, 267, 270, 271, 272, 273, 274, 275, 277, 278, 279, 280–281, 282, 283, 285, 286, 288–289, 290, 291, 292–293, 294, 295, 296, 297, 298, 299, 300, 301, 302–303, 308, 309, 310, 311, 312, 313, 314–315, 316, 317, 318, 319, 320, 320–321, 322, 323, 332–333, 336, 337, 338, 343, 81, 136, 137, 323, 332. © Stephen Webster
Olaf, Wipperfürth: pp.246–247. Olaf Wipperfürth/thelicensingproject.com
Wire Image: p.122. Photo by Denise Truscello/WireImage
Hannah Harley Young: p.329. © Hannah Harley Young

Amy Webster shot by Rankin
for his book F*ck Y*u

Published by Salma Editions, London

ISBN 978-0-9568738-4-2

A catalogue record for this book is available from The British Library.

Editor: Simon Mills
Designer: Rob Payne
Publishing Manager: Phoebe Adler
Printed by Graphicom, Verona, Italy

Lindsay Lohan wears
Stephen Webster
Superstud bracelets